Promoting Social Success

It   is fun to have
friends.

Promoting Social Success

A Curriculum for Children with Special Needs

by

Gary N. Siperstein, Ph.D.
Center for Social Development and Education
University of Massachusetts Boston

and

Emily Paige Rickards, M.A.
Oliver Wendell Holmes Society
Harvard Medical School, Boston

·P·A·U·L·H·
BROOKES
PUBLISHING CO®

Baltimore • London • Sydney

Paul H. Brookes Publishing Co.
Post Office Box 10624
Baltimore, MD 21285-0624

www.brookespublishing.com

Typeset by Integrated Publishing Solutions, Grand Rapids, Michigan.
Manufactured in the United States of America by
Sheridan Books, Inc., Fredericksburg, Virginia.

The *Promoting Social Success* curriculum was developed at the Center for Social
Development and Education (CSDE) with funding from the Joseph P. Kennedy,
Jr., Foundation and the U.S. Department of Education, Office of Special Educa-
tion Programs (U.S. Department of Education Grant No. H324C980167).

The case studies in this book are composites based on the authors' experiences.
In all instances, names and identifying details have been changed to protect
confidentiality.

Student drawing used by permission of the artist.
Photographs taken by Dan Small.
Illustrations by Ted Eiseman, Helmdean Noel, and Jamison Odone.

Second Printing, January 2009.
Library of Congress Cataloging-in-Publication Data

Siperstein, Gary N.
    Promoting social success : a curriculum for children with special needs /
by Gary N. Siperstein and Emily Paige Rickards.
    p. cm.
Includes bibliographical references.
ISBN-13: 978-1-55766-674-1
ISBN 1-55766-674-1
    1. Social skills—Study and teaching (Elementary).   2. Social skills in
children.   3. Children with mental disabilities—Education (Elementary).
I. Rickards, Emily Paige.   II. Title.
HQ783.S537 2003
302'.14'07—dc22

2003062600

British Library Cataloguing in Publication data are available from the British
Library.

Contents

Unit 3—Using Social Information: Noticing and Interpreting Cues

Unit 4—Planning What to Do: Problem Solving

Unit 5—Making and Keeping Friends: Social Knowledge

General Reproducibles

About the Authors

Gary N. Siperstein, Ph.D., Director, Center for Social Development and Education; Professor, University of Massachusetts Boston, 100 Morrissey Boulevard, Boston, MA 02125

Gary N. Siperstein is founder and Director of the Center for Social Development and Education (CSDE) at the University of Massachusetts Boston. CSDE is a research and training institute focused on improving the social and academic adjustment of children with learning problems who are at risk for academic and social failure. For more than 20 years, CSDE has been gathering data on the social functioning of children with special needs.

A professor at the University of Massachusetts Boston since 1976, Dr. Siperstein received his doctorate at the Ferkauf Graduate School of Psychology, Yeshiva University. He has published approximately 100 articles, chapters, and books on the social relationships and social development of children with disabilities. He has served as associate editor and editor of national journals and has received more than 20 research grants from federal agencies, including the National Institute of Child Health and Human Development (NICHD) and the U.S. Department of Education. Dr. Siperstein received the prestigious MERIT Award from NICHD for his work on the social aspects of mental retardation. Enhancing the social competence of children with disabilities in inclusive educational settings has been the focus of his most recent projects. Dr. Siperstein is presently President-Elect of the Division for Research of the Council for Exceptional Children (CEC).

Emily Paige Rickards, M.A., Program Officer, Oliver Wendell Holmes Society, Harvard Medical School, Medical Education Center, Room 263, 260 Longwood Avenue, Boston, MA 02115

Emily Paige Rickards' teaching experience ranges from fourth grade to the college level and includes the development of numerous professional development programs for teachers. She worked for many years with students with physical and mental disabilities and remains interested in education and curriculum development at all levels. After receiving her master's degree from Boston University, she worked as Research Assistant and Curriculum Specialist on the Promoting Social Success project at the Center for Social Development and Education at the University of Massachusetts Boston. She currently serves on the Educators Advisory Board for the Museum of Fine Arts, Boston; tutors adult learners in the Harvard Bridge to Learning and Literacy Program; and participates in efforts to include issues of diversity and culture in the medical school curriculum.

Preface

The *Promoting Social Success* curriculum was developed at the Center for Social Development and Education (CSDE) with funding from the Joseph P. Kennedy, Jr., Foundation and the U.S. Department of Education, Office of Special Education Programs. CSDE is a research and training institute dedicated to promoting quality education and social development program for students at risk for academic and social failure. For more than 20 years, CSDE has been gathering data on the social functioning of children with special needs. The ongoing research being done at CSDE informs the development of each program and intervention. In turn, the implementation of each program informs the development of new lines of research. The *Promoting Social Success* program grew from the desire to bridge the gap between research and practice and use data gathered about children's social functioning to help teachers such as yourself address the skill impairments of your students.

Acknowledgments

The *Promoting Social Success* program represents the culmination of more than 10 years of research and development in social skills and adjustment in children and has specifically resulted from a desire to help teachers address the social skill limitations found from data gathered about children's social functioning. As with any program, the *Promoting Social Success* curriculum would not have been possible if it were not for the tireless effort, support, and encouragement of numerous individuals.

Our heartfelt thanks to our colleagues at the Center for Social Development and Education (CSDE), each of whom contributed in his or her own unique way to the design, development, and implementation of this curriculum. We extend our thanks to James Leffert, whose research—beginning with his doctoral dissertation—helped set the foundation for the curriculum. We greatly appreciate the commitment and dedication of Laura Clary, who devoted many days, weeks, and years to helping design and implement the program in all of our pilot schools. We are grateful to Lori Legnon, Alfie Alschuler, and Chris Bucco for their help in writing and pilot testing many of the lessons in the curriculum.

We want to extend our gratitude to Dr. Mary Brady, who has gone above and beyond the duties asked of her during the final stages of the curriculum's development. As a professor in special education, Dr. Brady has been able to offer the perspective of both teachers and students. She has dedicated much of her energies in the last months of preparing this book to attending to the consistency of details and the quality of the content. The curriculum would not be what it is without her.

We appreciate the valuable insights from Barry Schneider, Margaret Beebee-Frankenberger, and Katherine Lane, who guided us in refining the curriculum and making sure that it not only covered all of the major aspects of children's social competence but also was "user friendly" for teachers in the classroom.

We are also indebted for the support and encouragement we received from the Directors of Special Education in the greater Boston area during the different phases of pilot testing and implementation of the curriculum. Particularly, we would like to thank Kay Seale and Joanne Malonson of the Brockton Public School System, Edward McCormack of the Everett Public School System, Pia Durkin of the Boston Public School System, and Gail Bernstein of the Medford Public School System. All of these administrators contributed their time and effort to ensure a successful evaluation of the curriculum.

In addition, we would like to thank the principals, school psychologists, and guidance counselors who also assisted project staff in implementing the *Promoting Social Success* curriculum in the following Boston, Brockton, and Everett, Massachusetts, schools:

- James Michael Curley Elementary

- Mather Elementary

- Charles Sumner Elementary

- Jackson-Mann Elementary

- Louis F. Angelo Elementary

- Oscar F. Raymond Elementary

- Edgar B. Davis Elementary

- Joseph H. Downey Elementary

- Joseph F. Plouffe Elementary

- Centre Elementary

We are forever grateful to the many teachers and their aides who helped make this all possible. Their belief in the curriculum and their valuable feedback have helped to ensure that the *Promoting Social Success* curriculum "works."

We recognize several external organizations that have given us their invaluable support. We acknowledge the visionary leadership of Mrs. Eunice Kennedy Shriver at the Joseph P. Kennedy, Jr., Foundation, which provided part of the funding for this curriculum. We thank Tom Hanley and Patricia Gonzales from the U.S. Department of Education, Office of Special Education Programs, whose encouragement and support over the past 10 years also helped make this curriculum possible. Finally, we recognize Mackenzie Cross, Jessica Allan, Erin Geoghegan, and Lisa Rapisarda from Paul H. Brookes Publishing Co., who worked hard to help smooth out the rough edges of the curriculum and put a shine on the lessons so that the entire curriculum sparkles.

Last, and most important, we are grateful for the opportunity to work with the many different children who participated in the project. Their eagerness to learn, willingness to try out new social skills, and excitement at being successful in making and keeping new friends was an inspiration to us all. We sincerely hope that all of the teachers who use the *Promoting Social Success* curriculum will experience the same inspiration from their students.

An Introduction to the *Promoting Social Success* Curriculum

WHY ARE SOCIAL SKILLS IMPORTANT?

Social skills are essential to a productive and satisfying educational experience. They are the building blocks on which a child's academic success and emotional well-being are founded, and they allow students to take full advantage of classroom instruction and activities. The development of appropriate social skills becomes even more important as more and more schools welcome students with special needs into inclusive classrooms. Students with special needs must adjust to the increased complexity of social demands found in inclusive settings, and general education students must adjust to a more heterogeneous classroom environment. Unfortunately, without social skills training, students with special needs often experience social rejection or isolation.

Achieving the social competence necessary to make and keep friends can be a catch-22 situation: Without basic social skills, children are unable to make and maintain friendships; yet it is within these peer relationships that children learn and practice ways of relating to one another. Simply put, without social skills, friends are hard to make; without friendships, social skills are hard to learn. Therefore, it is essential that students who have difficulty interacting appropriately with their peers receive explicit social instruction so they can begin building and practicing the social skills necessary to form beneficial interpersonal relationships. Social skills instruction helps students reach a level of social competence that they otherwise would be unable to obtain. The *Promoting Social Success* curriculum is designed to teach all children the skills they need to be socially successful, with particular emphasis on children with special needs.

Every day, teachers deal with the conflicts, emotional outbursts, changing alliances, and hurt feelings that so often characterize the social interactions of children. All of these events affect, and often interrupt, student learning. The more time you take to deal with conflicts and inappropriate behavior, the less time you have to devote to teaching actual subject matter. More and more, teachers just like you are using strategies such as cooperative groups and peer tutoring to improve the academic performance of students. These teaching strategies, however, require that students be able to interact with one another in collaborative and productive ways. Without basic social skills, students are unable to benefit from these learning experiences. Social skills instruction is a way of improving both the academic and social functioning of *individual* students and improving the interpersonal climate of the classroom for *all* students.

WHAT MAKES THE *PROMOTING SOCIAL SUCCESS* CURRICULUM UNIQUE?

We recognize that many teachers have tried one or even several programs that focus on improving their students' ability to get along with others. However, we believe that the *Promoting Social Success* curriculum, with its cognitive approach to social skills development, can make a difference for your students. Riley, the student whose drawing appears on the frontispiece and back cover, had difficulty making and maintaining friends within his peer group. The sentiment expressed in his drawing and the big smiles on the faces of the boys reflect Riley's idea of how it *might* feel to have friends. No one, especially not a child, should go through life without knowing what it feels like to have a friend.

Teachers already using the *Promoting Social Success* curriculum have offered positive feedback about the social skills their students have acquired:

"{Students} have become more aware of others' feelings and consider others more frequently when working or playing in groups." —third-grade teacher

"{A student} has begun to socialize much more and initiate contact with her peers. Before she would spend most time by herself." —fourth-grade teacher

"One student was being teased by others in an inclusion class. He was able to come up with different strategies for dealing with it, which came from the lessons on teasing." —third-grade teacher

There are many social skills curricula available, but the *Promoting Social Success* program is unique in its cognitive approach to social skills development. Most of the curricula used in elementary school classrooms since the 1980s attempt to address specific student interactions or behaviors, such as being a good listener, appropriately entering or leaving the room, and introducing oneself to others. These curricula can be useful if you are seeking help with common classroom situations. It is impossible, however, to create lessons that address every social interaction that children may encounter. The social world of children is simply too complex and contains too many variables to cover in one, or even several, curricula.

Rather than teaching children a set of prescribed behaviors, the *Promoting Social Success* program takes a broader perspective and focuses on the cognitive processes *behind* the behaviors. Just as reading programs focus on developing word attack and decoding skills that children can apply to any text, the *Promoting Social Success* curriculum focuses on developing cognitive skills that children can apply to any social interaction. With practice, these cognitive processes should ultimately be performed naturally without prompting. Through this program, you can help your students develop their ability to understand the emotional states of themselves and others, to better "read" social situations, and to determine appropriate social responses. The program develops students' social cognitive skills so that they become socially attuned thinkers and independent problem solvers as they interact with their peers.

Along with its unique cognitive approach to social skills instruction, the *Promoting Social Success* curriculum contains other special features that you can use throughout the various lessons, all of which are found in the General Reproducibles section at the end of the curriculum:

- **Body language photographs:** The body language photographs show real people expressing emotions with their bodies. The photographs allow students to identify and discuss the ways in which they can figure out what others are feeling by looking at their hands, arms, posture, and facial expressions. In combination with the feeling faces and the role-play situations (see p. 4) that are incorporated into many lessons, the body language photographs are an important tool in teaching students to correctly identify and interpret social cues.

- **Feeling faces:** An important component of many lessons in the *Promoting Social Success* curriculum, feeling faces depict the expressions of six different emotions and six emotional states. The emotions are: happy, sad, surprised, embarrassed, frustrated, and angry. The emotional states are: lonely, confused, nervous, scared, calm, and excited. Students use these faces as they think about their own emotional state and as they learn to identify the feeling states of others. The large faces are useful for showing to classes or groups. Students can use the smaller faces to create feelings books or to display on their desks the emotion that they are currently feeling. Students should feel free to color or otherwise personalize the small feeling faces. We encourage you to begin all *Promoting Social Success* lessons with the question, "How are you feeling?" to get students in the habit of using these feeling faces and monitoring their internal emotional states.

- **Parent newsletters:** The *Promoting Social Success* curriculum includes five parent newsletters. The first, *Introducing the Program,* is sent home to parents when you begin the curriculum; *The Calming Down Steps* is sent when you introduce the Stoplight Poster #1; and *Figuring Out Social Situations, Problem Solving,* and *Friendship* are sent at the beginning of each of the last three units of the *Promoting Social Success* curriculum. These newsletters will help parents understand the goals of the *Promoting Social Success* program and keep them informed about the skills and activities their child is working on. In addition, each newsletter gives suggestions for how parents can reinforce social skills at home, which is a critical part of the learning process.

- **Role-play footprints:** Role play is an essential part of the *Promoting Social Success* curriculum. Role play allows students to act out emotions and social interactions. It allows students to practice appropriate behaviors and allows the role-play audience to practice correctly interpreting what they observe. The role-play footprints are a tool that helps introduce students to role play. Stepping on and off the footprints helps students distinguish between times a person is pretending, or role playing, and times the person is not. Using the footprints provides a concrete beginning and end to the role play. As students become more familiar with role play, and as the role plays become more complex, the footprints may become unnecessary.

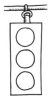

- **Stoplight posters:** These posters use stoplights to guide students through a series of calming down and problem-solving steps. Each student may color his or her own stoplight poster using the templates included in the General Reproducibles section at the end of the curriculum. You can display the posters somewhere in the classroom so that students can be easily reminded to "use the stoplight" when they are upset or angry. Used outside of the classroom as well, the posters create a "common language" for the school community to talk about the importance of calming down. Stoplight Poster #1 outlines the calming down steps next to the red light. The red light cues students to "Stop," "Keep Hands to Yourself," and "Take a Deep Breath." Stoplight Poster #2 outlines all of the problem-solving steps next to the yellow and green lights. The yellow light cues students to ask questions such as, "What is going on?" "What do I want to happen?" "What can I do?" The green light cues students to "Try my plan" and to evaluate the success of their plan with the question, "How did it go?" Taken as a whole, the red, yellow, and green lights provide students with a visual model for calming down and thinking through a problem before taking action.

Along with these general materials used throughout the program, many lessons incorporate other materials such as worksheets, photographs, and illustrations that are particular to that lesson—you can find these materials in the Reproducibles section for that lesson. (*Please note:* Many lessons require you to brainstorm various lists of ideas with your group of students [e.g., a list of feeling words, a list of times the students needed to be calmed down]—we strongly encourage that you keep copies of these lists, as you will need to refer to many of them in subsequent lessons.)

For your convenience, we have included a bibliography after the General Reproducibles section at the end of the curriculum. The *Promoting Social Success* curriculum uses popular, age-appropriate books as a means of engaging students in social skills instruction. We recognize, however, that you may not be able to obtain every book referenced in this curriculum; therefore, we have created a list of books that deal with issues of social competence, friendship, and emotional and behavioral regulation. Using the bibliography, you will be able to substitute comparable books for the ones mentioned in the lessons.

The *Promoting Social Success* curriculum also uses a variety of videos as tools to examine social interaction. Video is a medium that is familiar to students, and it allows them to repeatedly view important components of social interaction such as context, body language, and tone of voice. As such, we provide multiple suggestions for video clips in each lesson that uses video. If you are unable to acquire these particular videos, however, you should feel free to substitute clips of similar interactions from other videos.

IS THE *PROMOTING SOCIAL SUCCESS* CURRICULUM APPROPRIATE FOR MY STUDENTS?

The *Promoting Social Success* curriculum is designed to improve the social skills of students with special needs such as mild mental retardation and other learning difficulties,[1] along with their general education peers. The program is appropriate

---

[1] We are aware that terms used to refer to children who have below average intellectual abilities accompanied by adaptive behavior problems vary within some schools, using terms such as "mental retardation," "cognitive impairments," "learning problems," and, more recently, "intellectual disabilities."

Unit 1
Introductory Lessons

Coming Together to Form the Group
Introducing Role Play
Practicing Role Play
Introducing Problem-Solving Meetings
Practicing Problem-Solving Meetings

 Unit 2
Understanding Feelings and Actions: Emotional and Behavioral Regulation

Using Feeling Words
Identifying Happy Expressions
Understanding Sadness
The Difference Between Alone and Lonely
Understanding Fear
When Are We Surprised?
Understanding Love and Hate
Understanding Frustration
Understanding Anger
Feelings in Different Contexts
Different People Have Different Emotions
Understanding Emotional Intensity
What to Do When You Are Angry
Expressing Feelings in Appropriate Ways
Why Calming Down Is Important
Ways to Calm Down
Introducing the Red Light Calming Down Steps
Practicing the Calming Down Steps
Applying the Calming Down Steps
Reviewing the Calming Down Steps
What Helps Me Calm Down?
Reviewing Feeling Words

 Unit 3
Using Social Information: Noticing and Interpreting Cues

Introducing the Yellow Light Thinking Steps
Introducing Body Language
Interpreting Body Language
Interpreting Tone of Voice (Feelings)
Interpreting Tone of Voice (Sincerity)
Accident or On Purpose?
Identifying Intention
Is This Mean?
How to Tell When Someone Is Busy
Reacting to Other People
Reviewing Emotional Displays
Reviewing Social Situations

Figure 1. *Promoting Social Success* lessons by unit.

Figure 1. *(continued)*

 Unit 4
Planning What to Do: Problem Solving

What Does it Mean to Have Goals?

Identifying Goals

Practicing Identifying Goals

Generating Strategies to Solve a Problem

Practicing Generating Strategies

Generating Multiple Strategies

Assertive Problem-Solving Strategies

Using Compromise as a Strategy

Predicting Consequences

Practicing Strategy Selection

Introducing the Green Light Action Steps

How Did it Go?

What to Do If We Don't Reach Our Goal

Applying the Problem-Solving Steps

Reviewing Problem-Solving Skills

Unit 5
Making and Keeping Friends: Social Knowledge

What Makes a Good Friend?

The Ups and Downs of Friendship

The Importance of Trust

Give and Take

Encouraging Empathy

Communicating with Friends

Dealing with Rejection

Sharing Hurt Feelings with Friends

Coping with Teasing

The Importance of Forgiveness

Keeping Friends

The Importance of Compliments

for both self-contained and inclusive classrooms. School counselors might also find the *Promoting Social Success* curriculum useful for small-group sessions outside of the students' everyday classroom.

OVERVIEW OF THE CURRICULUM

The *Promoting Social Success* curriculum is organized into five units. Each unit focuses on a particular skill set that is necessary for appropriate social interaction. The curricular units, however, are not discrete entities. Skills that are introduced and practiced in one unit are revisited and extended in another. With the exception of Unit 5, which can be presented piece-meal throughout the curriculum if you wish, each unit builds on the last as more complex cognitive processes are addressed. The units proceed as follows (see Figure 1 for a listing of lessons by unit):

- Unit 1—Introductory Lessons

- Unit 2—Understanding Feelings and Actions: Emotional and Behavioral Regulation

- Unit 3—Using Social Information: Noticing and Interpreting Cues

- Unit 4—Planning What to Do: Problem Solving

- Unit 5—Making and Keeping Friends: Social Knowledge

Unit 1—Introductory Lessons

With the lessons in this unit, you will introduce students to the *Promoting Social Success* program, to each other, and to role play—an important educational technique utilized extensively in the *Promoting Social Success* curriculum. Two lessons in this unit also outline a format for cooperative problem-solving meetings. You can implement these two lessons at any point in the curriculum to set up regular problem-solving meetings and practice addressing real classroom situations.

Unit 2—Understanding Feelings and Actions: Emotional and Behavioral Regulation

Lessons in this unit are designed to help you increase students' emotional vocabulary. Together, you and your students will identify and practice the appropriate expression of a variety of emotions. Being able to identify one's own emotional state and express the emotions in healthy ways is a basic skill on which other skills build. Lessons in Unit 2 prepare students for the next unit in which students will be asked to perform the more difficult skills of noticing and interpreting the emotional states of others.

Lessons in Unit 2 also provide students with the framework for a method of self-control through a series of calming down steps. Behavioral regulation is an essential part of appropriate social interaction. We all have difficulty thinking clearly when we are upset. Children, especially children with mental retardation and other learning difficulties, often need explicit training on ways in which they can calm themselves down so that they can think more clearly about a problem. Lessons throughout the *Promoting Social Success* curriculum use the image of a stoplight to cue children to calm down, think about their situation, and solve their problem before they act. In this unit, the red light reminds students to "Stop," "Keep Hands to Yourself," and "Take a Deep Breath." The yellow and green light images will be used in subsequent units.

Unit 3—Using Social Information: Noticing and Interpreting Cues

Lessons in this unit encourage students to pay attention to the social cues around them and provide guided practice in the interpretation of these cues. Using the yellow light on the traffic signal, you will introduce students to the beginning step of the problem-solving model ("What is going on?"). Students will gather information about social situations using the social cues around them such as body language and tone of voice. Then, students will practice interpreting the behavior of others in lessons such as Is This Mean? and Accident or On Purpose? These lessons require students to integrate the social and emotional cues that they have gathered and make decisions about another person's intent.

Unit 4—Planning What to Do: Problem Solving

Lessons in this unit will guide you in presenting and practicing the remaining steps in the yellow light and proceeding to the green light—"Try Your Plan." Once a child has correctly "read" a social situation, the child must react appropriately. Lessons focus on identifying goals ("What do I want to happen?"), generating and selecting strategies ("What can I do?"), and evaluating problem-solving plans ("How did it go?").

Unit 5—Making and Keeping Friends: Social Knowledge

Lessons in this unit provide you and your students with opportunities to discuss and practice the social skills necessary to be a good friend. A child's social knowledge informs all aspects of his or her social interactions. The more a student understands about appropriate behaviors, the better able he or she will be able to work cooperatively with peers and solve social problems independent of adult intervention. You will be able to present these lessons as a unit after you finish Units 1–4, or you can present individual lessons from this unit at other times according to students' needs.

LAYOUT OF THE LESSON

Lessons in the *Promoting Social Success* instructional program are organized into seven sections. The sections are designed to identify the lesson's place within the wider curriculum, identify the purpose and outcomes of the lesson, and outline the discussions and activities that will take place. Lessons promote and encourage positive social interaction through role play and other interactive activities, while at the same time building essential cognitive skills through guided practice (see Figure 2 for a sample lesson). Each lesson plan contains the following sections:

- **Lesson title:** identifies the particular topic that will be addressed by the lesson

- **Purpose:** identifies the aim of the lesson—how the lesson will address the particular skill set in that unit. For example, the purpose of a lesson might be "to identify situations that are personally frustrating."

- **Students will:** outlines the behavioral expectations of students for the lesson. For example, "Students will: Complete a drawing activity that depicts a frustrating situation." The "Students will" section provides you with concrete products or measurable behaviors with which you can assess student progress.

- **Materials:** identifies the materials you need to implement the lesson. Many lessons are accompanied by stories and illustrations, feeling faces, or other materials.

- **Presentation of lesson:** describes the activities that will take place during the lesson. Most lessons are broken down into further parts such as "Discussion," "Story Activity," and "Wrap-up." These headings provide you with a guide for implementing the lesson. Lessons are not scripted, however, and you are encouraged to present lesson content in a way that is most appropriate to your own classroom and your own teaching style.

- **Alternative presentations:** provides you with the flexibility to implement a lesson with students of different ability levels. Two alternatives are suggested to replace, modify, or enhance the activities outlined in the "Presentation of Lesson" section. The "Challenging" presentation, often a discussion

	# Introducing Role Play
Identifies the topic addressed by each lesson →	

Identifies aim of lesson →

PURPOSE

To introduce the term *role play*

To familiarize students with the act of role playing

Provides behavioral expectations for students →

STUDENTS WILL

Enter the role of actor and present an idea to the group

MATERIALS

- Role-play footprints
- Tape

Outlines lesson activities →

PRESENTATION OF LESSON

Discussion

Introduce the group to the term *role play*. Explain to students that role play is an activity in which people pretend to be someone or something or pretend to do something. Role playing is like acting. Tape the role-play footprints to the floor and explain that whoever is doing the role play will stand on the footprints to indicate the beginning of the role play. The role play ends when the actor steps off the footprints (the footprints help make a concrete distinction between fantasy and reality).

Alerts teachers to go to the Reproducibles section at the end of the specific lesson for a handout

Role-Play Activity

Model a role play for the students. Stand on the footprints and act out your favorite animal. Have students guess which animal you are. When you step off the footprints, discuss with students how they guessed the animal, along with the importance of stepping on and off the footprints to signal the beginning and end of the role play.

Give each student a chance to role play his or her favorite animal, taking guesses from the rest of the group. You can have students participate in a second round of role playing using the category of a feeling or emotion. Model a role play using the emotion of sadness. When you step off the footprints, discuss with students how they guessed the emotion you were showing, focusing on how you used your face and body to convey this emotion.

Provides flexibility of presentation and easy adaptation to different learners →

ALTERNATIVE PRESENTATIONS

Fundamental

- *In addition to the materials already listed, you will need a stack of small feeling faces showing a variety of emotions.*

Present students with a stack of feeling faces showing different emotions. Each student picks a card and acts out the emotion that is on the card.

Alerts teachers to go to the General Reproducibles section at the end of the curriculum for a handout

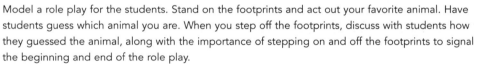

Challenging

- *In addition to the materials already listed, you will need chart paper and a marker or chalkboard and chalk.*

Present students with more challenging categories. Together, brainstorm a list of everyday activities such as brushing teeth, getting on the bus, or eating breakfast. Write this list under the heading "Things I Do Everyday" and have students choose a role play from this list to act out.

Gives hints to help reinforce and generalize skills →

THROUGHOUT THE DAY

- Encourage students to play Charades with their friends during free time to improve their role-playing skills.

Figure 2. Sample *Promoting Social Success* lesson.

question or topic, is meant to further explore the lesson's main idea. This presentation is often a good extension of the lesson for students with more highly developed cognitive abilities. The "Fundamental" presentation gives you suggestions for presenting the material to students with more basic cognitive abilities. These students may require additional opportunities to practice new skills, or they may need certain skills broken down into more fundamental components. For example, while discussing body language, it may be necessary to break the concept down into the elements of facial expression, posture, arm and hand positions, and so forth. Use these alternatives to facilitate your adaptation of lessons to particular groups and to maximize the benefit of a given lesson to any audience.

- **Throughout the day:** provides you with suggestions for reinforcing new skills throughout the school day. It is essential that children generalize the skills they learn during instructional time into other academic and nonacademic activities. For more information on the generalization of skills, please see the "Teachable Moments" section in this Introduction.

IMPLEMENTATION OF THE CURRICULUM

Where Do I Begin?

The units and lessons in the *Promoting Social Success* curriculum are arranged sequentially so that lessons that focus on complex skills follow lessons that focus on basic skills. We encourage you to begin the curriculum, however, at the point that is most appropriate for your students. It is a waste of valuable instruction time to extensively review skills that your students have mastered. For example, the arrangement of units is based on the assumption that children must first be calm and in control enough to attend to their social environment and really understand and navigate through a social situation. The lessons in Unit 3 that require students to interpret complex social cues build on the emotional and behavioral regulation skills addressed in Unit 2. Initial lessons provide scaffolding on which more complex skills can be introduced. However, if you are satisfied with your students' emotional vocabulary and their ability to exercise self-control, you may opt to skip the unit on emotional and behavioral regulation.

The question of how to accurately assess your students' abilities in these areas is a complicated one. In fact, researchers at the Center for Social Development and Education have been designing a formal, systematic assessment tool that will do just that. Until this tool is available, we suggest that you present one or two lessons in Unit 2 (e.g., Using Feeling Words), and use your own observations of student behavior to determine student ability. The appendix at the end of this Introduction provides a list of social cognitive skills and corresponding lessons.

In addition, there are lessons within the curriculum that do not need to be implemented in any particular order. The Introducing Problem-Solving Meetings lesson (Unit 1), for example, provides a wonderful opportunity for students to practice appropriate social interactions within a very structured environment. You can implement these meetings at any point during social skills instruction. Also, you can implement lessons in Unit 5 together after completing the other units or singly when a situation presents itself during the school day that might be aided by lesson content. For example, if you have a student who is experiencing misunderstandings with a peer, then you could present the Communicating with Friends (Unit 5) lesson to respond to the situation. You should feel free to structure the sequence of these lessons according to the needs of your students.

How Often and For How Long?

The implementation of a lesson in the *Promoting Social Success* curriculum generally takes between 30 and 45 minutes. We encourage you to make time for lessons on a daily basis; however, a once-a-week lesson may be supplemented by taking advantage of teachable moments throughout the week (for more information, see the "Teachable Moments" section).

The amount of time needed to implement the entire curriculum will depend on where in the curriculum you begin, the frequency of lesson implementation, and whether you choose to implement each lesson or to use individual lessons on an as-needed basis.

What Is the Ideal Implementation of the *Promoting Social Success* Curriculum?

Ideal implementation of the *Promoting Social Success* curriculum is an instruction schedule that results in the acquisition, practice, and generalization of social skills throughout the school day. To this end, we encourage a weekly schedule consisting of

- One whole-group lesson

- One small-group lesson for students experiencing particular social skill difficulties

- One problem-solving meeting

- Appropriate teachable moments

Figure 3 shows a suggested weekly instruction schedule.

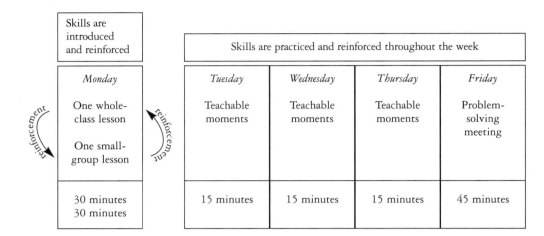

Figure 3. Suggested weekly instruction schedule.

As mentioned previously, the movement toward inclusion means that it is increasingly important for both special and general education teachers to focus on social skills. Students with special needs are more frequently participating in general education settings for some or all of the school day. These placements challenge students to navigate increasingly complex social interactions, progress academically, and become truly "included" in the social life of the classroom.

Combination of Whole-Group and Small-Group Lessons

The *Promoting Social Success* program has been successfully piloted in both self-contained and inclusive settings. Regardless of the type of classroom, we found that ideal instruction consisted of a combination of small-group and whole-group lessons. This combination allows you to target particular social or behavioral issues and focus on the inclusion of particular students into a wider social environment. The weekly whole-group and small-group lessons can be implemented in a variety of ways. You can use small-group lessons to introduce concepts that will be covered in a whole-group lesson, thus allowing your students who need extra help with their social skills to act as "experts" among their peers. For example, students who experience the Introducing Body Language lesson (Unit 3) in a small group can act as experts when the whole group works on the Interpreting Body Language lesson (Unit 3). Alternatively, you can use small-group lessons to further practice skills learned during a whole-group lesson. For example, the Practicing Strategy Selection lesson (Unit 4) may provide a small group of students with additional skill reinforcement after the Predicting Consequences lesson (Unit 4).

Problem-Solving Meetings

Problem-solving meetings are a wonderful opportunity for students to practice their problem-solving skills in a structured setting. Held each week, problem-solving meetings increase student accountability for the social dynamic of the group and encourage students to generate and select problem-solving plans that do not rely on your authority. The delayed nature of this procedure (students must wait until the problem-solving meeting time to discuss the problem) allows students to cool off and evaluate the importance of the problem over time. Problem-solving meetings can be time-consuming and can raise sensitive issues about the behavior and social standing of students in the group. Given time, however, they can be an important part of creating a group community. You can implement problem-solving meetings at any point in the *Promoting Social Success* curriculum (the earlier in the school year, the better), but they become particularly relevant during the problem-solving lessons in Unit 4 as students become more proficient at identifying goals, generating and selecting strategies, and so forth.

Teachable Moments

Teachable moments are those unplanned opportunities outside of formal instructional time in which you can reinforce and practice the skills presented in the *Promoting Social Success* lessons. For example, when you are upset with the behavior of a student or the group, you can model the calming down steps. Or, when a student is having difficulty understanding his or her peers, you can guide the student to more accurately read the social situation. Teachable moments are perhaps the most powerful tool available to you in terms of making social skills a priority in the group.

General Instructional Strategies

There are a number of tried and true instructional strategies that, if used, can maximize the effect of the *Promoting Social Success* curriculum on your students' social functioning. In combination with the lesson activities and materials, these strategies can help students acquire the cognitive skills necessary to be socially successful.

1. *Social skill acquisition requires social interaction.* During lessons, encourage as much appropriate social interaction as possible. While students are completing an activity, encourage them to interact, share, and talk with one another. These interactions may provide you with valuable teachable moments to reinforce skills.

2. *Repeat, repeat, repeat.* Children with mental retardation or other learning difficulties need multiple opportunities to learn and practice new skills. The combination of small-group and whole-group lessons provides some of the necessary repetition. Do not hesitate, however, to repeat lessons or to present the same information in different ways.

3. *Use concrete examples.* Many children have difficulty understanding hypothetical situations. In discussions, use names of familiar people to illustrate your point. Have students act out appropriate and inappropriate ways of behaving. The more concrete you make the information, the more likely students will comprehend it.

4. *Use consistent language.* Using the language contained in the lessons (e.g., the "calming down steps") throughout the day will help students internalize the lesson content and will help students to generalize what they learn during lessons to other parts of their day. "Think alouds" (e.g., "Which would be the best strategy for me to pick?") help children identify opportunities to practice the skills they have been learning.

5. *Model appropriate social skills.* As mentioned in our discussion of teachable moments, it is very important that you model the skills that students are learning. Naming the calming down steps as you use them in a frustrating situation is a simple, yet effective way of reinforcing this particular skill.

DEVELOPMENT OF THE CURRICULUM

Theoretical Framework

The *Promoting Social Success* program uses the Social Information Processing (SIP) model, developed by Crick and Dodge (1994), as its framework. This model has informed the development of social skills curricula for varied populations of children (Elias et al., 1997; Kusche & Greenberg, 1994). Simply stated, the SIP model illustrates the cognitive steps that guide our behavior during social interactions. Successful completion of these cognitive steps generally results in socially appropriate behavior. For most of us, the cognitive steps occur naturally, without intervention or instruction. However, some children, particularly some children with special needs, have difficulty processing social information. When children do not complete the cognitive steps, or complete them without a certain degree of accuracy, socially inappropriate behavior can result. Many students such as Riley (the boy who created the artwork on the frontispiece and back cover) need additional help with specific cognitive func-

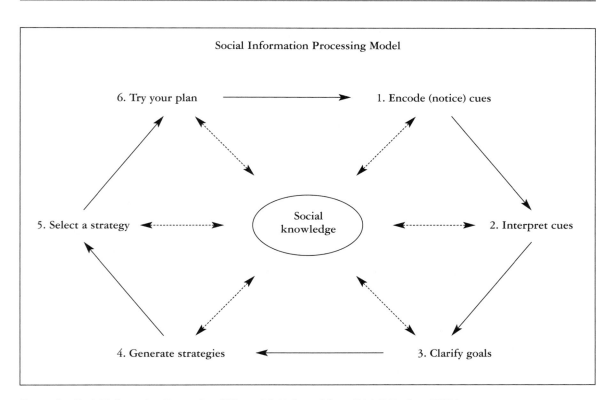

Figure 4. Social Information Processing (SIP) model. (Adapted from Crick & Dodge, 1994.)

tions such as emotion recognition, social perception, strategy generation, and consequential reasoning. Figure 4 shows the adapted version of the SIP model.

The cognitive processes depicted in the SIP model are cyclical in nature—they do not have clear beginning and end points. However, for clarity's sake, we will discuss them in the order they appear in the model.

1. *Encode (notice) cues:* First, in any social situation we take in, or "encode," the social cues around us. These cues include ones that we gather from people around us, such as facial expressions, body language, and tone of voice. Social cues also include environmental cues, such as the setting of the social interaction (an office setting versus a party, for example). Encoding these cues simply means that we give them our attention; they enter our awareness.

2. *Interpret cues:* Second, we assign meaning to the cues we have encoded. We take the information we have gathered and come to a conclusion about the social interaction/situation.

3. *Clarify goals:* Once we have interpreted the social cues, we need to clarify what it is we want to happen. What results do we want from this particular social interaction?

4. *Generate strategies:* Now that we know what our goals are, how will we solve our problem? The ability to generate an array of strategies to solve a given problem is an important skill.

5. *Select a strategy:* Once we have a variety of strategies from which to choose, we need to pick one that will help us reach our goal(s).

6. *Try your plan:* Next, we try our plan. If the plan is not successful, then, the cognitive process must begin again. New social cues need to be encoded and interpreted, and a new plan of action may need to be made.

In the center of the SIP model is our memory storehouse about social interactions. The knowledge about social rules and norms that influences each cognitive process is in this storehouse. As children make and maintain friendships and practice their social skills, this storehouse of social knowledge grows. It allows children to learn from their relationships and put new knowledge to use in future friendships.

You will notice that the SIP model does not address emotional and behavioral regulation that corresponds with the lessons in Unit 2 of the *Promoting Social Success* curriculum. Although the original SIP model did not account for the emotional aspect of social cognitive functioning, later models (Lemerise & Arsenio, 2000) do include descriptions of how important emotional regulation is to cognitive processing. For this reason, and because our own experience teaching children told us that it is essential for them to be aware of—and be able to regulate—their own emotional experiences, we included lessons that focus on these issues in Unit 2.

Applying the Social Information Processing Model

The SIP model can help us better understand what goes through our minds during social interactions. Figure 5 examines a particular social situation using the SIP model.

Social Information Processing "Mistakes"

None of us will execute these steps with accuracy and precision at all times. We all have embarrassing stories about the time we made a joke at an inappropriate moment or the time we reacted with anger to someone's "rudeness" only to realize later that we had misunderstood the person's intentions. Children with special needs or other learning difficulties, however, have a tendency to make social "mistakes" with more frequency than most people. For example, when Robert, a fourth-grade boy with mental retardation, was shown an illustration

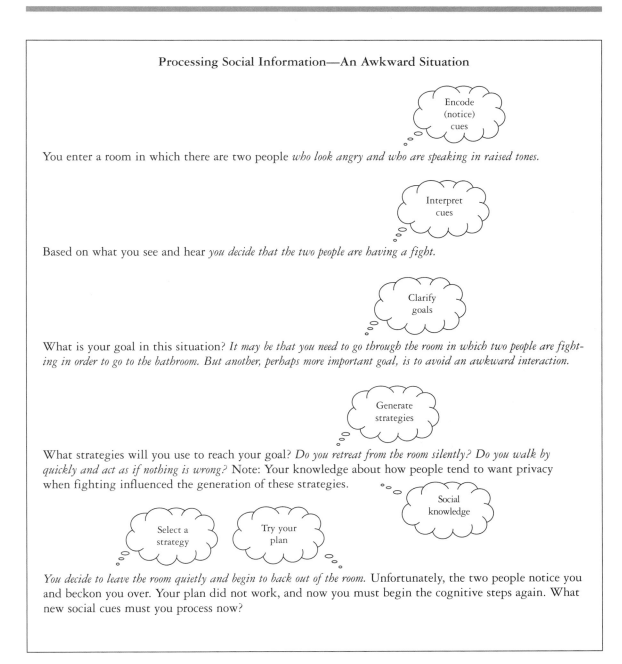

Figure 5. Applying the Social Information Processing (SIP) model.

similar to Figure 6 and asked, "What is going on in this picture?" Robert replied, "The girls are fighting." Robert made social information processing errors on several levels. First, Robert failed to encode the relevant cues—he did not notice the girl sitting by herself and her sad expression. In doing so, Robert completely missed what we might consider the social "main idea" of the picture, namely that the girl was left out of the game. Lessons in Unit 2 and 3 will help students such as Robert be more aware of the dynamics of social situations.

Figure 6. Illustration. (Adapted form Childswork/Childsplay Conflict Resolution Problem-Solving Cards)

Robert also made an error in Interpreting cues. Although he noticed the action of the girls' arms and legs, he misinterpreted the emotional tone of the situation. He concluded that the girls were fighting instead of playing. There are several explanations for this conclusion. One is that he simply did not attend to the facial expressions of the girls (i.e., he did not notice/pay attention to their expressions). A second explanation is that he did see the smiles and yet still failed to include these social cues in his interpretation of the situation. Perhaps, for example, his memory storehouse contained memories of soccer games that involved a great deal of fighting, and these memories wrongly influenced his interpretation of the girls' game. Again, lessons in Unit 2 and 3 will help students such as Robert be more aware of the dynamics of social situations.

The tendency to interpret social situations with a negative bias (the kind of bias that leads to a "fighting" rather than a "playing" interpretation) is not unique to Robert. In fact, research shows that children with learning difficulties often interpret social interactions as being more negative than the social cues would indicate. For example, if one child knocks over the blocks of another, the child with learning difficulties is likely to interpret the first child's intentions as being "mean." Even in the presence of an auditory cue that would indicate an accident (e.g., an apology—"Oops, sorry"), the child with learning difficulties will still often construe the situation as being a negative or hostile one.

This negative bias can greatly influence the child's ability to interact appropriately with his or her peers because, as in Robert's case, any interactions carried out by the student will be undertaken with a false understanding of the social dynamic. Were Robert to attempt to join the social interaction, he might do so in a manner that was appropriate to a fight (i.e., with aggression), rather than to a peaceful game of soccer. The *Promoting Social Success* curriculum addresses this negative bias through skill-building exercises in which children are encouraged to pay attention to social cues and make accurate interpretations about the emotional states and intentions of others.

Children, especially children with mental retardation or other learning difficulties, often make "mistakes" in other areas of the SIP model as well:

- *Incompatible goals:* Many children have difficulty keeping socially oriented goals in the forefront of their minds. For example, Sherri may really want to remain friends with the other girls at the table, but when faced with a shortage of magic markers, she will forsake her social goal in order to fulfill her desire for the limited resources available. In other words, she may snatch the last marker and have difficulty sharing. The lessons in Unit 5 will help keep Sherri focused on her more socially oriented goals.

- *Reliance on a single strategy:* Children with special needs or other learning difficulties often do not exhibit an ability to generate a variety of strategies to solve a problem. Children with mental retardation or other learning difficulties tend to rely on one or two strategies and apply them to just about every problem more frequently than their peers without disabilities. For example, children with mental retardation are likely to appeal to an adult to solve a problem whether there are other strategies that they could try on their own that might be more successful. According to Leffert and Siperstein (2002), this application may be due to a feeling of powerlessness to influence others in terms of social wishes. However, it may also be due to a desire to rely on an adult's superior abilities to "read" social situations. If this is in fact the case, then it behooves us to improve the child's skill in that area in order to reduce his or her reliance on adults. Lessons such as Assertive Problem-Solving Strategies or Using Compromise as a Strategy in Unit 4 might be good resources in this instance. (See appendix for a complete list of social cognitive skills by lesson.)

CONCLUSION

Perhaps the most important thing we learned as we implemented the *Promoting Social Success* curriculum with more than 400 students was that children such as Riley and Robert sorely need our help. The *Promoting Social Success* curriculum is important because these children are so often overlooked in classrooms full of students with more obvious and more clamorous problems. But the development of social skills plays an enormous role in the academic and emotional futures of young people. We worked with Riley and Robert to build and reinforce their social cognitive abilities and also to provide them with a classroom environment that recognized the importance of positive peer relationships. With the *Promoting Social Success* program, we as educators can offer the same to other students. The *Promoting Social Success* curriculum is an effective tool in creating a more socially competent student and a more socially accepting classroom.

REFERENCES

Crick, N.R., & Dodge, K.A. (1994). A review and reformulation of social-information-processing mechanisms in children's social adjustment. *Psychological Bulletin, 115,* 74–101.

Elias, M.J., Zins, J.E., Weissberg, R.P., Frey, K.S., Greenberg, M.T., Haynes, N.M., et al. (1997). *Promoting social and emotional learning: Guidelines for educators.* Alexandria, VA: Association for Supervision and Curriculum Development.

Kusche, C.A., & Greenberg, M.T. (1994). *The PATHS Curriculum.* Seattle: Developmental Research and Programs.

Leffert, J.S., & Siperstein, G.N. (2002). Social cognition: A key to understanding adaptive behavior in individuals with mild mental retardation. In L.M. Glidden (Ed.), *International review of research in mental retardation* (Vol. 25, pp. 135–182). San Diego: Academic Press.

Lemerise, E.A., & Arsenio, W.F. (2000). An integrated model of emotion process and cognition in social information processing. *Child Development, 71,* 107–118.

APPENDIX

Social Cognitive Skills by Lesson

Social Cognitive Skills	Unit 1	Unit 2	Unit 3	Unit 4	Unit 5
The student recognizes, communicates, and identifies causes of own emotions.	Coming Together to Form the Group Introducing Role Play	Using Feeling Words Understanding Sadness The Difference Between Alone and Lonely Understanding Fear When Are We Surprised? Understanding Love and Hate Understanding Frustration Understanding Anger Different People Have Different Emotions Understanding Emotional Intensity Ways to Calm Down Applying the Calming Down Steps What Helps Me Calm Down? Reviewing Feeling Words			The Ups and Downs of Friendship Sharing Hurt Feelings with Friends The Importance of Forgiveness
The student distinguishes between levels of emotional intensity.		Understanding Love and Hate Understanding Emotional Intensity			
The student calms down in socially appropriate ways.	Introducing Problem-Solving Meetings Practicing Problem-Solving Meetings	Introducing the Red Light Calming Down Steps Practicing the Calming Down Steps Applying the Calming Down Steps Reviewing the Calming Down Steps		Applying the Problem-Solving Steps Reviewing Problem-Solving Skills	The Importance of Forgiveness

Social Cognitive Skills	Unit 1	Unit 2	Unit 3	Unit 4	Unit 5
The student identifies and interprets contextual cues.		Using Feeling Words Feelings in Different Contexts What to Do When You Are Angry Expressing Feelings in Appropriate Ways Ways to Calm Down Practicing the Calming Down Steps	Introducing the Yellow Light Thinking Steps Introducing Body Language Accident or On Purpose? Identifying Intention Is This Mean? How to Tell When Someone is Busy Reviewing Emotional Displays Reviewing Social Situations	Applying the Problem-Solving Steps Reviewing Problem-Solving Skills	What Makes a Good Friend? The Ups and Downs of Friendship Encouraging Empathy Coping with Teasing
The student identifies the feelings of others through facial expressions.	Introducing Role Play Practicing Role Play	Using Feeling Words Identifying Happy Expressions Understanding Fear Understanding Frustration Understanding Anger Feelings in Different Contexts Introducing the Red Light Calming Down Steps Reviewing Feeling Words	Introducing the Yellow Light Thinking Steps Introducing Body Language Interpreting Body Language Accident or On Purpose? Identifying Intention Is This Mean? Reacting to Other People Reviewing Emotional Displays Reviewing Social Situations		The Ups and Downs of Friendship Encouraging Empathy Coping with Teasing
The student identifies the feelings of others through body language.	Introducing Role Play Practicing Role Play	Using Feeling Words Understanding Frustration Understanding Anger Feelings in Different Contexts Introducing the Red Light Calming Down Steps	Introducing the Yellow Light Thinking Steps Introducing Body Language Interpreting Body Language Accident or On Purpose? Identifying Intention Is This Mean?		The Ups and Downs of Friendship Encouraging Empathy Coping with Teasing

Social Cognitive Skills	Unit 1	Unit 2	Unit 3	Unit 4	Unit 5
			Reacting to Other People Reviewing Emotional Displays Reviewing Social Situations		
The student identifies the feelings and sincerity of others through tone of voice.		Using Feeling Words Feelings in Different Contexts	Interpreting Tone of Voice (Feelings) Interpreting Tone of Voice (Sincerity) Identifying Intention Reviewing Emotional Displays Reviewing Social Situations		Coping with Teasing
The student interprets cues from multiple sources (e.g., body language, facial expression) simultaneously.			Introducing the Yellow Light Thinking Steps Introducing Body Language Interpreting Tone of Voice (Feelings) Interpreting Tone of Voice (Sincerity) Accident or On Purpose? Identifying Intention Is This Mean? How to Tell When Someone is Busy Reacting to Other People Reviewing Emotional Displays Reviewing Social Situations	Applying the Problem-Solving Steps Reviewing Problem-Solving Skills	Coping with Teasing
The student interprets the intent of others based on cues.			Accident or On Purpose? Identifying Intention Is This Mean? How to Tell When Someone is Busy Reviewing Social Situations		Give and Take Dealing with Rejection Coping with Teasing

Social Cognitive Skills	Unit 1	Unit 2	Unit 3	Unit 4	Unit 5
The student recognizes when available cues are insufficient to make an interpretation.			Accident or On Purpose? Is This Mean? Reviewing Social Situations		Coping with Teasing
The student predicts the emotional impact of own actions on others.		Different People Have Different Emotions What to Do When You Are Angry Practicing the Calming Down Steps			What Makes a Good Friend? The Importance of Trust The Importance of Compliments
The student identifies desired outcomes in social situations.	Introducing Problem-Solving Meetings Practicing Problem-Solving Meetings	Why Calming Down is Important Ways to Calm Down Practicing the Calming Down Steps		What Does it Mean to Have Goals? Identifying Goals Practicing Identifying Goals Applying the Problem-Solving Steps Reviewing Problem-Solving Skills	Dealing with Rejection
The student understands concept of "goal" and identifies multiple goals.				What Does it Mean to Have Goals? Identifying Goals Practicing Identifying Goals Applying the Problem-Solving Steps Reviewing Problem-Solving Skills	
The student identifies goals which promote social success.	Introducing Problem-Solving Meetings Practicing Problem-Solving Meetings			What Does it Mean to Have Goals? Identifying Goals Practicing Identifying Goals Applying the Problem-Solving Steps Reviewing Problem-Solving Skills	

Social Cognitive Skills	Unit 1	Unit 2	Unit 3	Unit 4	Unit 5
The student identifies assertive, accommodating, and other strategies to achieve desired outcomes.	Introducing Problem-Solving Meetings Practicing Problem-Solving Meetings	Understanding Sadness The Difference Between Alone and Lonely Ways to Calm Down Reviewing the Calming Down Steps What Helps Me Calm Down?		Generating Strategies to Solve a Problem Practicing Generating Strategies Generating Multiple Strategies Assertive Problem-Solving Strategies Using Compromise as a Strategy Applying the Problem-Solving Steps Reviewing Problem-Solving Skills	Communicating with Friends Keeping Friends
The student predicts consequences of actions.		What to Do When You Are Angry Why Calming Down is Important Ways to Calm Down Introducing the Red Light Calming Down Steps Practicing the Calming Down Steps		Predicting Consequences Practicing Strategy Selection Applying the Problem-Solving Steps Reviewing Problem-Solving Skills	The Importance of Trust Keeping Friends
The student evaluates desirability of consequences.		What to Do When You Are Angry Introducing the Red Light Calming Down Steps Practicing the Calming Down Steps		Predicting Consequences Practicing Strategy Selection What to Do If We Don't Reach Our Goal Applying the Problem-Solving Steps Reviewing Problem-Solving Skills	The Importance of Trust Give and Take Keeping Friends
The student selects strategies which promote social success.	Introducing Problem-Solving Meetings Practicing Problem-Solving Meetings	What to Do When You Are Angry Introducing the Red Light Calming Down Steps Practicing the Calming Down Steps	Reacting to Other People	Practicing Generating Strategies Assertive Problem-Solving Strategies Predicting Consequences	Dealing with Rejection The Importance of Compliments

Social Cognitive Skills		Unit 1		Unit 2		Unit 3		Unit 4		Unit 5
				What Helps Me Calm Down?				Practicing Strategy Selection		
								What to Do If We Don't Reach Our Goal		
								Applying the Problem-Solving Steps		
								Reviewing Problem-Solving Skills		
The student evaluates the success of problem-solving plan.								Introducing the Green Light Action Steps		
								How Did it Go?		
								What to Do If We Don't Reach Our Goal		
								Applying the Problem-Solving Steps		
								Reviewing Problem-Solving Skills		

Introductory Lessons

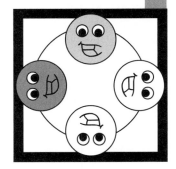

Coming Together
to Form the Group

PURPOSE

To establish the rules of the group when participating in *Promoting Social Success* activities

To have students get to know each other in new ways

STUDENTS WILL

Discuss/generate at least one appropriate rule for the group

Complete a list of their favorite things

MATERIALS

- Index cards

- Pencils

- One manila folder for each student

- Crayons/markers

- *Promoting Social Success* Parent Newsletter: *Introducing the Program*

PRESENTATION OF LESSON

Discussion

Explain to students that the group will meet once per week (or once per day) to talk about things having to do with feelings, friends, and problems that students have in school. Explain that they will also be participating in fun activities on these topics.

Discuss the need to have rules for the group. Begin the discussion by asking students to reiterate their everyday classroom rules. Discuss whether these rules still apply to the *Promoting Social Success* group, even if the group is pulled out from the general classroom. Then ask students to generate a list of appropriate rules. The final list of rules will depend on the classroom but might include versions of the following:

- Keep your desk clear.

- Stay seated unless otherwise directed.

- Use good listening skills (make eye contact, no talking, no fidgeting).

- Respect opinions of others.

- Follow directions.

Write out a list of these rules for the next meeting and make copies so that each student has his or her own list. You might also have a discussion about the consequences of misbehaving during group time.

Writing Activity

Pass out an index card and pencil to each student. Ask the students in the group to put their names on the card and number the card one through six, leaving enough space for answers. Ask the students to list their favorite

1. Animal

2. Color

3. TV show

4. Sport

5. Thing to do with friends

6. Thing to do at recess

When everyone has completed a card, go around the group and have each student share his or her favorite thing by category (everyone says what their favorite TV show is, everyone says what their favorite color is, and so forth). If student attention is waning, then try to vary the format of the activity. You could ask for volunteers to share their favorites, switching the order in which the group shares; take a poll by asking for a show of hands (How many people put baseball as their favorite sport? How many people put kickball?); or ask students to make the noise of their favorite animal for others to guess. You might also vary the categories and ask the students about their favorite subject, book, or food. One way to encourage student attention and cooperation is to ask students to repeat

the favorite item of another student (see the "Challenging" Alternative Presentation).

Wrap-Up

As a closing activity, have students decorate and write their names on the manila folders with crayons or markers. Find a place in the room where students can put the folders. They should bring these folders to each lesson and store any handouts in them.

ALTERNATIVE PRESENTATIONS

Fundamental

- *In addition to the materials already listed, you will need a bag of M&Ms (or any other small treat).*

When establishing rules for the group, provide students with a list of rules on the board that you would like the group to discuss. For the writing activity, if students are unable to write down their favorites, suggest that they write down first initials of their answer, or allow them to share verbally when it is their turn. You can also have the students pick between five and 10 M&Ms, and for each one they eat, they must share something about themselves.

Challenging

Play a memory game in which the students state their favorite thing in a particular category along with the favorite thing named by each student that went previously. For example, a student's response might be, "My favorite animal is a lion, Steve's is a raccoon, April's is an elephant," and so forth.

THROUGHOUT THE DAY

- Post the list of rules in the appropriate place in the classroom.

- Send home the *Promoting Social Success* Parent Newsletter: *Introducing the Program.*

General

Introducing Role Play

PURPOSE

To introduce the term *role play*

To familiarize students with the act of role playing

STUDENTS WILL

Enter the role of actor and present an idea to the group

MATERIALS

- Role-play footprints

- Tape

PRESENTATION OF LESSON

Discussion

Introduce the group to the term *role play*. Explain to students that role play is an activity in which people pretend to be someone or something or pretend to do something. Role playing is like acting. Tape the role-play footprints to the floor and explain that whoever is doing the role play will stand on the footprints to indicate the beginning of the role play. The role play ends when the actor steps off the footprints (the footprints help make a concrete distinction between fantasy and reality).

Role-Play Activity

Model a role play for the students. Stand on the footprints and act out your favorite animal. Have students guess which animal you are. When you step off the footprints, discuss with students how they guessed the animal, along with the importance of stepping on and off the footprints to signal the beginning and end of the role play.

Give each student a chance to role play his or her favorite animal, taking guesses from the rest of the group. You can have students participate in a second round of role playing using the category of a feeling or emotion. Model a role play using the emotion of sadness. When you step off the footprints, discuss with students how they guessed the emotion you were showing, focusing on how you used your face and body to convey this emotion.

ALTERNATIVE PRESENTATIONS

Fundamental

- *In addition to the materials already listed, you will need a stack of small feeling faces showing a variety of emotions.*

Present students with a stack of feeling faces showing different emotions. Each student picks a card and acts out the emotion that is on the card.

Challenging

- *In addition to the materials already listed, you will need chart paper and a marker or chalkboard and chalk.*

Present students with more challenging categories. Together, brainstorm a list of everyday activities such as brushing teeth, getting on the bus, or eating breakfast. Write this list under the heading "Things I Do Everyday" and have students choose a role play from this list to act out.

THROUGHOUT THE DAY

- Encourage students to play Charades with their friends during free time to improve their role-playing skills.

Practicing Role Play

PURPOSE

To practice role-playing situations

To increase student comfort with role play

STUDENTS WILL

Enter the role of actor and present a situation to the group

MATERIALS

- Stack of role-play cards (cut out prior to class)

- Role-play footprints

- Tape

PRESENTATION OF LESSON

Discussion

Review the previous role-playing lesson with students. Review the meaning of the term *role play* (when you pretend to be someone or something else; when you act something out) along with the importance of stepping on and off the role-play footprints to signal the beginning and end of the role play.

Role-Play Activity

Explain to students that this time they will be doing role plays that involve more than one person and that instead of guessing, the rest of the group is going to help figure out what the role play should look like. Present one of the situations from the role-play cards (e.g., playing a board game with a friend) and discuss the various roles with students. Key questions might include

- What kinds of things do we do when we are playing a board game?

- What kinds of things do we say to each other?

Model the role-play situation yourself with a volunteer, using the suggestions the group provides. Be sure to stand on the role-play footprints to begin the role play.

Continue through the role-play cards, discussing the roles in each situation first, then assigning students different roles. Each student should participate in at least one role play. Focus on appropriate social interactions, encouraging students to be friendly and polite.

ALTERNATIVE PRESENTATIONS

Fundamental

- *In addition to the materials already listed, you will need index cards, safety pins, and crayons/markers.*

Create tags to be worn by the people in the role plays by writing the name of the character being portrayed (e.g., "Waiter") and drawing an accompanying picture; pin the name tag to the student performing the role play. Allow the group to continue giving suggestions ("Pretend you're pouring coffee!") during the role play to guide the student. Repeat one or two of the situations with different students instead of acting out a new situation each time.

Challenging

Encourage students to come up with their own role-play situations. Give volunteers a moment or two to decide how they will portray the situation before they present to the group.

THROUGHOUT THE DAY

- Role play a problem or situation that the group has experienced. Discuss the students' reactions and ways to solve the problem.

- Encourage students to play Charades with their friends during free time to improve their role-playing skills.

LESSON REPRODUCIBLE

calling a friend on the telephone	playing basketball with a friend
ordering lunch from a server	playing a board game with a friend
meeting a new student	asking a teacher for help

Introducing Problem-Solving Meetings

PURPOSE

To introduce the purpose and procedures of problem-solving meetings

To decrease the classroom teacher's role in solving student problems

To increase the sense of community within the classroom and provide a forum in which to deal with social problems

To increase students' problem-solving skills

The delayed nature of this problem-solving procedure allows students to cool off and evaluate the importance of the problem over time.

STUDENTS WILL

Practice following the rules and procedures of problem-solving meetings and participate in solving a real problem

MATERIALS

- Small slips of paper

- Pen or pencil

- Shoe box with slit in lid (this will be the group's problem-solving box)

- Small object to identify speaker

- Problem-Solving Meeting Rules poster (you will make this prior to the lesson, see following section)

PRESENTATION OF LESSON

Prior to the Lesson

- Briefly review any particular problems that are relevant to the group (e.g., students being noisy after recess, students not raising their hands before speaking in class).

- Write your name and a brief description of the problem on a piece of paper, and put it in the problem-solving box to use as an example.

- Identify a location for the problem-solving box and for the circle of chairs that the students will use when participating in group meetings.

- Identify an appropriate object to pass around the circle (e.g., a small stuffed animal) that will identify the speaker (only the person who is holding the object may speak).

- Create a poster that lists the rules of the problem-solving meetings; title the poster "Problem-Solving Meeting Rules" and list the three rules listed in the "Discussion" section.

Discussion

Explain to students that they are going to become group problem solvers and take part in problem-solving meetings. The group will meet once (or twice) a week to solve the problems that students have during the day. Today, as an example of how the meetings are run, the group will discuss a problem that you, the teacher, are having.

Display the box and slips of paper and discuss proper use. Explain that students should put their name on the paper and write a brief description of a problem they are having. They should do this during a free moment in the day, not during the lesson. The lid should remain on the box and problems put through the slot. Identify the location of the box in the room.

Discuss the three rules for problem-solving meetings using the Problem-Solving Meeting Rules poster:

1. Always keep six feet on the floor (four chair legs, two student legs).

2. Keep your hands in your lap.

3. Use good listening skills (look at the speaker, only talk when you have the object).

Discuss the proper way to move chairs into a circle. Ask students for ideas about how to best move into a circle (e.g., moving quickly and quietly, holding chair safely, following directions). This is an important discussion as the circle formation sets the tone of the meeting. It is a good idea to ask the students to move in sections—the front of the room forming one part of the circle, then the back of the room forming another part, and so forth. Practice this once or twice before continuing with the problem solving.

Problem-Solving Meeting

Once in a circle, remind students of the rules, then move on to the first stage of the meeting: compliments. Each student will be given the opportunity to compliment another group member when the object is passed to him or her. Briefly discuss compliments and the kinds of things students might say about their peers (see The Importance of Compliments lesson in Unit 5 for further discussion). Emphasize compliments concerning actions (something kind that someone did) or character (a nice quality in someone, something a person is good at) over compliments concerning looks (clothing, hair) or possessions (toys, games).

The teacher begins the compliment process, perhaps complimenting someone on how quietly he or she carried a chair into the circle. Model and explain good passing of the object (pass, not toss), and continue around the circle with compliments. Students may be reluctant to offer compliments at the first meeting, but it is still important to practice passing the speaker object correctly.

After the compliments process, move on to the second stage of the meeting: problem solving.

- Take the slip of paper from the problem-solving box. *(At this point, only your sample problem should be in the box.)*

- Ask the person whose name is on the slip if he or she still feels that it is a problem (you may have to remind the student what he or she wrote). If the answer is no, put the problem aside and pull out another slip. If the answer is yes, continue with the procedure. *(Because the group is using your sample problem as an example, your answer should be yes, the issue is still a problem.)*

What Is Going On?

- Give the student the option of explaining the problem or having you read it aloud. *(Explain to students the problem you are having.)*

What Do I Want to Happen?

- Ask the student to identify his or her goal. *(Explain your goal to the students. For example, "I want my students to settle down after recess and get ready to work.")*

- Once the problem is read or explained, pass the speaker object around the circle one time allowing response (particularly if the problem concerns another student) and discussion. Students may have reactions to, or additional information about, the problem that they would like to share.

What Can I Do?

- Pass the speaker object around one time to generate possible solutions for the problem. Feel free to include your own ideas. Write down each idea.

- Read all of the ideas aloud once, asking students to think about which is the best solution.

- Pass the speaker object around the circle a final time, asking each student to pick a solution that best solves the problem. Tally the votes.

- Read the tally of the votes and check with the owner of the problem to see if he or she feels that the problem has been solved.

- Move on to the next slip of paper, or remind students of proper chair-moving procedures and dismiss in sections.

Things to Remember

- Encourage students to use positive and nonaccusatory language.

- Insist that students not speak unless they are holding the speaker object. If students need more discussion of a problem, pass the speaker object around the circle an additional time.

- The structure of the meetings is very important, especially in the first few meetings. It gives students a framework with which to approach problem solving and encourages thoughtful, nonaccusatory problem solving. As time goes on, the students will be able to apply this procedure to problems outside of the problem-solving meetings.

Thank students for their cooperation, and remind them to use the box during the week. It is important that meetings be held on a regular and frequent basis. Pick an appropriate time once or twice per week and stick with it. Repetition will make the process more comfortable.

   Note: You may not have time to complete this whole procedure during the first meeting. Try to complete as much as possible and schedule another session as soon as possible to complete the process. A natural break may be after the compliments but before the problem-solving procedure.

ALTERNATIVE PRESENTATION

There are no alternative presentations for this lesson. Students of almost all ability levels should be able to participate to some extent.

THROUGHOUT THE DAY

- Try to remove yourself from the role of problem solver during the week. Unless the problem is serious enough to warrant immediate attention, tell students at every opportunity to, "Put it in the box!"

Practicing Problem-Solving Meetings

PURPOSE

To practice implementing problem-solving meetings

To decrease the classroom teacher's role in solving student problems

To increase the sense of community within the classroom and provide a forum in which to deal with social problems

To increase students' problem-solving skills

The delayed nature of this problem-solving procedure allows students to cool off and evaluate the importance of the problem over time

STUDENTS WILL

Practice following the rules and procedures of the problem-solving meetings and participate in solving a real problem

MATERIALS

- Problem-solving box

- Small slips of paper

- Pen or pencil

- Small object to identify speaker

- Steps for Facilitating Problem-Solving Meetings list

- Problem-Solving Meeting Rules poster (from the Introducing Problem-Solving Meetings lesson)

PRESENTATION OF LESSON

Prior to the Lesson

Assess whether students have been using the problem-solving box. If not, write down a problem that has occurred in the classroom and place it in the box for discussion.

Discussion

Ask students if they have any questions or concerns about using the problem-solving box. Review the rules on the poster and the proper chair-moving procedure.

Problem-Solving Meeting

- Direct students to move into the problem-solving circle in sections. Do not hesitate to ask them to repeat this procedure more than once if they are louder or more disorderly than necessary.

- Practice the compliments and problem-solving procedures (see the Steps for Facilitating Problem-Solving Meetings list).

- Dismiss students in sections.

- Thank students for their cooperation and remind them to use the box during the week.

It is important that meetings be held on a regular and frequent basis. Pick an appropriate time once or twice per week and stick with it. Repetition will make the process more comfortable.

ALTERNATIVE PRESENTATION

There are no alternative presentations for this lesson. Students of almost all ability levels should be able to participate to some extent.

THROUGHOUT THE DAY

- Try to remove yourself from the role of problem solver during the week. Unless the problem is serious enough to warrant immediate attention, tell students at every opportunity to, "Put it in the box!"

LESSON REPRODUCIBLE

Steps for Facilitating Problem-Solving Meetings

- Once students are assembled, pass the speaker object around the circle one time for compliments.

- Take a slip of paper from the problem-solving box.

- Ask the person whose name is on the slip if he or she still feels that it is a problem (you may have to remind the student what he or she wrote). If the answer is no, put the problem aside and pull out another slip. If the answer is yes, continue with the procedure.

What Is Going On?

- Give the student the option of explaining the problem or having you read it aloud.

What Do I Want to Happen?

- Ask the student to identify his or her goal.

- Once the problem is read or explained, pass the speaker object around the circle one time allowing response (particularly if the problem concerns another student) and discussion. Students may have reactions to, or additional information about, the problem that they would like to share.

What Can I Do?

- Pass the speaker object around one time to generate possible solutions for the problem. Feel free to include your own ideas. Write down each idea.

- Read all of the ideas aloud once, asking students to think about which is the best solution.

- Pass the speaker object around the circle a final time, asking each student to pick a solution that best solves the problem. Tally the votes.

- Read the tally of the votes and check with the owner of the problem to see if he or she feels that the problem has been solved.

- Move on to the next slip of paper, or remind students of proper chair-moving procedures and dismiss in sections.

Things to Remember

- Encourage students to use positive and nonaccusatory language.

- Insist that students not speak unless they are holding the speaker object. If students need more discussion of a problem, pass the speaker object around the circle an additional time.

- The structure of the meetings is very important, especially in the first few meetings. It gives students a framework with which to approach problem solving and encourages thoughtful, nonaccusatory problem solving. As time goes on, students will be able to apply this procedure to problems outside of the problem-solving meetings.

Understanding Feelings and Actions

EMOTIONAL AND BEHAVIORAL REGULATION

Using Feeling Words

PURPOSE

To introduce a variety of feeling words

To increase students' emotional vocabularies

STUDENTS WILL

Generate examples of feeling words

Identify the feeling words used in the book *Today I Feel Silly & Other Moods that Make My Day* by Jamie Lee Curtis

Identify how they feel at the time of the lesson

MATERIALS

- *Today I Feel Silly* by Jamie Lee Curtis

- Chart paper and a marker or chalkboard and chalk

- One set of small feeling faces per student

- One set of large feeling faces for the teacher

PRESENTATION OF LESSON

Discussion

Explain to students that over the next few weeks the group will be talking a lot about feelings and that it is important to know what words to use when talking about feelings. Brainstorm a list of feeling words together, and write them on the chalkboard or chart paper. The list may include words such as *happy, sad, angry, lonely, frustrated,* and so forth. You may need to prompt students by asking them questions such as

- How would you feel if you were about to go to a party?

- How would you feel if you were home alone and heard a strange noise?

Story Activity

Read *Today I Feel Silly* to your students once from beginning to end. Then, read it again, pausing after each page to write down any feeling words that the students hear in the story. Add these words to your brainstorm list if they are not already listed.

Wrap-Up

As a closing activity, distribute a set of small feeling faces to each student. Identify each feeling together by showing a large feeling face and having students hold up the corresponding small feeling face. Have students demonstrate the emotion they are feeling at the time of this lesson by placing the appropriate feeling face on their desk (students may also pick a face and place it in a more private spot). Students can also draw a picture of themselves and how they are feeling at the time of the lesson. Remind students that the group will be talking more about some of the feelings on the list during the next few lessons.

General

ALTERNATIVE PRESENTATIONS

Fundamental

Begin with a few examples of feeling words (e.g., *happy, sad, angry*), instead of brainstorming. Read the book slowly, writing a list of feeling words from the story as you go.

Challenging

Have students pick an emotion from the list of words that the group has generated and tell about a time they felt that way and why. Discuss the way in which some feelings are enjoyable (happiness, excitement), while others are more uncomfortable (sadness, anger, frustration). Key questions might include

- How is feeling [emotion] different from feeling [emotion]?

- How does it feel inside when you are [emotion]?

- Do you think it is still okay to have those uncomfortable feelings? Why or why not?

THROUGHOUT THE DAY

- Label the emotions you feel throughout the day and have the student do the same, using the large and small feeling faces, respectively. This will help the students recognize a number of different emotions and the real-life situations in which they might arise.

- Display the list of feeling words in the classroom and refer to the feeling terms during lessons throughout this unit.

Identifying Happy Expressions

PURPOSE

To identify faces showing happy expressions through common characteristics

To differentiate between happy expressions and other facial expressions

STUDENTS WILL

Identify and select pictures with happy expressions

Assemble a collage of magazine photos showing happy facial expressions

MATERIALS

- One large happy feeling face

- Role-play footprints

- Tape

- Chart paper and a marker or chalkboard and chalk

- Stack of magazines (enough so each student has one)

- Poster board

- Markers

- Scissors

- Glue

PRESENTATION OF LESSON

Discussion

Show the large happy feeling face to the group and model a happy expression while stepping on the role-play footprints. When you step off the footprints, ask students to identify the emotion you were showing and explain how they came to this conclusion. On the chalkboard or chart paper, write down a list of characteristics that are common to a happy expression (e.g., smile, crinkled eyes, head up). Compare a magazine picture showing a happy face to one showing some other emotion. Discuss the differences between the two (e.g., mouth, eyes, head position), and create a second list of characteristics that are common to the other expression. Ask students to demonstrate a happy face, making sure that the parts of their face are similar to the happy face in the picture.

General

Collage Activity

Explain to the students that they will be making a happy collage. First, have students write the word *happy* in the middle of a piece of poster board, or assist those who cannot. Then give each student a magazine and ask him or her to find pictures showing people with happy expressions. Have the students cut out these pictures and glue them onto their own collage. Remind students about the characteristics of happy expressions, and encourage them to help each other identify appropriate pictures in magazines.

Wrap-Up

Close the lesson with a review of characteristics of a happy expression. Have each student share his or her collage and tell about a time he or she felt happy. This activity can be done using the footprint cutouts. Have the students describe a time they felt happy, then have them step on the footprints to demonstrate what they looked like when they felt this way (mini role play).

ALTERNATIVE PRESENTATIONS

Fundamental

Assist students in selecting appropriate magazine pictures for their personal happy collages by asking them questions about specific pictures. Key questions might include

- What is it about that person's face that makes you think he or she is happy?

- Is that person smiling?

- Is that why you think this person is happy?

Provide any necessary assistance with the cutting and gluing tasks.

Challenging

Make individual happy collages as well as one large emotion poster. Encourage students to find pictures depicting emotions other than happiness, and have the students glue them to a large poster board. Be sure to label the emotion displayed in each picture, and discuss the characteristics of that facial expression.

You can also discuss with students pictures in which the person's expression is neutral or ambiguous. Explain that sometimes it isn't possible to figure out what a person is feeling by looking at his or her face. In these cases, we need to look for other clues, such as the person's body language or what is happening around him or her.

THROUGHOUT THE DAY

- Note aloud the characteristics of happy faces in class materials (e.g., books, worksheets), and verbally identify students with happy facial expressions.

- Have students bring in photographs from home to add to their collages.

- Remind students to identify and display how they are feeling using their set of small feeling faces.

Understanding Sadness

PURPOSE

To identify situations that may cause sadness

To generate coping strategies for dealing with sadness

STUDENTS WILL

Generate at least one example of a situation that can cause sadness

Generate at least one coping strategy

Complete the drawing activity

MATERIALS

- Large sad feeling face

- Role-play footprints

- Tape

- Chart paper and a marker or chalkboard and chalk

- What Can I Do When I'm Sad? title page and blank book pages

- Crayons/markers

PRESENTATION OF LESSON

Discussion

Begin the lesson by showing the large sad feeling face. Stand on the role-play footprints and demonstrate a sad expression and posture. When you step off of the footprints, ask students to describe what emotion you were displaying and what it was about the way you looked that told them you were feeling sad (e.g., head down, eyes looking down). Write the word *sad* on the chalkboard or chart paper. Discuss sadness. Key questions might include

- How does it feel inside when you are sad?

- What kinds of things make you sad?

Together, brainstorm a list of things we do when we are sad, either to express our emotion (cry) or to make ourselves feel better. Discuss with students good strategies for dealing with sadness (ones that do not hurt others and cheer us up) versus strategies that are not as good (ones that hurt others or that end up making us more upset). Examples of good strategies might include

- Writing in a journal

- Talking to a parent or friend

- Listening to music

- Playing a sport

- Giving someone a hug

- Having a snack

Examples of strategies that are not so good might include

- Running away from home

- Locking yourself in a room

- Being mean to your little sister or brother

- Breaking something

Drawing Activity

Explain that the group is going to make a book about being sad. Ask each student to pick one of the strategies from the list that he or she would actually use or try (each strategy can be used more than once by different students) and give each student a blank page from the What Can I Do When I'm Sad? book template. Have the students illustrate their coping strategy (e.g., they might draw a picture of themselves listening to music) and fill in the sentence at the bottom of the page, "When I'm sad, I can ___." Gather together all of the pages and staple them into a book.

Wrap-Up

As a closing activity, ask students to review what they learned about sadness. Summaries should include some mention of what people look like when they are sad, what it feels like inside, situations that can cause us to be sad, and coping strategies for dealing with sadness.

ALTERNATIVE PRESENTATIONS

Fundamental

- *In addition to the materials already listed, you will need* Today I Feel Silly and Other Moods that Make My Day *by Jamie Lee Curtis.*

On (approximately) page 24, the character is feeling sad. Use the picture in the book to ground your discussion of sadness. Discuss how the character looks, why she is feeling sad, and what she could do to make herself feel better. During the bookmaking activity, assist students in completing the sentence at the bottom of the page.

Challenging

Have students think about ways to help each other when another group member is feeling sad. Come up with a group plan of ways to support each other and make students more comfortable with expressing sadness.

THROUGHOUT THE DAY

- Display the book the students made about being sad in an accessible place and encourage students who are having a bad day to use the strategies included in the book.

- Remind students to identify and display how they are feeling using their set of small feeling faces.

What can I do when I'm sad?

When I'm sad, I can _____ .

The Difference Between Alone and Lonely

PURPOSE

To identify the characteristics of, and differences between, the feelings/states of being *alone* and being *lonely*

To identify coping strategies for dealing with loneliness

STUDENTS WILL

Identify at least one activity that they like to do alone, one example of a time they felt lonely, and one coping strategy for dealing with loneliness

Complete a picture of the *One Lonely Day* story character enacting that strategy

MATERIALS

- Chart paper and a marker or chalkboard and chalk

- Large lonely feeling face

- *One Lonely Day* story and illustrations

- Drawing paper

- Crayons/markers

PRESENTATION OF LESSON

Discussion

Explain to students that today you will be discussing two new feeling words. Write the word *alone* on the chalkboard or chart paper and ask students to describe what it means. Write student responses next to the word (possible definitions include "being by yourself" and "when no one else is around"). Discuss with students whether they think being alone is a good thing or a bad thing. Key questions might include, Do you like being by yourself sometimes? Why or why not?

Explain that some people like to do things by themselves, without other people around. For example, some people like to read a book or make chocolate chip cookies. Ask students key questions such as

- What kinds of things do you like to do when you are by yourself?

- How do you feel when you are doing these things by yourself?

Show the large lonely feeling face and write the word *lonely* on the chalkboard or chart paper. Ask students to describe what it means. Write student responses next to the word (possible definitions include "what you feel when you don't want to be alone" and "when you want to play with or talk to someone else but no one is around").

Explain that when we talk about being alone and reading a book, we should think about how we might feel then. Someone might like what he or she is doing and doesn't feel badly being by him- or herself. But sometimes, when people are alone, they don't feel good about it. They might want to go outside to play with other people but no one else is around. Then they may feel lonely. Ask your students, "Can any of you think of times when you felt lonely?"

Story Activity

Read the story, *One Lonely Day*. Discuss how Marnie looks in the second illustration. Ask the students what it is about her face and body that tells us that she is feeling lonely. The story asks students to come up with ideas of how Marnie can make herself feel less lonely. Write down these responses (possibilities include go to the park where there are other kids, ask her mother to do a special activity with her, write a letter to a friend, and so forth). When you are finished reading the story, ask students what Marnie did to make herself feel better.

Drawing Activity

Have each student draw a picture of Marnie using one of the strategies he or she generated.

Wrap-Up

As a closing activity, ask students to review what they learned about being alone and feeling lonely. Summaries should include some mention of the difference between alone and lonely, what people look like when they are lonely, what lonely feels like inside, situations that can cause us to be lonely, and coping strategies for dealing with loneliness.

ALTERNATIVE PRESENTATIONS

Fundamental

- *In addition to the materials already listed, you will need* Today I Feel Silly *by Jamie Lee Curtis.*

On (approximately) page 17, the character is feeling lonely. Use the picture in the book to ground your discussion of loneliness. Discuss how the character looks, why she is feeling lonely, and what she could do to make herself feel better. During the drawing activity, have students draw a picture of a time they felt lonely, instead of drawing a picture about Marnie.

Challenging

Discuss with students the connection between loneliness and sadness, which you discussed in the previous lesson (loneliness is a type of sad feeling—being sad because you are alone).

THROUGHOUT THE DAY

- Check with students who are by themselves during recess or other recreational activities to see if they just want to be alone or if they are feeling lonely. If students report feelings of loneliness, guide them in selecting a strategy to deal with these feelings.

- Remind students to identify and display how they are feeling using their set of small feeling faces.

LESSON REPRODUCIBLE

Marnie looked around her bedroom and sighed. She was tired of playing video games, and her mom wouldn't let her watch any more TV. She could read her new books, but she didn't really feel like it. What she really wanted to do was go outside and play soccer, but that wasn't any fun by herself. Marnie sat on the edge of her bed and tried to figure out why she felt kind of unhappy inside (show illustration #1).

"What is going on?" Marnie asked herself. "Why am I feeling this way?" Suddenly Marnie knew what it was she was feeling—she was lonely! There was no one around for her to play with, and Marnie didn't really want to be by herself right now. Being lonely is what you feel when you want to be with other people. Marnie felt a little better already just by figuring out what was going on inside of her.

Marnie hopped off the bed and went to get something to drink. "Okay, what do I want to happen?" she asked herself as she sat at the kitchen table (show illustration #2). She played with the edge of the placemat and thought, "I think I'd like my friend Owen to come over and play soccer with me. That's what I'd really like to happen right now." Marnie finished her drink.

Say to students: *Now that Marnie has decided what she wants to happen, she has to figure out what to do. If you were Marnie, what would you do to solve her problem? (Have your students generate strategies for achieving Marnie's goal.) Those are some great ideas! Now let's see what Marnie decided to do to solve her problem.*

Marnie's friend Owen lived in an apartment a few floors above Marnie's apartment. Marnie and Owen were such good friends that they usually didn't bother calling each other on the telephone, they just ran up or down the stairs to visit the other one. Marnie decided that the best plan was to ask her mother if she could go upstairs to Owen's apartment and if the two of them could go outside and play soccer in the courtyard. So that's just what she did.

Marnie ran upstairs and knocked on Owen's door (show illustration #3). When Owen opened the door, Marnie could barely speak, she had run so fast. "Do, do you want to go out and play soccer?" Marnie gasped. Owen nodded, he just needed to put his sneakers on, then he'd be ready. It turned out that he had been feeling kind of lonely too. The two friends ended up kicking around the soccer ball all afternoon until they got called in for dinner (show illustration #4).

As she came inside holding the muddy soccer ball, Marnie thought happily, "This turned out to be a great day after all!" (show illustration #5).

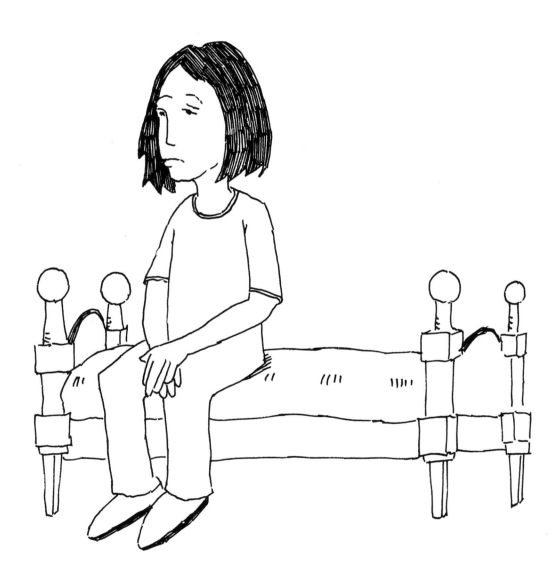

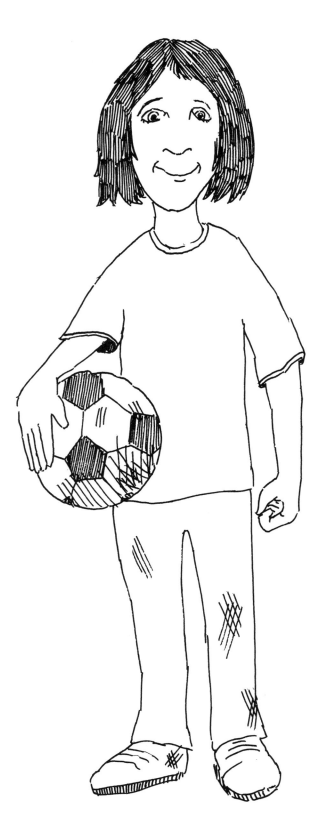

Unit 2: The Difference Between Alone and Lonely

Understanding Fear

PURPOSE

To identify situations that may cause fear

To generate coping strategies for dealing with fear

STUDENTS WILL

Generate at least one example of a situation that can cause fear

Generate at least one coping strategy

Complete the drawing activity

MATERIALS

- Large scared feeling face

- Role-play footprints

- Tape

- Chart paper and a marker or chalkboard and chalk

- *There's a Monster Under My Bed* by James Howe

- Drawing paper

- Crayons/markers

PRESENTATION OF LESSON

Discussion

Begin the lesson by showing the large scared feeling face. Stand on the role-play footprints and demonstrate a scared expression and posture. When you step off of the footprints, ask students to describe what emotion you were dis-

General

playing and what about the way you looked told them you were feeling scared. Write the word *scared* on the chalkboard or chart paper.

Discuss the feeling of being scared. Key questions might include

- How does it feel inside when you are scared?

- What kinds of things make you scared?

Story Activity

Read and discuss *There's a Monster Under My Bed.* Key questions to generate discussion might include

- Does being scared mean that you are a baby? (Simon was afraid of looking like a baby if he called out to his parents.)

- What can you do when you're scared?

Drawing Activity

Show students the last page of the story and ask them to draw a picture of something that they would think was scary if it were under their bed.

Wrap-Up

As a closing activity, ask students to review what they learned about fear. Summaries should include some mention of what people look like when they are scared, what it feels like inside, situations that can cause us to be afraid, and coping strategies for dealing with fear.

ALTERNATIVE PRESENTATIONS

Fundamental

Have students role-play situations in which they have been scared. Encourage students to use their facial expressions and body language to communicate fear to the audience.

Challenging

Encourage students to discuss fears that are more social in nature (e.g., walking into a room of people you don't know, having to make new friends, being scared that others don't like you). Give students the choice of drawing something that would scare them if it were under their bed or drawing something that makes them feel scared in general (or if this seems potentially embarrassing, you might have them draw something of which they used to be scared).

THROUGHOUT THE DAY

- Discuss with parents and students any particular fears the student has, especially school-related fears. This information might act as material for follow-up lessons about fear.

- Remind students to identify and display how they are feeling using their set of small feeling faces.

UNIT 2

When Are We Surprised?

PURPOSE

To identify situations that may cause surprise

STUDENTS WILL

Generate at least one example of a situation that can cause surprise

MATERIALS

- Large surprised feeling face

- Role-play footprints

- Tape

- Chart paper and a marker or chalkboard and chalk

- *No Jumping on the Bed!* by Tedd Arnold

PRESENTATION OF LESSON

Discussion

Begin the lesson by showing the large surprised feeling face. Stand on the role-play footprints and demonstrate a surprised expression and posture. When you step off of the footprints, ask students to describe the emotion you were displaying and what it was about the way you looked that told them you were feeling surprised. Write the word *surprised* on the chalkboard or chart paper.

Story Activity

Read *No Jumping on the Bed!* to students, stopping periodically to discuss the surprised expressions and body language of the different characters. Also discuss with the students what they feel inside when they are surprised.

Role-Play Activity

Ask students for examples of situations that might cause someone to feel surprised. Examples might include

- Walking in to a surprise party

- Finding money in the street

- Having a pop quiz at school

- Making an unexpected goal or basket

Write down the examples generated by students. Explain to students that you will be role playing some of the situations listed. Begin by reviewing the meaning of a role play (pretending to be someone or something else, acting something out) and the significance of the role-play footprints (to signal the beginning and end of the role play). Ask students for suggestions of the kinds of things that someone in the first situation might do or say, then, together with a volunteer, model a role play of the first situation. Repeat this process with each situation, making sure that each student has a chance to participate in at least one role play.

Wrap-Up

As a closing activity, ask students to review what they learned about surprise. Summaries should include some mention of what people look like when they are surprised, what it feels like inside, and situations that can cause us to be surprised.

ALTERNATIVE PRESENTATIONS

Fundamental

- *In addition to the materials already listed, you will need index cards, safety pins, and crayons/markers.*

Create tags to be worn by the people in the role plays by writing the name of the character being portrayed (e.g., birthday girl) and drawing an accompanying picture; pin the name tag to the student performing the role play. Allow the group to continue giving suggestions ("Pretend you're blowing out your birthday candles!") during the role play to guide the student. Repeat one or two of the situations with different students instead of acting out a new situation each time.

Challenging

Encourage students to come up with additional situations when people might feel surprised. Have students role play these situations. Give volunteers a moment or two to decide how they will portray the situation before they present it to the group. Discuss with students the difference between being scared and being surprised. Key questions might include

- What is the difference between being scared and being surprised?

- Which feeling is more comfortable? Why?

THROUGHOUT THE DAY

- Identify and discuss surprising events that occur in or outside of school.

- Remind students to identify and display how they are feeling using their set of small feeling faces.

Understanding Love and Hate

UNIT 2

PURPOSE

To introduce love and hate as the two extremes on an emotional continuum

To elicit information about student experiences with these emotions

STUDENTS WILL

Visually demonstrate the intensity of their feelings about a certain object or subject by writing the names of those objects or subjects in different areas of a feelings meter

MATERIALS

- Copies of the feelings meter (one per student and one for teacher)

- Chart board and a marker or chalkboard and chalk

- Large paper clips

- Subject cards

- Magazines

- Glue

- Scissors

- Love–Hate collage templates

PRESENTATION OF LESSON

Discussion

Explain to students that today you will be discussing two new feeling words and that the group is going to talk about how people can feel different ways about things. For instance, if someone really likes cats, you could say that he or she loves cats. But, if someone doesn't like cats at all, you could say that he or she hates cats. To generate discussion, ask your students to share some things they love and then some things they hate.

Next, show your students the feelings meter and read what it says (*love, like, dislike, hate*). Write the word *cats* at the love end of the spectrum of your meter. Explain to students that people who really love cats would put them at the love end of the spectrum, like you, but people who really hate cats would put them at the other end.

Write the word *love* on the chalkboard or chart paper, and ask students to describe what it means. Write student responses next to the word. Possible definitions include, "When we really, really like something" and "What we feel for our mother and father." Then write the word *hate* on the chalkboard or chart paper and ask students to describe what it means. Write student responses next to the word. Possible definitions include, "The opposite of love" and "What we feel toward something we really don't like." Discuss how the two words are related. Key questions might include

- How are these two words related to each other?

- Are there any feelings in between love and hate?

Feelings Meter Activity

Pass one feelings meter to each student and explain that there are other feelings in between love and hate. Go over the rest of the terms on the meter, eliciting examples of things students feel that way about for each term. After you explain the meter, pass out the paper clips. Hold the subject cards in a fan and ask a student to pick a card. Read the subject and ask each student to put a paper clip on the meter to indicate how he or she feels about that subject. Repeat for additional subjects, having the students move their paper clips accordingly. Make sure to give each student at least one turn to pick a card. Encourage students to look at the variety of answers their classmates give for each subject.

Wrap-Up

As a closing activity, ask students to make a collage that shows things that they love, things that they hate, and several things in between. Have students cut out pictures from magazines and glue them onto the Love–Hate collage template.

ALTERNATIVE PRESENTATIONS

Fundamental

- *In addition to the materials already listed, you will need crayons/markers.*

Simplify the feelings meter by eliminating one or both of the terms in between love and hate. Have students draw a picture of one thing that they love and one thing that hate on the Love–Hate collage template rather than doing the collage activity.

Challenging

Have students read the subject cards themselves and make up their own subjects rather than using the cards. Discuss with students how feelings change in intensity at different times or in different situations. Key questions might include

- Can you love something one day and not like it the next?

- Why do you think this happens?

Students can also write a list of things that they love and hate on the Love–Hate collage template rather than doing the collage activity.

THROUGHOUT THE DAY

- Encourage students to identify and label the intensity of their feelings toward different activities, things, and people. Model this process yourself.

- Remind students to identify and display how they are feeling using their set of small feeling faces.

LESSON REPRODUCIBLES

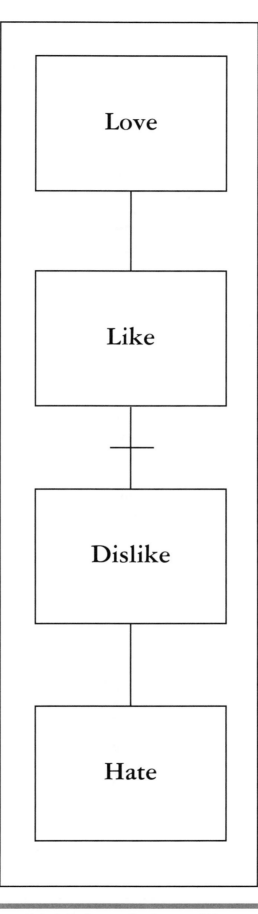

presents	pizza	homework
sisters	snow	reading
family	ice cream	flowers

dogs	swimming	friends
field trips	being sick	tests
brothers	movies	baseball

LOVE–HATE COLLAGE TEMPLATE

Something
I
love

Something
I
hate

Understanding Frustration

PURPOSE

To identify situations that are personally frustrating

STUDENTS WILL

Identify one situation that is personally frustrating

Complete a drawing of this situation

MATERIALS

- Large frustrated feeling face

- Role-play footprints

- Tape

- Chart paper and a marker or chalkboard and chalk

- *Alexander and the Terrible, Horrible, No Good, Very Bad Day* by Judith Viorst

- Crayons/markers

PRESENTATION OF LESSON

Discussion

Begin the lesson by showing the large frustrated feeling face. Stand on the role-play footprints and demonstrate a frustrated expression and posture. When you step off of the footprints, ask students to describe the emotion you were displaying and what it was about the way you looked that told them you were feeling frustrated. Write the word *frustrated* on the chalkboard or chart paper. Discuss the meaning of the word. Write student responses next to the word. Possible definitions include, "When you're trying to do something and you can't" and

General

"When things aren't going the way you want them to." Discuss how it feels inside when you are frustrated.

Story Activity

Read *Alexander and the Terrible, Horrible, No Good, Very Bad Day* and discuss the frustrating things that happened to Alexander throughout the day.

Timeline Activity

On a lengthwise piece of chart paper, draw a timeline like the one below.

morning   lunch   after school   bedtime

Have students come up with examples of frustrating things that have happened to them at different points throughout the day (especially frustrating episodes concerning friends and maintaining friendships), and write a brief description of these things along the timeline. Have students complete drawings along the timeline that illustrate these frustrating events.

Wrap-Up

As a closing activity, ask students to review what they learned about frustration. Summaries should include some mention of what people look like when they are frustrated, what it feels like inside, and situations that can cause people to be frustrated. Explain to students that in future lessons you will be talking more about anger and frustration and how people can deal with these feelings.

ALTERNATIVE PRESENTATIONS

Fundamental

- *In addition to the materials already listed, you will need drawing paper.*

The idea of a timeline might be too complicated for some groups. Brainstorm a list of frustrating events that have happened to students and have them illustrate these events. Compile the drawings into a Very Bad Day book in a chronological order according to when they occurred during the day.

Challenging

Reread the last three sentences of the book. Discuss with students the idea that sometimes just managing to get through a bad day is a coping strategy. Key questions might include

- Why do you think Alexander's mother said that to him?

- How do you think Alexander might feel in the morning?

- Why is it that bad days feel like they go on forever?

THROUGHOUT THE DAY

- Compile a list of examples of situations that have been frustrating for students in the classroom. This list could be helpful for reviewing frustration as a concept and for identifying needs of particular students.

- Identify times during the day that you are feeling frustrated. Describe to students how you are feeling and why. Model appropriate coping strategies.

- Remind students to identify and display how they are feeling using their set of small feeling faces.

Understanding Anger

PURPOSE

To become more familiar with anger

To recognize the feeling of anger in oneself and in others

STUDENTS WILL

Participate in the discussion about how anger makes people feel

Complete the drawing activity

MATERIALS

- Large angry feeling face

- Role-play footprints

- Tape

- Chart paper and a marker or chalkboard and chalk

- *When I'm Angry* by Jane Aaron

- Drawing paper

- Crayons/markers

PRESENTATION OF LESSON

Discussion

Begin the lesson by showing the large angry feeling face. Stand on the role-play footprints and demonstrate an angry expression and posture. When you step off of the footprints, ask students to describe the emotion you were displaying and

General

what it was about the way you looked that told them you were feeling angry. Write the words *angry* and *mad* on the chalkboard or chart paper.

Story Activity

Read *When I'm Angry*. Discuss with students how being angry makes you feel inside. Refer back to pages (approximately) 13–20, and write down the different ways anger can make people feel (big and strong and important, like hitting or shouting mean words, like nobody is listening, like you want to cry). Key questions might include

- The character says that being angry makes him feel different ways sometimes, how does it make you feel inside?

- Why do you think feeling angry can be scary sometimes?

Drawing Activity

Have students draw and share a picture of a time they felt angry.

Wrap-Up

As a closing activity, ask students to review what they learned about anger. Summaries should include some mention of what people look like when they are angry, what it feels like inside, and situations that can cause people to be angry.

ALTERNATIVE PRESENTATIONS

Fundamental

The discussion about how being angry feels inside may be difficult for these students. You may need to focus on how the character's face and body look and feel when he is angry. By discussing the clenched fists and jaw, you may be able to teach that people feel tense and unhappy when angry. Model an angry posture yourself and then have students demonstrate the emotion as well. Key questions during their demonstrations might include

- How do your face and body feel?

- Do you feel relaxed, or do you feel all tight inside?

Challenging

Discuss with students the idea that sometimes people hide their feelings and that we may not be able to tell what emotion they are feeling. Key questions might include

- How could you tell that the character in the book was feeling angry?

- Are there ever times when people feel angry but do not show it?

- How can you let people know what you are feeling?

THROUGHOUT THE DAY

- Encourage students to go beyond simply labeling their emotions to actually describing the more complex issues of how it feels to experience these emotions. Recognizing student anger in all its forms—whether it is expressed through tears, misbehavior, or withdrawal—should help teachers and students deal with this emotion.

- Identify times during the day when you are feeling angry. Describe to students how you are feeling and why. Model appropriate coping strategies.

- Remind students to identify and display how they are feeling using their set of small feeling faces.

Feelings in Different Contexts

PURPOSE

To review feeling words and their meanings within a particular context

To identify situations or events that may cause different emotions

STUDENTS WILL

Provide a definition/description for each feeling word picked and make a connection between that feeling and a particular situation

MATERIALS

- Any visual aids that reflect the chosen contexts in the game

- Stack of small feeling faces

- Small prizes for the game, such as stickers (optional)

- Role-play footprints

- Tape

- Fill in the Feelings worksheet

PRESENTATION OF LESSON

Discussion

Explain to students that you will be reviewing feelings by playing a game. The game will consist of several rounds. For each round, the students will have to provide answers about emotions that occur within a specific context. Possible contexts to use include

- Playing basketball

- Shopping at the mall

- Taking a spelling test

- Playing in the park

It is preferable to choose a context that is personally relevant and of interest to the students. Feel free to use a different context from the ones that are provided here and to change the context for each round of the game (after each student has had one or two turns).

Prior to beginning the game, students might benefit from a visualization exercise in which they are encouraged to picture the context and think of all the things they know about that particular situation. For example, you might say to your students, "Picture a basketball court. There are two baskets and lots of people watching the game. The players are running up and down the court dribbling the ball and shooting into the nets. Pretend that you are one of those players."

You might also present visual reminders, such as a basketball or a picture of a basketball.

Game Activity

Each student will

- Pick a feeling face

- Give a description of the feeling ("Frustrated is when you're trying to do something and you can't")

- Give an example of when a person might experience this feeling within the predetermined context ("A person might feel frustrated in a basketball game when he or she misses both free throws")

If your group is big enough, this game can be played in teams, with the teams receiving points for each appropriate answer. Encourage students to listen to and respect the ideas of others. Students can also receive helper points for assisting another student in coming up with an appropriate answer. Prizes can be given for having the most points, following the rules of the game, and exhibiting good behavior.

Wrap-Up

Role play one of the situations. In the middle of the action, have students freeze and describe how they are feeling at that moment.

ALTERNATIVE PRESENTATIONS

Fundamental

Use a more limited number of emotions and have students pick out the appropriate feeling face from a selection of faces when given an event. Within the context of a basketball game, for example, a student might be asked to pick out the face that best shows how he or she would feel if he or she just made a basket. You may also need to limit the number of different contexts.

Challenging

Have students come up with their own contexts and use more complex emotions, such as disappointed and embarrassed.

THROUGHOUT THE DAY

- At different times during the day, ask students to identify what they are feeling at that moment and why they might be feeling that way. This will help students practice examining and verbalizing their feelings within a variety of contexts.

- Have students complete the Fill in the Feelings worksheet for morning work or homework.

- Remind students to identify and display how they are feeling using their set of small feeling faces.

LESSON REPRODUCIBLE

Name _____ Date _____

Read the story. Complete the sentence with one of the words in the box.

excited	sad	happy
confused	scared	angry

1. "He took my pencil without even asking me!" thought Mark. "I can't believe he did that! He isn't my friend anymore."

   Mark is feeling _____.

2. Juanita could not figure out what was going on. Her friends were not speaking to her and she didn't know why. "I wonder what they are thinking?" she thought to herself.

   Juanita is feeling _____.

3. "I am having such a good day today!" thought Jen. "I got an A on my science test, and I got picked first to play soccer!" Jen had a big smile on her face.

   Jen is feeling _____.

4. Terry's best friend moved away. Terry does not know if he will get to see his friend again. He walked outside but couldn't find anything he wanted to play with.

   Terry is feeling _____.

5. Sherita was home alone. She lay in bed listening to all the noises in her house. She wished that her mother would come back. Sherita shivered as she heard another noise.

   Sherita is feeling _____.

6. Richard couldn't wait until Friday night! He was going to spend the night at his friend's house, and they were going to camp out in the back yard. Richard couldn't sit still because he was thinking about it all day long.

   Richard is feeling _____.

Different People
Have Different Emotions

 UNIT 2

PURPOSE

To explore the concept that different people may feel different emotions in the same situation

STUDENTS WILL

Convey their own emotional reaction to hypothetical situations using Yes/No signs

Participate in a discussion about the answers given by the group

MATERIALS

- Chart paper and a marker or chalkboard and chalk

- Large scared, angry, excited, and sad feeling faces

- Role-play footprints

- Tape

- Yes/No signs (cut in half before handing out to students)

PRESENTATION OF LESSON

Discussion

Before beginning the lesson, write the words *scared*, *angry*, *excited*, and *sad* on the chalkboard or chart paper. Show the large feeling faces to the students and discuss the meanings of the terms, modeling the appropriate facial expression and body language for each emotion using the role-play footprints. Elicit examples from students when they have felt these emotions.

General

Introduce the idea that different people can feel different emotions in the same situations. Perhaps use the example of being scared of mice. Ask the students to raise their hands if they would be scared if a mouse were to run across the floor. There should be some variety in their response, but if not, use the less obvious example of being scared of dogs or black cats.

Survey Activity

Explain to the students that you are going to read a list of questions and that they will get to answer the questions by holding up a sign. Demonstrate this using the question about the mouse. Hand out the Yes/No signs, and answer any questions about the process.

Read the list of questions below, allowing time for students to respond. After each question, tally the responses on the chalkboard or chart paper, noting whether there was general agreement or a lot of disagreement in the students' responses. Be sure to point out that there are some things that tend to make everyone feel a certain way (getting hit often causes anger) and some for which there is a great deal of variability (flying may only scare some people). You do not have to ask every question. Assess the level of interest and proceed accordingly.

1. Would you feel scared if you were home all alone?

2. Would you feel scared if you moved to a new school?

3. Would you feel scared if you had to get up in front of people and sing?

4. Would you feel scared if your room was dark at night?

5. Would you feel scared if you flew on a plane?

6. Would you feel angry if someone borrowed your crayons without asking?

7. Would you feel angry if someone hit you on purpose?

8. Would you feel angry if your brother or sister got more ice cream than you?

9. Would you feel angry if your friend played with someone else?

10. Would you feel angry if you had a babysitter one night?

11. Would you feel excited if you had a peanut butter sandwich in your lunch?

12. Would you feel excited if you were going to a birthday party?

13. Would you feel excited if it was time to go to school?

14. Would you feel excited if you got to use the computer?

15. Would you feel excited if your grandmother came to stay with you?

16. Would you feel sad if your pet got sick?

17. Would you feel sad if you lost your homework?

18. Would you feel sad if your teacher was absent one day?

19. Would you feel sad if you forgot your lunch?

20. Would you feel sad if you didn't get picked to play kickball?

Wrap-Up

Review a question for which there was variability in response and discuss why it might be important to realize that others might not feel the same as you do. For example, if someone is scared or sad, you could comfort him or her. If someone else is angry, you might want to give him or her some time alone. If someone else is excited about something, you don't want to disappoint him or her. Bring up two volunteers who had different responses to one of the questions and pose the question, "Who is right?" Other key questions for discussion might include

- Is there a right answer?

- How do you feel if someone says you're wrong or teases you about how you feel?

- What can you do if this happens?

As a closing activity, role play a situation in which people are experiencing different emotions. Use one of the situations listed previously and encourage students to demonstrate their emotions using their faces and bodies.

ALTERNATIVE PRESENTATIONS

Fundamental

If student attention wanes or your particular group requires a more active lesson, post the Yes/No signs in two different areas of the classroom. Ask students to stand under or near the appropriate sign for each question.

Or, instead of asking, Would you feel . . . if . . . , ask students to pick the feeling face that best shows how they would feel in that particular situation ("How would you feel if . . .?").

Challenging

Have students come up with their own questions for the rest of the group. Focus on misunderstandings that occur in the classroom because students do not anticipate the emotional reactions of others (e.g., students who are reacting differently to report cards). Survey the classroom ("Would you feel scared on report card day?"). Then use this example as the subject of a role play (one student excitedly sharing his or her report card and asking other less excited students about theirs), and discuss ways in which the misunderstanding could be avoided. Repeat the role play, but now have the characters assume a new understanding of other people's feelings (the excited student checking with classmates to see if they are upset).

THROUGHOUT THE DAY

- Point out situations in which people may be feeling a variety of emotions.

- Encourage students to assess the emotional state of their classmates as they interact.

- Remind students to identify and display how they are feeling using their set of small feeling faces.

LESSON REPRODUCIBLE

YES

NO

Understanding Emotional Intensity

PURPOSE

To introduce the idea that people experience emotions of varied intensity

To introduce the idea that different people have feelings of different intensity about the same situation

STUDENTS WILL

Create a feelings thermometer and demonstrate understanding of the concept by answering questions about the intensity of their emotions

MATERIALS

- Chart paper and a marker of chalkboard and chalk

- Completed feelings thermometer (for an example)

- Feelings thermometer template

- Scissors

- Red paper clips/clothespins for each student

- Lists of questions

- Large thermometer drawn on chart paper or the chalkboard

- Squares of red paper for each student

- Tape

PRESENTATION OF LESSON

Discussion

Using the example of a basic emotion such as sad or angry, discuss how you can feel the emotion with different levels of intensity. Key questions might include

- Are there times when you feel a little bit angry?

- What are some of those times?

- Are there times when you feel *really* angry?

- What are those times?

Brainstorm a list of words that people might use to describe the extremes of specific emotions (*grumpy-angry-furious, nervous-scared-terrified, content-happy-delighted*), and write this list on the chalkboard or chart paper. Tell students that today you will be making a feelings thermometer.

Assess the students' knowledge of thermometers and their uses. Key questions might include

- What is a thermometer?

- What does a thermometer measure?

- What does it mean when the mercury is at the bottom or top of the thermometer?

Thermometer Activity

Show the completed thermometer and demonstrate how it is used to display the strength of different emotions. Explain to students that if they want to show that they are only a little angry, they would put the red clip down toward the bottom of the thermometer. If they want to show that they are very angry, they would put the red clip up toward the top of the thermometer.

Next, pass out the feelings thermometer templates and have students color them and cut them out. Once the thermometers are finished (and, ideally, laminated), begin asking students the feeling questions about being scared, angy, and sad on the How Would You Feel If. . . . worksheets. With a large group, begin by asking questions of the whole group and have students share their answers by using their thermometers. Then split the group into pairs and have them ask each other the questions.

Wrap-Up

Conclude the activity with a group thermometer. Have students respond to new questions that are not on the list (e.g., "How scared would you be to go to the dentist?") by taping a red square of paper onto the large thermometer (drawn on chart paper or on the chalkboard) in the appropriate area. The red squares graphically depict the concept that different people can have feelings of different intensity about the same situation.

ALTERNATIVE PRESENTATIONS

Fundamental

- *In addition to the materials already listed, you will need role-play footprints.*

This lesson may need to be divided into more than one session. The first session might entail a discussion of emotional intensity using role plays to illustrate situations evoking emotions of differing intensity. The second session might focus on the construction of the thermometers and a more limited, perhaps more teacher directed, use of them in answering questions.

Challenging

The three-step gradation of feelings (Very, A Little, Not at All) can be adapted to a gradation with finer distinctions for higher-functioning groups.

THROUGHOUT THE DAY

- Make use of these thermometers during conflicts in order to help students assess and communicate the intensity of their feelings.

- Remind students to identify and display how they are feeling using their set of small feeling faces.

LESSON REPRODUCIBLES

1. You had to go down into a really dark basement?

2. Someone threatened to hurt you?

3. You did something wrong and had to go to the principal's office?

4. You were left alone in the house at night?

5. You had to go to a new school where you didn't know anyone?

6. Your best friend found out that you lied to him or her?

7. You got lost in a big department store?

8. You heard gunshots outside your house?

9. You had to take a big math test?

10. You had to go on an airplane?

11. You were watching a horror movie?

12. The lights went out?

13. You thought your friends were mad at you?

14. You and your brother or sister got in a big fight?

15. You saw a big spider?

16. Your teacher yelled at the class?

17. You lost your winter coat and you thought your mom would be mad at you?

18. You had to get a shot at the doctor's office?

19. Someone had on a scary costume on Halloween?

20. An older student pushed you?

1.   Someone took your pencil without asking?

2.   You didn't get any dessert with your lunch?

3.   You didn't get to watch the television show you wanted to?

4.   Someone made fun of you during gym class?

5.   Your teacher always called on someone else?

6.   You got a bad grade on your test?

7.   You couldn't find your hat?

8.   Your friend didn't want to play the board game you wanted to play?

9.   Your mom punished you for something you didn't do?

10.   Your father didn't show up when he said he would?

11.   You couldn't go to the park because it was raining?

12.   No one would listen to you?

13.   The class party got cancelled because people weren't behaving?

14.   You were the last person picked for a kickball team?

15.   Someone called you a bad name?

16.   Someone made fun of your clothes?

17.   Other people were teasing your friend?

18.   Your mom wouldn't let you go outside and play?

19.   There were no magic markers left, so you didn't get any?

20.   You never got a turn to be a line leader?

1. Your best friend said that you weren't his or her best friend anymore?

2. You had to move away and leave your house?

3. Your dog or cat got sick?

4. You made your mother upset?

5. Your teacher yelled at you?

6. You didn't get a part in the class play?

7. Someone made fun of the way you look?

8. You thought your mom liked your brother or sister better than she liked you?

9. Your grandmother died?

10. You missed your favorite television show one night?

11. You lost your new watch?

12. You didn't get any Valentine's Day cards?

13. Your friend moved to another school?

14. Your aunt didn't come over like she said she would?

15. You missed your basketball game because you were sick?

16. You got into trouble for fighting with your brother or sister?

17. Someone said that they didn't want to play with you?

18. No one came to your birthday party?

19. You thought your teacher didn't like you?

20. You spilled food on your clothes?

Promoting Social Success: A Curriculum for Children with Special Needs by Gary N. Siperstein & Emily Paige Rickards
© 2004 by Paul H. Brookes Publishing Co. Inc. All rights reserved.
www.brookespublishing.com   1-800-638-3775

What to Do When You Are Angry

PURPOSE

To differentiate between feelings and behaviors

To introduce the qualitative judgment that all feelings are okay to have, but that all behaviors are not necessarily okay

To identify positive ways to express uncomfortable emotions such as anger and frustration

STUDENTS WILL

Correctly categorize at least one behavior (that is an expression of anger or frustration) as being either appropriate (okay) or inappropriate (not okay)

MATERIALS

- Large angry and frustrated feeling faces

- Chart paper and a marker or chalkboard and chalk

- Poster board with columns labeled "Okay" and "Not Okay"

- Action cards

- Strategies to Deal with Emotions worksheet

PRESENTATION OF LESSON

Discussion

Show the large angry and frustrated feeling faces. Briefly review the terms *angry* and *frustrated.* Write the words on the chalkboard or chart paper, and ask students to describe what they mean. Write the student responses next to the words.

General

Discuss the fact that all feelings are okay to have, including the uncomfortable ones such as being angry, frustrated, sad, and scared. Key questions might include

- How many of you have felt all of these emotions?

- Is it okay to feel all of these emotions? Why or why not?

Visually demonstrate this concept on the chalkboard or chart paper:

Feelings

↓

Okay

Make the distinction between feelings and behaviors either by discussion or by a brief role play (angry feeling [facial and body expression] versus angry behavior [pushing someone]). Explain to students that it is okay to feel these emotions, but sometimes when we are really angry or frustrated (refer back to the feeling intensity thermometers completed in the previous lesson), we do things that are not okay. Visually demonstrate this concept on the chalkboard or chart paper:

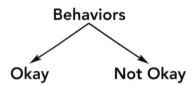

Behaviors

Okay   **Not Okay**

Discuss with students a rule that we can use to determine whether a behavior is okay or not okay when you are angry or frustrated. Key questions might include

- What kinds of things do people do when they are angry?

- What happens when they do these things?

- How do you like to be treated by other people?

The final version of the rule should be similar to the following: It is not okay to behave in a way that might hurt someone else or yourself (hurting someone includes hurt feelings as well as physical harm). Asking, "Could someone get hurt?" can act as a guide when making the decision about behaviors.

Okay/Not Okay Activity

Place the action cards on the table, action side down. Pick up one of the cards and read the action aloud. Ask, "Could someone get hurt?" If the answer is no, have a student tape the card on the "Okay" side of the chalkboard. If the answer is yes, the student should tape the card on the "Not Okay" side. Continue through the rest of the cards, reading the action and taping the card on the correct side of the chalkboard.

If your students have difficulty deciding where the card belongs, remind them to ask the question, "Could someone get hurt?" to help them decide.

Wrap-Up

As a closing activity, ask students to review what they learned about behaviors that are okay and not okay. Summaries should include some mention of what makes a behavior inappropriate (the possibility of someone getting hurt).

ALTERNATIVE PRESENTATIONS

Fundamental

The concepts in this lesson may need to be broken down into several lessons. The first lesson should focus on the difference between feelings and behaviors. The second lesson should focus on a rule to use to decide if a behavior is appropriate (okay). The third lesson should focus on using that rule to make determinations in specific instances (using the behavior/action cards).

Challenging

Have students come up with their own examples of appropriate (okay) and inappropriate (not okay) behaviors.

THROUGHOUT THE DAY

- Students need to have their emotions validated and recognized even when their behaviors are inappropriate. Practice using such statements as, "I know that you are angry with me right now, but you are not allowed to kick people" or "I know that you are angry right now. Maybe a good thing for you to do is pound on this pillow."

- Have students complete the Strategies to Deal with Emotions worksheet for morning work or homework.

- Remind students to identify and display how they are feeling using their set of small feeling faces.

Lesson

LESSON REPRODUCIBLES

Listen to good music	Have a snack	Talk to your parents
Count to 10 slowly	Run around outside	Walk away
Yell at someone	Go to a quiet place	Punch a pillow

Punch a wall	Throw a dish	Push your friend
Slam the door	Poke holes in your shirt	Kick your dog
Read a book	Rip up blank paper	Rip up a book

Name _____ Date _____

Circle the emotion you had and the strategy you used to cope with that emotion. Have your parent or teacher sign the paper when you are done.

Feeling I had   What I did

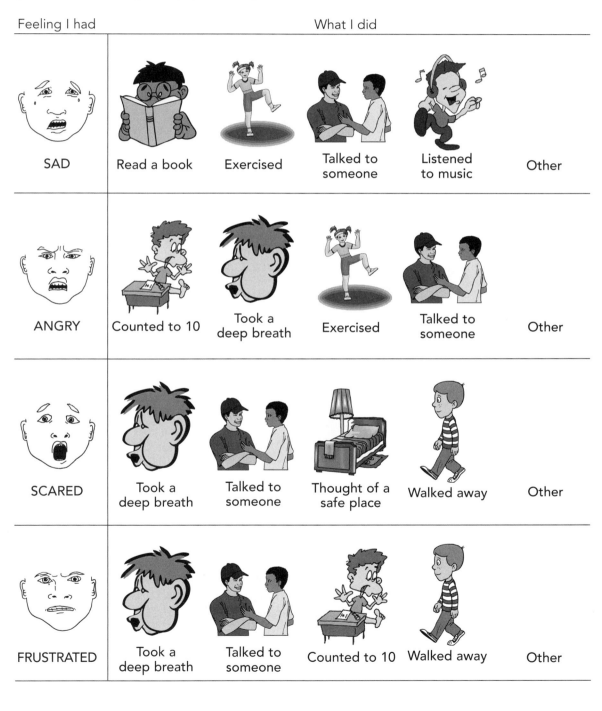

SAD	Read a book	Exercised	Talked to someone	Listened to music	Other
ANGRY	Counted to 10	Took a deep breath	Exercised	Talked to someone	Other
SCARED	Took a deep breath	Talked to someone	Thought of a safe place	Walked away	Other
FRUSTRATED	Took a deep breath	Talked to someone	Counted to 10	Walked away	Other

Parent/Teacher initials _____

Expressing Feelings in Appropriate Ways

PURPOSE

To review the qualitative judgment that all feelings are okay to have but that not all behaviors are necessarily okay

Note: This lesson reviews concepts introduced in the What to Do When You Are Angry *lesson but also asks students to evaluate behaviors related to emotions other than anger and frustration. This evaluation taps into students' social knowledge regarding appropriate behavior.*

STUDENTS WILL

Make at least one accurate determination as to whether a behavior is okay and provide a reasonable rationale for that determination

MATERIALS

- Chart paper and a marker or chalkboard and chalk

- Okay/Not Okay signs (cut in half before handing out to students)

- Pictures ("Yelling at Someone," "Drawing a Mean Picture," "Breaking Someone's Pencil," "Taking Someone's Ball," "Punching a Pillow," and "Telling Dad You're Frustrated")

- Expressing Feelings Role-Play Situations list

- Role-play footprints

- Tape

PRESENTATION OF LESSON

Discussion

Review the idea that all feelings are okay to have, including the uncomfortable ones such as being angry, sad, and scared. Key questions might include

- How many of you have felt all of these emotions?

- Is it okay to feel all of these emotions? Why or why not?

Visually demonstrate this concept on the chalkboard or chart paper:

Review the distinction between feelings and behaviors either by discussion or by a brief role play (angry feeling [facial and body expression] versus angry behavior [pushing someone]). Explain that it is okay to feel any emotion, but that some behaviors are not okay. Visually demonstrate this concept on the chalkboard or chart paper:

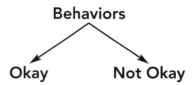

Hand out Okay/Not Okay signs, or have the students make their own (signs should be on separate pieces of paper—students may become confused by a sign with words on both sides).

Okay/Not Okay Activity

Begin by showing the pictures to students. Ask the students to describe what is going on in each picture and how the people in the picture are feeling. For each behavior depicted, have students hold up their signs to indicate if they think it is an okay behavior or not.

After reviewing the pictures, create a table on the chalkboard or chart paper that has two columns ("Okay" and "Not Okay"). Using the list of behaviors that follows, read each behavior to the students and have them tell you which column to place each behavior in. Review with students the rule that we use to determine whether a behavior is okay or not okay when you are angry or frustrated (it is not okay to behave in a way that might hurt someone else or yourself—hurting someone includes hurt feelings as well as physical harm), and make sure students give a rationale for their decisions each time. Write a brief description of each behavior in the proper column.

Okay and Not Okay Behaviors

1. Steven is upset, so he is trying to calm down and relax a little. Is that an okay thing to do? Why or why not?

2. Randy feels mad, so he is hitting his brother. Do you think that is an okay thing to do? Why or why not?

3. Marie feels angry, so she is crumpling up some old magazines she found. Is that an okay thing to do? Why or why not?

4. Jason feels mad, so he is letting his friend know how he feels. He is saying, "I feel very mad at you right now." Is that an okay thing to do? Why or why not?

5. Shannon feels happy, so she gives a stranger a big hug. Is that an okay thing to do? Why or why not?

6. Keisha feels angry, so she is tearing up another girl's notebook. Is that an okay thing to do? Why or why not?

7. Wendell is excited, so he calls his friend on the telephone. Is that an okay thing to do? Why or why not?

8. Barry feels angry, so he is fighting with one of the kids in his class. Is that an okay thing to do? Why or why not?

9. Quentin is excited, so he jumps up and yells in the library. Is that an okay thing to do? Why or why not?

10. Amanda is mad, so she is making fun of her cousin and calling him "stupid." Is that an okay thing to do? Why or why not?

11. Crystal is unhappy, so she is fooling around during class and bothering other students. Are those okay things to do? Why or why not?

12. Daniel is mad at his friends, so he is going to play by himself for a while. Is that an okay thing to do? Why or why not?

13. Robert feels mad, so he is throwing stones at a dog. Is that an okay thing to do? Why or why not?

14. José is mad, so he is drawing a picture about what happened that made him angry. Is that an okay thing to do? Why or why not?

15. Rosa feels happy, so she does a cartwheel in the backyard. Is that an okay thing to do? Why or why not?

16. Laura feels sad, so she runs away from home without telling anyone. Is that an okay thing to do? Why or why not?

17. Gail is upset with her mother, so she is telling her mother, "I'd like to talk to you about why I'm angry right now." Is that an okay thing to do? Why or why not?

18. Christina is happy, so she laughs when someone else makes a mistake. Is that an okay thing to do? Why or why not?

Role-Play Activity

Using the Expressing Feelings Role-Play Situations list, have students role play situations in which one character is feeling angry or frustrated. The audience must decide if the character's behavior is okay or not okay.

Wrap-Up

As a closing activity, ask students to review what they learned about behaviors that are okay and not okay. Summaries should include some mention of what makes a behavior inappropriate (the possibility of someone getting hurt).

ALTERNATIVE PRESENTATIONS

Fundamental

You may need to illustrate the behaviors on the list with a brief role play. If student attention wanes or your particular group requires a more active lesson, post Okay/Not Okay signs in two different areas of the classroom. Ask students to stand under or near the appropriate sign for each behavior.

Challenging

Have students come up with their own examples of appropriate (okay) and inappropriate (not okay) behaviors. Encourage students to discuss behaviors that are not easily categorized as okay or not okay. Some examples of these behaviors might be

- Yelling loudly in frustration

- Hugging someone that you know slightly

- Not letting someone play with you

- Telling the teacher when someone does something to you

THROUGHOUT THE DAY

- Identify times during the day that you are feeling angry or frustrated. Describe to students how you are feeling and why. Model appropriate (okay) coping strategies and behaviors.

- Students may need corrective feedback regarding inappropriate behaviors such as hugging strangers.

- Remind students to identify and display how they are feeling using their set of small feeling faces.

LESSON REPRODUCIBLES

Okay

Not
Okay

YELLING AT SOMEONE

Unit 2: Expressing Feelings in Appropriate Ways

DRAWING A MEAN PICTURE

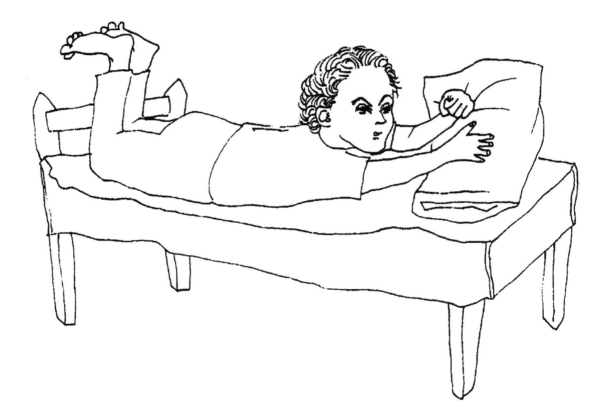

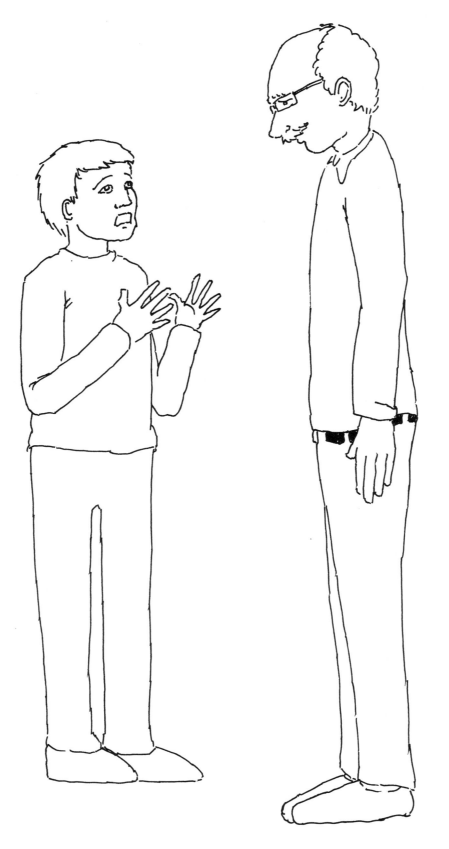

Role-Play Situations

Role Play #1:
Characters: Julie, her teacher, her classmate

Julie had a bad morning, and she comes to school feeling angry. She goofs off during class, interrupting her teacher and bothering her classmates.

Role Play #2:
Characters: Linda, her friend, another student

Linda and her friend are walking to class and another student bumps into Linda by accident. All of Linda's homework papers fall to the floor. Linda yells at the student, "Stupid! Watch where you're going!"

Role Play #3:
Characters: Sara, her mother, her brother

Sara's mother yells at Sara because she has not cleaned up her room. Sara feels angry. She stomps into the other room and pushes her brother as she walks by him and says, "Get out of my way!"

Role Play #4:
Characters: Maria, her teacher, her classmate

Maria's teacher tells her that she has to stay in for recess to finish her homework. Her classmate teases her by saying, "Ha, ha, you missed recess!" Maria is angry. She takes a blank piece of paper and rips it up.

Role Play #5:
Characters: Mario, Joe, the teacher

Joe grabs Mario's pencil without asking Mario if he can borrow it. Mario tells Joe that he doesn't like what Joe did and takes a deep breath to calm himself down.

Role Play #6:
Characters: Alex, his father, the dog

Alex's father sends Alex to bed early, and he misses his favorite television show. Alex tears up his father's newspaper and throws the pieces at the dog.

Role Play #7:
Characters: John, his friend, his other friend

John gets into a fight with two of his friends. He tells them that he's mad at them and walks away to play by himself.

Why Calming Down Is Important

PURPOSE

To define what it means to *calm down*

To provide a rationale for the importance of calming down and how calming down can have a positive impact on students' lives

To predict the consequences of certain behaviors

STUDENTS WILL

Participate in the discussion

Complete the drawing activity

MATERIALS

- Chart paper and a marker or chalkboard and chalk

- *Johnny and a Busy Santa Claus* story and illustrations

- *Melody the Kickball Queen* story and illustrations

- Drawing paper

- Crayons/markers

PRESENTATION OF LESSON

Discussion

Write *calm down* on the chalkboard or chart paper. Ask students to explain what this phrase means. Write student responses next to the words. Key questions might include

- What does it mean when someone says for you to calm down?

- When do your mother and father tell you that you need to calm down?

Explain to students that people need to calm down sometimes when they are angry or frustrated and sometimes when they are too excited or being too loud. Explain that calming down is a way to be less upset or to "chill out." It is important for people to have their feelings under control before they can start to deal with any problems in the best possible way.

Story Activity

Explain to the students that today you are going to read them two stories. They are going to be special stories, each with two endings. The stories are about times when someone is upset and angry because something happens that he or she does not like. In one ending, the character calms down, and in the other ending, the character does not calm down.

Read *Johnny and a Busy Santa Claus*. Ask students to summarize the events that occurred in the two endings. Discuss with the students what was different about the two endings. What did Johnny do differently, and how did that make a difference?

Read *Melody the Kickball Queen*. Ask students to summarize the events that occurred in the two endings. Discuss with students what Melody did differently in the two endings and what happened because of her actions. Emphasize the benefits of calming down (e.g., friendly relationships with classmates, spending enjoyable time with a parent, avoiding trouble with teachers).

Drawing Activity

Have students think of a time when they got upset. Have students draw a picture or write a story describing what happened when they calmed down or what would have happened if they had been successful at calming down.

Wrap-Up

As a closing activity, ask students to review what they learned about why calming down is important. Summaries should include some mention of avoiding trouble and maintaining good relationships with others.

ALTERNATIVE PRESENTATIONS

Fundamental

* *In addition to the materials already listed, you will need role-play footprints and tape.*

This activity may need to be split into two lessons. Read one story for each lesson. Summarize the events of each ending. Role play the story two times, once with each ending. Discuss with students why calming down was important for that character, and have students pick one ending to illustrate.

Challenging

Have students make up a third story with their own two endings. Have students illustrate what happens when the character does calm down and what happens when the character does not calm down.

THROUGHOUT THE DAY

- After an upsetting incident has occurred, have students think about what might have happened if they had calmed down. Or, if students successfully calmed down, congratulate them and ask them what they think might have happened if they had not calmed down. This will help them stay aware of the positive and negative effects of their actions.

- Remind students to identify and display how they are feeling using their set of small feeling faces.

LESSON REPRODUCIBLES

Johnny loved Christmas. It was his favorite time of year. Everyone in his family was home around Christmas, and they all got presents for each other. However, Johnny always got his best present from Santa Claus. Santa always knew just what he wanted the most. This was not magic, though, because Johnny got to tell Santa every year what he wanted (show illustration #1). Johnny and his mom would go to the Meadowbrook Mall where Santa stayed every year for one weekend before Christmas.

This year Johnny was very excited because he knew just what he wanted, and he couldn't wait to tell Santa. He could barely sit still as they drove to the mall to tell Santa his wish. Johnny's mom told him they would have to hurry because she had an important doctor's appointment to go to after they met with Santa. When they got to the mall and went into Santa's workshop, Johnny's heart sank. There was a long line of kids waiting to tell Santa what they wanted for Christmas (show illustration #2). It was going to take too long to wait in the line! Johnny's mom had to go to the doctor's office. Johnny's mom told him that they had to leave but that he could write Santa a letter with her help, and they would leave it for Santa right by the fireplace on Christmas Eve (show illustration #3). Johnny was upset (show illustration #4). This is not what he had been hoping for; he had been so excited that he would talk to Santa in person.

Ending 1: Johnny could feel himself getting upset because things weren't turning out the way he wanted them to. He took a deep breath and tried to relax his body a little bit. He said to his mom, "I really wish I got to talk to Santa Claus. I feel all disappointed and mad." Johnny's mom was very proud of Johnny for calming down and telling her how he felt.

That evening Johnny and his mom got to spend some special time together writing a fun letter to Santa. Johnny got to practice his writing. He was happy that he wrote a letter to Santa, even though he was disappointed that he didn't get to talk to him in person.

Ending 2: (Re-read paragraph just before first ending.) "No, no, no!" said Johnny. "I want to talk to Santa." Johnny was yelling and pulling on his mother's arm. The other kids in line, and even Santa, were looking at him because he was making such a big fuss. Johnny didn't notice. He was too upset to think about what he was doing.

When Johnny's mom finally dragged him out of the mall, Johnny started to feel embarrassed. He had been so loud and rude in front of all those kids and Santa Claus. And to make things worse, his mother was angry with him and didn't let him play with the box of toys at the doctor's office.

JOHNNY AND A BUSY SANTA CLAUS ILLUSTRATION #2

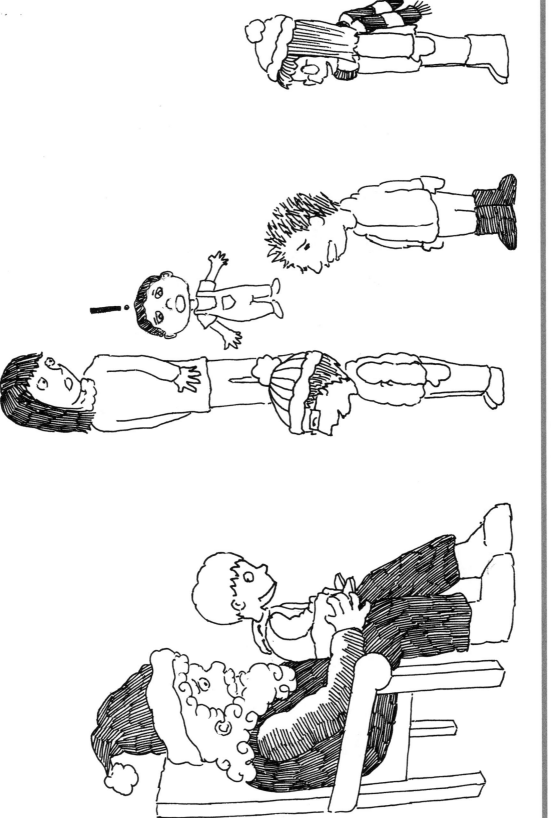

Unit 2: Why Calming Down Is Important

Melody was an excellent kickball player and loved to play kickball. She would practice every day after school by kicking the ball inside her garage against the garage door (show illustration #1). She would also practice throwing and catching against the garage door. When she was playing a real game, she kicked the ball over the outfielders' heads almost every time. She would run around the bases before anyone was even close to the ball.

During the winter there was too much snow for the kids to play kickball at school. Melody would dream about the first warm spring day when they could go outside and play kickball again. The winter seemed like it would never end.

Finally, one warm day in April, the teacher told the class that they could go outside for recess and play kickball. Melody was so excited. She knew that she was the best player in the class. She was proud of being the best player because she practiced so much at home. It was something that she worked hard to accomplish.

When they were outside, the teacher chose two captains to pick teams, Gary and Jim. All of the students waited against the backstop to be chosen on a team (show illustration #2). Melody was certain she would be chosen first. Gary got to choose first. Instead of picking Melody, he picked Paul. Gary and Paul were best friends. Melody was upset. She was a much better player than Paul. Why did Gary choose Paul first? Then it was Jim's turn to choose a player. Jim's best friend was Bob, and Jim picked him. Melody was furious.

Ending 1: When Melody was upset, she knew that taking deep breaths and counting to 10 actually helped her calm down. Melody took a deep breath and told herself to calm down. She would end up being chosen eventually. As she was counting to herself, she heard her name being called. Jim had chosen her for his team.

After all of the kids had been picked for a team, they started the game. Melody's team was up first. Melody was so excited and happy. She could barely wait to get up and kick the ball. When it was her turn to kick the ball, Melody blasted the ball (show illustration #3). It went over the fence, and she got a home run!

Ending 2: (Re-read paragraph just before first ending) Melody started to yell at Gary and Jim. "You don't know how to pick teams. You are both stupid. I hope you both lose!" Melody's teacher, Mr. Benson, did not let his students use that kind of language. He wanted all of the students to be kind to each other. Mr. Benson took Melody away from the students and the kickball game and told her to sit on the bench (show illustration #4). He told her that she was not going to be able to play kickball today because she could not control her temper. Melody was very angry and disappointed. She had messed up her first chance to play kickball and now she had to watch everyone else play.

MELODY THE KICKBALL QUEEN ILLUSTRATION #1

Unit 2: Why Calming Down Is Important

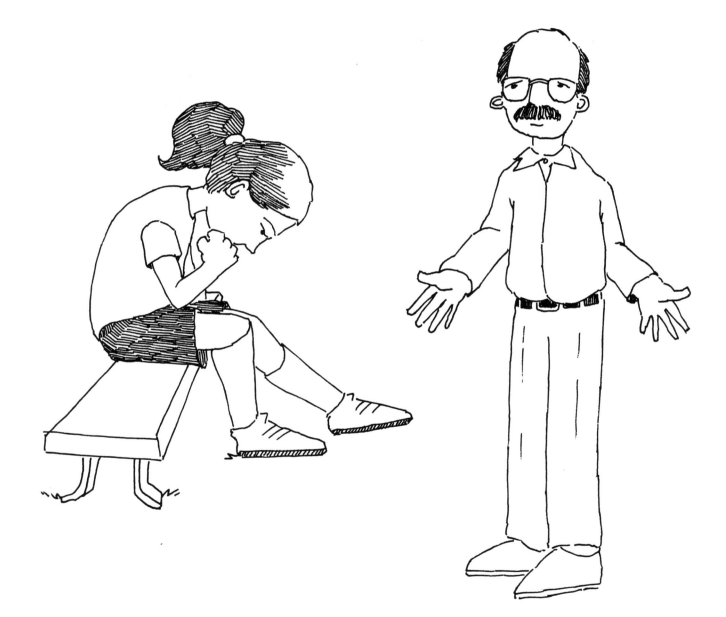

Unit 2: Why Calming Down Is Important

Ways to Calm Down

PURPOSE

To identify situations that cause students to become upset and/or excited

To identify strategies that will help students calm down

STUDENTS WILL

Identify at least one situation that has upset them

Identify at least one strategy for calming down

MATERIALS

- Chart paper and a marker or chalkboard and chalk

- *When I'm Angry* by Jane Aaron

- Calming Down worksheet

- Crayons/markers

PRESENTATION OF LESSON

Discussion

Review with students what it means to *calm down*. Key questions might include

- What does it mean when someone says for you to calm down?

- When do your mother and father tell you that you need to calm down?

Explain to students that people need to calm down sometimes when they are angry or frustrated and sometimes when they are too excited or being too loud. Explain that calming down is a way to be less upset or to "chill out." It is important for people to have their feelings under control before they can start to deal with any problems in the best possible way. Make a list on the chalkboard or chart paper of examples of when students have been upset or excited and have had to calm down. Label this list "Times I Needed to Calm Down."

Story Activity

Show *When I'm Angry* (also used in the Understanding Anger lesson in this unit) to students and explain that you will be reading the book again today, but this time you want them to listen for the ways the character calms himself down. When you are finished reading, ask students for examples of how the character calmed himself down. Make a list of strategies the character used under the heading "Ways to Calm Down." Your list should contain the following strategies:

- Talked to his mom and told her how he felt

- Let his toys do the shouting

- Was by himself

- Had something to eat

- Looked at a book

When the list of strategies from the book is complete, ask students for other ideas that might help people calm down. Add these suggestions to the list.

Drawing Activity

Have students complete the Calming Down worksheet. On the left side of the paper, have students draw and label a picture of a time they were upset or excited. On the right side of the paper, have students draw a picture of themselves using one of the calming down strategies. Students should be encouraged to use the lists they generated as guides.

ALTERNATIVE PRESENTATIONS

Fundamental

- *In addition to the materials already listed, you will need role-play footprints and tape.*

Students may need you to model the use of a calming down strategy. Prior to the drawing activity, pick a situation in which someone is likely to become overly excited, and role play the use of a calming down strategy (e.g., getting into an argument with a friend and going off by yourself before you say something you'd regret).

Challenging

Have students identify the best calming down strategies for each situation in the "Times I Needed to Calm Down" list. Go through the list of situations and have them discuss what calming down strategy might be most appropriate in each situation (e.g., listening to music or making a snack might not work at school, but counting to 10 would be appropriate). Connect the chosen strategy, or strategies, to the situation with a bright colored marker.

THROUGHOUT THE DAY

- Post the list of calming down strategies in the classroom and refer to it when needed.

- Remind students to identify and display how they are feeling using their set of small feeling faces.

LESSON REPRODUCIBLE

Name _____ Date _____

Complete the sentences below and draw a picture for each.

I needed to calm down when _____

_____

[ ]

To calm myself down I _____

_____

Introducing the
Red Light Calming Down Steps

PURPOSE

To introduce and practice the three steps for calming down

STUDENTS WILL

Complete the calming down reminder cards

MATERIALS

- List of calming down strategies generated in the Ways to Calm Down lesson

- Stoplight posters #1 and #2

- Crayons/markers

- Blank index cards

- Role-play footprints

- Tape

- Using the Calming Down Steps worksheet

- *Promoting Social Success* Parent Newsletter: *The Calming Down Steps*

PRESENTATION OF LESSON

Discussion

Review with students the list of calming down strategies generated in the Ways to Calm Down lesson. Explain to students that although there are many strategies that people use to calm down, this lesson is going to focus on one way in particular because it can help in almost every situation.

Pass out copies of Stoplight poster #1. Have each student appropriately color the stoplight red, yellow, and green. Discuss the meaning of the red, yellow, and green lights, both in the real world (stop, slow down, go) and in terms of needing to calm down (stop and calm down, slow down and think, go try your plan). Key questions might include

- What does it mean when you see a red/yellow/green light?

- What do you think a red light might mean if we are angry or excited?

On this poster, the red light tells us to stop and calm down. Explain to students that you will be focusing on the calming down steps next to the red light for the next few lessons and that later you will be discussing the steps next to the yellow and green lights. (You can show them Stoplight poster #2 at this point so that they understand that there are more steps to come.) Display the posters around the room or in other areas easily accessible to students.

Together read, discuss, and practice the three steps for calming down. Key questions might include

- Why is it important to keep your hands to yourself?

- How does taking a deep breath help you calm down?

Reminder Card Activity

The Stoplight posters may be too large for students to display on their desks; however, small reminder cards can be taped in the corner of students' desks or tables to act as personal reminders of the calming down steps. Reminder cards could also be carried with students as they move throughout the school day. Hand out the index cards and explain to students that the cards are going to act as reminders to help them calm down when needed. Students should number the cards 1, 2, 3 and copy down the three steps for calming down from the poster. Whenever they are upset or overexcited, they can look at or pull out the cards to remind themselves of how to calm down.

Wrap-Up

As a closing activity, use a role play to model the way in which students can use their reminder cards. For example, you are playing in the living room of your house and running around the room. Your mother yells for you to calm down, so you take out your card to remind yourself how to do this. Demonstrate the three steps.

ALTERNATIVE PRESENTATIONS

Fundamental

Students who cannot read will need additional practice of the three steps. Have students practice the three steps throughout the day and week. Students can create reminder cards with drawings of the stoplight on them.

Challenging

Discuss with students why these three steps are appropriate for almost any situation. Encourage students to come up with their own ideas of situations in which they can utilize the reminder cards and the three steps. Role play these situations.

THROUGHOUT THE DAY

- Using the three calming down steps in real-life situations is a very hard thing to teach. It is important that the red light be referred to, and rewards given for performing the calming down steps, during the regular school day. Encourage students to use their reminder cards.

- Model the calming down steps yourself when you are upset.

- Have students complete the Using the Calming Down Steps worksheet for morning work or homework.

- Remind students to identify and display how they are feeling using their set of small feeling faces.

- Send home the *Promoting Social Success* Parent Newsletter: *The Calming Down Steps* and a copy of Stoplight poster #1.

LESSON REPRODUCIBLE

Name _____ Date _____

Directions: Circle one picture that describes a time when you were upset. Then draw a picture of yourself calming down.

I was upset when...

I argued with someone   I got in trouble   Someone teased me

I got in a fight   Other:

Then I Calmed Down!

The Calming Down Steps Are:

1. Stop

2. Keep Hands to Yourself

3. Take a Deep Breath

Here is a picture of me calming down.

```


```

Parent/Teacher initials _____

What happened? _____

Practicing the
Calming Down Steps

UNIT 2

PURPOSE

To practice the three steps for calming down in a role-play situation

To identify the importance of calming down by examining consequences of behavior

STUDENTS WILL

Participate in at least one role play

Practice the three steps for calming down

MATERIALS

- Stoplight poster #1

- Calming Down Steps Role-Play Situations list

- Role-play footprints

- Tape

PRESENTATION OF LESSON

Discussion

Using Stoplight poster #1, review with students the meaning of the red light and the three steps for calming down.

General

Role-Play Activity

Explain to students that today they will be performing role plays from the Calming Down Steps Role-Play Situations list. Each role play will be performed two times, once to illustrate what can happen if you don't calm down and once to illustrate what can happen if you do calm down.

Perform one of the role plays with yourself as the main character first, then allow students to reenact the scene. Modeling the role play yourself first will give students ideas for possible actions and dialogue and will help prevent students from becoming too carried away with their role play anger.

After each role play, discuss the consequences of the character's actions and how taking the time to calm down was beneficial to him or her.

Wrap-Up

Practice the three calming down steps as a group.

ALTERNATIVE PRESENTATIONS

Fundamental

Perform only one of the role plays and stop after the first ending (when the character remains upset) to summarize the events. Have students predict what might have happened if the character had used the three steps for calming down and then role play their suggestions. Summarize the events of the second ending, when the character calms down.

Challenging

Have students come up with their own role-play situations. Discuss two possible endings first, then have the students enact the situations.

THROUGHOUT THE DAY

- Cue students to use the three steps for calming down with reminders such as, "Red light!" or "Go to the stoplight!"

- After an upsetting incident has occurred, have students think about what might have happened if they had calmed down. Or, if students successfully calmed down, congratulate them and ask them what they think might have happened if they had not calmed down. This will help them stay aware of the positive and negative effects of their actions.

- Model using the steps yourself when you are upset.

- Remind students to identify and display how they are feeling using their set of small feeling faces.

LESSON REPRODUCIBLE

Role-Play Situations

Role Play #1:

Students are on the playground at recess and have just finished up a kickball game. One student is unable to find his jacket where he left it.

a) The student accuses teammates of stealing the jacket. The other students become angry and walk away, leaving the student without friends and still without the jacket.

b) The student uses the three steps for calming down and thinks out loud about what could have happened to the jacket and about the best way to solve the problem. The student asks his teammates to help search for the jacket, and it is discovered that someone took it by mistake thinking that it was hers.

Role Play #2:

A student is told by her mother that she cannot ride her bike today because she did not do her chores.

a) Angry and resentful, the student defies her mother and takes off on her bike. When she returns, she gets in more trouble and is not allowed to play outside at all.

b) The student uses the three steps for calming down and thinks out loud about her choices and which is the best thing to do. She decides to do her chores quickly and then ask again for permission to ride her bike.

Role Play #3:

A group of students is running around outside on the playground. Some of the students begin to throw rocks against the building.

a) The student joins in the rock throwing. When another student is hurt by a piece of rock, all the students throwing rocks get in trouble.

b) The student uses the three steps for calming down and thinks out loud about what might happen if she were to join the other students and throw rocks. She goes to play with other friends and is praised by a teacher for playing nicely.

Applying the Calming Down Steps

PURPOSE

To reinforce and practice the three steps for calming down

STUDENTS WILL

Correctly perform the three steps for calming down when cued to do so

MATERIALS

- Stoplight poster #1

- Role-play footprints

- Tape

- Chart paper and a marker or a chalkboard and chalk

PRESENTATION OF LESSON

Discussion

Review with students that people need to calm down sometimes when they are angry or frustrated and sometimes when they are too excited or being too loud. Calming down is a way to be less upset or to "chill out." It is important for people to have their feelings under control before they can start to deal with any problems in the best possible way. Review some of the situations that students previously identified as causing anger or excitement.

Role-Play Activity

Using Stoplight poster #1, practice the calming down steps with students. Ask students how they would feel if there were no gym/PE that day because it was snowing. Have students show you how they would feel using their faces and bodies.

Most of your students will most likely look very upset. Explain to students that feeling upset is sometimes a signal that we need to calm down. Perform the three steps for calming down together, and ask your students how they feel when you are done. Have your students show you how they feel with their faces and bodies.

Note that most of your students look much calmer after completing the calming down steps. Have your students brainstorm a list of fun things to do during your open gym period, and list these activities on the chalkboard or chart paper.

Next, have your students pretend that they have just finished a great game during their open gym time. During the game everyone was running around and having fun. Ask your students how they would feel after this game. Have your students show you how they would feel using their faces and bodies.

Explain to students that it is now time to get back to work, so they will need to calm down. Practice the three steps for calming down together. Ask your students how they feel after completing the calming down steps and have them show you with their faces and bodies.

Remind your students that it is important to calm down so that they can think clearly. Explain to the students that you will be focusing on solving problems using the steps next to the yellow and green lights in more detail later on.

Simon Says Activity

Play a game very similar to Simon Says. You will be asking students to perform an action, such as running in place, by saying, "Simon says, run in place." Students will then perform the action until you say, "Red light!" At this time, the students must say and perform the three steps for calming down and wait for the next command. If you fail to mention "Simon says" and simply say something such as, "Run in place," then the students are to remain still (and calm). Any student who begins the action by mistake is "out" and will rejoin after one action.

Wrap-Up

Students may become too rowdy during the game. This can be an excellent opportunity to apply the calming down steps to real-life arousal. Require students to perform the three steps and calm down before moving onto your next activity.

ALTERNATIVE PRESENTATIONS

There are no alternative presentations for this lesson. Students of all abilities should be able to participate in the activities to some extent.

THROUGHOUT THE DAY

- Make an ongoing attempt to refer to Stoplight poster #1 throughout the day during periods of arousal. Transitions after recess, gym, and lunch are often difficult. Use the three steps for calming down to ease these transitions.

- Provide positive feedback or rewards to students who practice the steps, either independently or when directed.

- Remind students to identify and display how they are feeling using their set of small feeling faces.

Reviewing the Calming Down Steps

PURPOSE

To reinforce and practice the three steps for calming down

STUDENTS WILL

Correctly perform the three steps for calming down when cued to do so

MATERIALS

- Stoplight poster #1

- I Used the Calming Down Steps! worksheet

PRESENTATION OF LESSON

Prompt the students to think of a situation that might result in a need to calm down. Verbalize the situation and then ask the students the cue question, "Okay, you have just . . ., and you are very upset/excited. What do you do?" Use the Stoplight poster #1 as a visual reminder. Examples may include, "You have just . . ."

General

- Had an argument with another student

- Come in from recess

- Had a bad day

ALTERNATIVE PRESENTATION

For All Groups

If the students are having difficulty, practice the steps repeatedly together. Set the stage again by verbalizing a situation ("Okay, you have just . . . , and you are very upset/excited . . .") and asking "What do you do?"

THROUGHOUT THE DAY

- Discuss with students their use of the three steps at home or other places outside of school.

- Have students complete the I Used the Calming Down Steps! worksheet for morning work or homework.

- Remind students to identify and display how they are feeling using their set of small feeling faces.

LESSON REPRODUCIBLE

Name _____ Date _____

I got upset when _____

_____

Then, I used the calming down steps. They are:

1. _____

2. _____

3. _____

After I was calm, I _____

_____

Here is a picture of what I did after I calmed down.

What Helps Me Calm Down?

PURPOSE

To reinforce the identification of emotions in oneself and reinforce the identification of situations that may cause emotional arousal

To identify people and places that may aid in the calming down process

STUDENTS WILL

Complete a Chill Out book

MATERIALS

- Finished Chill Out book example

- Blank Chill Out book pages

- Crayons/markers

- Stapler

PRESENTATION OF LESSON

Prior to the lesson

Make your own Chill Out book to use as an example for the group.

Discussion

Explain that today, and perhaps for the next few meetings, the group will be making Chill Out books. The books will illustrate different aspects of calming down such as where students go to calm down and who can help them when they need to calm down.

Book Activity

Show a finished example of a Chill Out book, and go through each page explaining your drawings. Call special attention to the details of the drawings such as facial expressions, labeling of people and places, and so forth. Hand out crayons/markers and blank Chill Out book pages for each student.

Wrap-Up

As a final activity, decorate book covers and have each child share a favorite page (if large group) or whole book (if small group or group with good attention span).

ALTERNATIVE PRESENTATIONS

Fundamental

Instead of presenting students with a complete book, address each page individually.

Challenging

Have students read and discuss their books with a younger student.

THROUGHOUT THE DAY

- Encourage students to share the books with other teachers or adults so that the adults are aware of students' safe places and people.

- Add finished Chill Out books to classroom libraries or have children take them home to share with parents.

- Remind students to identify and display how they are feeling using their set of small feeling faces.

LESSON REPRODUCIBLE

Chill Out Book

by _____

Draw a picture of your face and body when you are angry or upset.

Draw a picture of your face and body when you are calm and relaxed.

Draw a picture of something that happened that made you upset or angry.

What happened? _____

Draw a picture of a place you go when you are upset or angry.

Where did you go? _____

Draw a picture of people who could help you calm down.

Who could help you calm down?
_____

Draw a picture of yourself using the three steps to calm down.

The three steps for calming down are:

1. _____

2. _____

3. _____

Reviewing Feeling Words

PURPOSE

To review a variety of feeling words

To review emotions as conveyed through facial expressions

STUDENTS WILL

Provide at least one example of a feeling word during the brainstorm

Participate in the game activity and identify emotions using written and pictorial cues

Provide examples of times they felt particular emotions

MATERIALS

- Chart paper and a marker or chalkboard and chalk

- List of feeling words from Using Feeling Words lesson (optional)

- Sets of small feeling face cards (cut out one set for every three to four students) with two of each feeling

- Tape

PRESENTATION OF LESSON

Discussion

Explain to students that today's activity will review many of the feelings that the group has discussed. Brainstorm a list of feeling words together and write this list on the chalkboard or chart paper, or refer to the list of feeling words from the Using Feeling Words lesson. Together, choose approximately 10 emotions that the group has dealt with in previous lessons.

Game Activity

Play Memory with the small feeling faces that correspond with the 10 emotions that your group has chosen. Place the feeling faces (two of each emotion) face down on the table. Each student takes a turn picking two faces, identifying the emotions conveyed in each. If the cards match, the student keeps the pair and gives an example of a time he or she felt that emotion. Then the student takes a second turn. If the cards do not match, the student puts the faces back down and the game moves on to the next person. Repeat until all cards have been matched.

Wrap-Up

It may be possible to play multiple games with your group. During the final game, have students who find feeling face pairs tape one of the faces next to the appropriate word on the brainstormed list and give an example of a time when he or she felt that emotion. Display the poster (if your list is on chart paper) with the words and faces in the classroom.

ALTERNATIVE PRESENTATIONS

Fundamental

Have students take turns "going fish"—picking one face at a time from the pile and giving the appropriate response. Or, play the matching game with a reduced number of pairs.

Challenging

Vary the responses that students must give when they find a pair. Instead of having them give an example of a time they felt that emotion, ask them to respond to one of the following prompts:

- Show me what someone might look like if they were feeling [emotion]. (Facial expression or body language)

- What can you do if you are feeling [emotion]? (Coping strategy)

- Why/when might you make someone else feel [emotion]? (Causes of emotions)

THROUGHOUT THE DAY

- Label the emotions that you and the students feel throughout the day, applying feeling words to real-life situations. This will help the students recognize a number of different emotions and the situations in which they might occur.

- Remind students to identify and display how they are feeling using their set of small feeling faces.

Unit 2: Reviewing Feeling Words

Using Social Information

NOTICING AND INTERPRETING CUES

UNIT 3

Introducing the
Yellow Light Thinking Steps

PURPOSE

To introduce Step #4 on Stoplight poster #2

To review the identification of feelings in oneself and in others

STUDENTS WILL

Identify at least one emotion displayed in movie clip

Identify a problem they have experienced

Identify the feelings of others and of themselves within the context of that
problem

MATERIALS

- Stoplight poster #2

- Role-play footprints

- Tape

- *Fantasia* video or other movie clip

- TV/VCR

- Chart paper and a marker or chalkboard and chalk

- *Promoting Social Success* Parent Newsletter: *Figuring Out Social Situations*

PRESENTATION OF LESSON

Discussion

Briefly review the three steps for calming down, then explain to the group that today you are going to move on to the yellow light on Stoplight poster #2. Ask the class what they think yellow might mean. Key questions might include

- What does it mean when you see a yellow light?

- What do you think a yellow light might mean if you have calmed down but you still have a problem?

Reiterate to students that the red light on the stoplight poster tells us to stop and calm down. Explain to them that yellow equals going slowly, which equals thinking. Once people are calm, they need to think about things so that they can figure out what is going on and what to do. Tell your students that you are going to spend the next few weeks on Step #4 next to the yellow light. Pass out copies of Stoplight poster #2. Have each student appropriately color the stoplight red, yellow, and green.

Explain that once you are calm, you need to ask yourself, "What is going on?" One way to figure out what is going on is to pay attention to what other people are feeling. Knowing how other people are feeling can give you important information about what to do.

Role-Play Activity

Role play a situation in which someone approaches you and asks you to play a game. You respond, "I don't want to play." Respond once with a sad tone of voice and sad body language. Respond a second time with an angry tone of voice and angry body language. Discuss why it is important for the other student to figure out how you are feeling and how the student might react differently in the two situations.

Video Activity

Show a clip from *Fantasia* (or another movie that presents a character feeling different emotions), pausing periodically to have students identify the emotions being displayed. At different points in *Fantasia*, Mickey is tired, frustrated, happy, scared (for a good deal of the clip), and sorry. Discuss with students how they knew Mickey was feeling those particular emotions. What were the cues that told students how Mickey was feeling?

Discussion

Once the clip is finished, tell students that it is sometimes harder to identify feelings when you are having a problem than when someone else is having a problem. When a problem happens to you, you might be too upset or confused to think clearly. But, when you are having a problem, it is important to identify your own feelings as well as those of others. Write the questions, "What am I feeling?" and "What are others feeling?" on the chalkboard or chart paper.

Ask students for examples of problems that have happened to them. Have students answer the two questions on the chalkboard for that particular problem. Model this process first yourself (for example, "I once got yelled at by my boss at work. I felt upset and like I was going to cry. I think my boss was feeling tired and cranky."). Go around the group and share answers.

Wrap-Up

End the lesson by reviewing Step #4 on Stoplight poster #2 and reiterating that a good way to figure out what is going on is to pay attention to what you are feeling and to what other people are feeling.

ALTERNATIVE PRESENTATIONS

Fundamental

Have students use their set of small feeling faces to describe their own and others' emotions.

Challenging

Discuss with students the importance of paying attention to the emotions of others. Key questions might include

- How does paying attention to the emotions of others help you figure out what is going on?

- If you wanted to ask your teacher for help with something, why might it be important to pay attention to how he or she is feeling?

- What would you do differently if your teacher was angry/happy/sad?

THROUGHOUT THE DAY

- When problems occur, remind students to gather information by paying attention to their own feelings and the feelings of others.

- Remind students to use the three steps for calming down on Stoplight poster #1.

- Send home the *Promoting Social Success* Parent Newsletter: *Figuring Out Social Situations* and a copy of Stoplight poster #2.

Introducing Body Language

PURPOSE

To review Step #4 on Stoplight poster #2

To introduce and define the term *body language* as it relates to Step #4

STUDENTS WILL

Give plausible explanations as to what is happening in several pictures using the characters' body language as clues

MATERIALS

- Stoplight poster #2

- Chart paper and a marker or chalkboard and chalk

- Role-play footprints

- Tape

- Series of photographs showing body language

- Pictures depicting problem situations ("Tracking Mud in the House," "Finding Out a Grade," "Waiting for the Principal," "Giving Her Flowers," and "Watching from a Window")

PRESENTATION OF LESSON

Discussion

Review Steps #1–4 on Stoplight poster #2. Emphasize to students that once they are calm, they need to think about things so they can figure out what is going on and what to do. Once they are calm, they need to ask themselves, "What is going on?" Explain to students that one way to figure out what is going on is to pay attention to what they are feeling and to what other people are feeling.

Write the term *body language* on the chalkboard or chart paper. Ask students if anyone knows what it means. Break down the term into its two parts, and explain to students that body language is like talking with your body.

Role-Play Activity

Explain to students that people use body language to show others how they are feeling. For example, people can tell others they are sad by using words or their bodies.

Using the role-play footprints, model a sad face and body—drooping shoulders, bringing head down, exhibiting a sad expression, kicking aimlessly at the floor, and so forth. Ask students to guess how you are feeling and to identify the specific characteristics of your pose that led them to their conclusion. Model an angry pose and ask students what you are telling them with your body language.

Explain that you can figure out how people are feeling based on how they look, which can help you figure out what is going on.

Body Language Activity

Show students the body language photographs. Ask them to describe how the person might be feeling, and ask them how the person's body language acted as clues. Focus on facial expression, posture, head tilt, and so forth as they relate to each photograph.

Next, show students the pictures depicting different problem situations, and explain that they are going to use the people's body language to help figure out what is going on in each picture. Have students describe what is going on using the characters' body language as clues.

Wrap-Up

Review and practice Steps #1–4 on Stoplight poster #2.

ALTERNATIVE PRESENTATIONS

Fundamental

This lesson may need to be broken down into two lessons. The first lesson should focus on an examination of the photographs and modeling of expressive poses. The second lesson should focus on the pictures and the interpretation of the characters' body language.

Challenging

Discuss the importance of paying attention to the body language of others. Key questions might include

- How does paying attention to others' body language help you figure out what is going on?

- If you wanted to ask your father for help with something, why is it important to pay attention to how he looks?

- What would you do differently if your father looked busy/angry/tired? (Role play these situations.)

THROUGHOUT THE DAY

- Ask students to examine both their own body language and that of others during conflicts or when involved in social interactions.

- Have students bring photographs from home that show people expressing emotions with their body language.

LESSON REPRODUCIBLES

Unit 3: Introducing Body Language

Interpreting Body Language

PURPOSE

To explore the concept of body language as it relates to expressing emotions

UNIT 3

STUDENTS WILL

Accurately identify emotions displayed in photographs and in physical
demonstrations

MATERIALS

- Role-play footprints

- Tape

- Series of photographs showing body language

- Body Language Role-Play Situations list

- Stoplight poster #2

PRESENTATION OF LESSON

Discussion

Review the concept of body language with the students (body language is like
talking with your body).

Remind students that they can figure out how other people are feeling
based on how the other people look. Knowing how other people are feeling can
give the students important information about what to do.

Using the role-play footprints, model for students how a person communi-
cates with body language. Display sadness—drooping shoulders, bringing head
down, exhibiting a sad expression, kicking aimlessly at the floor, and so forth.
Ask students to guess how you are feeling and to identify the specific characteristics of your pose that led them to their conclusions.

Review the body language photographs and ask students to describe how each person might be feeling and how the person's body language acted as clues. Focus on facial expression, posture, head tilt, and so forth, as they relate to each photograph.

Role-Play Activity

Explain to the students that you will be practicing using body language during some role-play situations. Have students act out several situations from the Body Language Role-Play Situations list. When you say "freeze," have the group discuss what emotions the actors are conveying with their bodies.

Wrap-Up

Review and practice Steps #1–4 on Stoplight poster #2.

ALTERNATIVE PRESENTATIONS

Fundamental

Students may have difficulty in the role-play situations without more practice modeling individual emotions first. Have students select an emotion to act out and have the rest of the group guess what emotion they are showing. This can be done in a game format—have students stand in a circle and decide on an emotion (e.g., sad, mad). Instruct the students to close their eyes while you walk around the circle and tap one student on the shoulder. The student you tapped will use his or her body to display the emotion the group chose. Instruct the students to open their eyes. Students then try to identify which person is displaying the particular emotion.

Challenging

- *In addition to the materials already listed, you will need the artist/statue cards, the emotions cards (surprised, sad, angry, excited, scared), and safety pins.*

Have students play a Statues game in which partners are given a card with a particular emotion. One partner is designated as the artist, the other as the statue. Pin the role cards onto the students' shirts. The artist molds the statue into a pose that displays that emotion. The statue should be instructed to hold any position or expression designed by the artist.

THROUGHOUT THE DAY

- Ask students to examine their own body language and that of others during conflicts or when involved in social interactions.

- Play Feeling Charades during a free period. Have students model body language that depicts a certain emotion while their classmates guess the emotion.

LESSON REPRODUCIBLES

Role-Play Situations

Role Play #1:

Your best friend tells you that she has found a new best friend and doesn't want to play with you any more.

Role Play #2:

You and your friend are playing on the beach.

Role Play #3:

A group of kids are playing a game. You want to join them, but you are worried that they may not want you to play.

Role Play #4:

Your teacher just handed back a math test. One of your classmates is teasing you because you got a bad grade.

Role Play #5:

It is your birthday, and someone throws a surprise party for you.

Role Play #6:

It is your birthday. You get many presents, but you do not get the one thing that you really wanted.

statue	artist	artist
sad	surprised	statue
scared	excited	angry

Interpreting
Tone of Voice (Feelings)

PURPOSE

UNIT 3

To teach students to consider tone of voice when evaluating the mood of another person

STUDENTS WILL

Identify an emotional tone of voice versus a neutral tone of voice (during activity with first and second sets of recordings)

Identify individual emotions conveyed by tone of voice (during activity with third set of recordings)

MATERIALS

- Tape of recordings (to be recorded prior to the lesson, see next section)

- Stoplight poster #2

- Chart paper and a marker or chalkboard and chalk

- Set of large feeling faces

- Tape player

- Blank audiotape

PRESENTATION OF LESSON

Prior to the Lesson

Record yourself or someone else saying the series of statements below. Be sure to use the appropriate emotional tone of voice. Remember to record each statement twice (once in a neutral tone, once in an angry or excited tone) for Sets A and B.

List of Recorded Statements

Set A: Angry versus not angry

- "Emily, I'd like you to come over here, now." (first = neutral, second = angry)

- "I don't want you to go to the store." (first = neutral, second = angry)

- "It's my turn. I was here first." (first = angry, second = neutral)

Set B: Excited versus not excited

- "The circus is coming to town." (first = excited, second = neutral)

- "I'm going to the movies tonight." (first = neutral, second = excited)

- "Recess is in 10 minutes." (first = excited, second = neutral)

Set C: Which emotion do you hear?

- "I miss my father. I wish I could be with him." (sad)

- "I don't understand my math homework." (frustrated)

- "Ahhh! A mouse just ran across the floor." (scared/surprised)

- "I can't wait until my birthday party." (happy/excited)

- "I can't believe you broke my favorite toy." (angry)

- "I'm going to be late for school because I have to wait in this line." (frustrated)

- "I don't want to go in there. It's dark in there." (scared/nervous)

- "I wish you could come over today, I miss you." (sad)

Discussion

Review with students Step #4 on Stoplight poster #2. Explain to students that today you are going to be talking about another clue (in addition to body language) that they can use to help figure out what is going on. Write *tone of voice* on the chalkboard or chart paper, and ask students if they know what it means. Explain that tone of voice is how someone sounds when they are speaking and that you can often tell how someone is feeling from their tone of voice.

Repeat the following in a neutral tone and in an angry tone, and ask students to describe the difference: "I want some cookies."

Tape Recording Activity

The first set of recordings deals with an angry tone of voice. Show the large angry feeling face. Listen to the first two recordings (of the same statement). Ask students to tell you which of the statements sounded angry and how they could tell. Repeat for the second and third statements.

The second set of recordings deals with an excited tone of voice. Display the large excited feeling face. Listen to the first two recordings (of the same statement). Ask students to tell you which statement sounds excited and how they could tell. Repeat for the second and third statements.

For the third group of recordings, you will be asking the students to identify the emotion conveyed in the tone of voice. To prepare for this, display the large angry, frustrated, sad, scared, happy, and excited feeling faces. Play the statements for the students and ask them to identify the emotion conveyed.

Wrap-Up

As a closing activity, ask students to record their own tone of voice statements. Practice an angry statement as a group, focusing on tone of voice, then ask for a volunteer to record the statement. Practice a scared statement as a group, and allow another student to record his or her voice. Repeat with other emotions until all students are on tape, then play the recordings to the group.

ALTERNATIVE PRESENTATIONS

Fundamental

When identifying emotions, have students hold up or point to the appropriate feeling face. Or, hold up two possible faces and ask them to choose which is appropriate.

Challenging

Have students come up with their own statements to record. Discuss with students the difference between emotions conveyed by content ("I'm so happy that you're here") and emotions conveyed by tone of voice ("You're here!" said in a happy tone). Key questions might include

- How did you know that I was happy?

- Did I say any words that let you know how I felt?

- What was it about the way I spoke that let you know I was happy?

THROUGHOUT THE DAY

- Reinforce interpreting tone of voice by asking the students to examine both their own tone of voice and that of others during conflicts or when requesting something.

- Allow students to use the tape recorder during free periods (e.g., center time). Have students pick a feeling face and record themselves using that tone of voice.

Interpreting Tone of Voice (Sincerity)

PURPOSE

To teach students to consider tone of voice when evaluating the sincerity of another person

STUDENTS WILL

Determine the sincerity of statements using tone of voice as a cue

MATERIALS

- Mean It/Don't Mean It signs (cut in half before handing out to students)

- Tape player

- Tape of recordings (to be recorded prior to the lesson, see next section)

- Blank audiotape

PRESENTATION OF LESSON

Prior to the Lesson

Record yourself or someone else saying the series of statements listed below and on the following page. Be sure to use the appropriate sincere or sarcastic tone of voice. Remember to record each statement twice for Set A (once in a sincere tone, once in a sarcastic tone).

List of Recorded Statements

Set A: Which one sounds sincere (Mean It)?

- "Great job on your art project!" (first = Mean It, second = Don't Mean It)

- "I'm really sorry I bumped into you." (first = Mean It, second = Don't Mean It)

- "Sorry I pushed you." (first = Don't Mean It, second = Mean It)

- "You did a nice job on your book report." (first = Mean It, second = Don't Mean It)

- "Nice hat!" (first = Don't Mean It, second = Mean It)

- "I am sorry I forgot your birthday." (first = Don't Mean It, second = Mean It)

- "This is just great! I can't believe this." (first = Mean It, second = Don't Mean It)

Set B: Mean it or Don't mean it?

- "I know I'm taking a long time; I am sorry, geesh." (Don't Mean It)

- "Mr. Benson said to say I'm sorry." (Don't Mean It)

- "Oh yeah, I love Barney!" (Mean It)

- "This is just great! I can't believe this." (Don't Mean It)

Discussion

Review with students what *tone of voice* means. Explain that tone of voice is how someone sounds when they are speaking and that you can often tell how someone is feeling from his or her tone of voice. Tone of voice can also tell us whether someone really means what he or she is saying.

Repeat the following sentence two times, once in a very sincere manner, the next time in a very insincere, sarcastic manner: "Great job on your art project!" Discuss the two statements with students. Explain that sometimes the words that people say do not match what they really mean (the second time you read the sentence, you weren't really complimenting someone's art project). But, if we pay attention to the person's tone of voice, we can often tell whether they really mean what they are saying. Key questions might include

- What was the difference between those two sentences?

- Which one sounded like I really meant what I was saying?

- What was it that made me sound like I meant it/didn't mean it?

Tape Recording Activity

Explain to students that you are going to play some sentences for them on the tape recorder. The first set of recordings present the same sentence twice, once in a sincere tone, once in a sarcastic tone. Have students identify when the person sounds as if he or she means what he or she says by holding up the Mean It sign.

The second set of recordings presents one statement in either a sincere or sarcastic tone. Students will identify a sincere tone by holding up the appropriate sign (Mean It) or a sarcastic tone by holding up the appropriate sign (Don't Mean It). Practice this by repeating "Great job on your art project" in sincere and sarcastic tones.

Play the recorded sentences and have students make their determinations.

Wrap-Up

As a closing activity, have students practice and record statements in sincere and insincere tones ("I'm sorry I bumped into you"). Explain that it is important to pay attention to our own tone of voice, as well as others' tone of voice. If we want people to believe us, then we need to make sure we sound as if we mean what we say.

UNIT 3

ALTERNATIVE PRESENTATIONS

Fundamental

Students might need statements to be repeated more than once in order to determine sincerity.

Challenging

Have students come up with their own sincere and sarcastic statements to record.

THROUGHOUT THE DAY

- Reinforce interpreting tone of voice by asking the students to examine their own tone of voice and that of others during conflicts or when requesting something.

- When people in the classroom say they are sorry, bring it to the attention of the students. Discuss the tone of voice and whether the person seemed to mean it. Encourage sincere apologies.

LESSON REPRODUCIBLE

Mean It

Don't
Mean It

Accident or On Purpose?

PURPOSE

To introduce the concept of intention using the categories of "Accident" and "On Purpose"

To reinforce the connection between emotions and events

STUDENTS WILL

Identify events in pictures as being an accident or as happening on purpose, using cues in the pictures

MATERIALS

- Chart paper and a marker or chalkboard and chalk

- Role-play footprints

- Tape

- Accident or On Purpose? pictures

PRESENTATION OF LESSON

Discussion

Write the words *accident* and *on purpose* on the chalkboard or chart paper. Ask students if they can explain the difference between an accident (when you didn't mean for something to happen) and something that is done on purpose (when you meant for something to happen). Discuss the fact that it is sometimes hard to tell if things were an accident or if they were done on purpose. Model this dilemma by role playing a situation in which you run into someone because you are looking the other way. Did you shove him or her on purpose or was it an accident? Explain that the group will be working on how to figure out whether something was an accident.

Pictures Activity

Show the students each of the Accident or On Purpose? pictures (or groups of pictures). Ask the students if the actions in the pictures were an accident or whether the person involved meant for them to happen (on purpose). Discuss the clues that the students used to come up with their answers. Be sure to include the following in your discussion:

* Facial expressions

* Body language

* Contextual clues (things in the environment)

Role-Play Activity

Explain that students will line up behind you and then, as the students walk forward, you will pretend to trip and disrupt the line. Act this out with students, then sit back down and discuss how they felt. Key questions might include

* Did I disrupt the line on purpose? How did you know?

* How did you feel when you were jostled even though you knew it was an accident?

* What could the line leader have done to make you feel better?

Wrap-Up

Explain to students that most of the time we can figure out if something was an accident or not by looking for clues. It is important to gather information about the situation before reacting. Review the kinds of clues that you used during the pictures and role-play activities.

ALTERNATIVE PRESENTATIONS

Fundamental

Limit the number of pictures to discuss. Compare and contrast a set of pictures depicting an accident with a set depicting something that was done on purpose by focusing on the clues students use to determine intent.

Challenging

Discuss with students how to handle situations when they are unsure if someone meant to hurt them. What can they do to gather information? How should they react?

THROUGHOUT THE DAY

- Label events that happen in the classroom as being accidental or on purpose. Ask students to identify which category an event may fit into and the cues that lead them to this conclusion.

LESSON REPRODUCIBLES

ACCIDENT OR ON PURPOSE? #3A

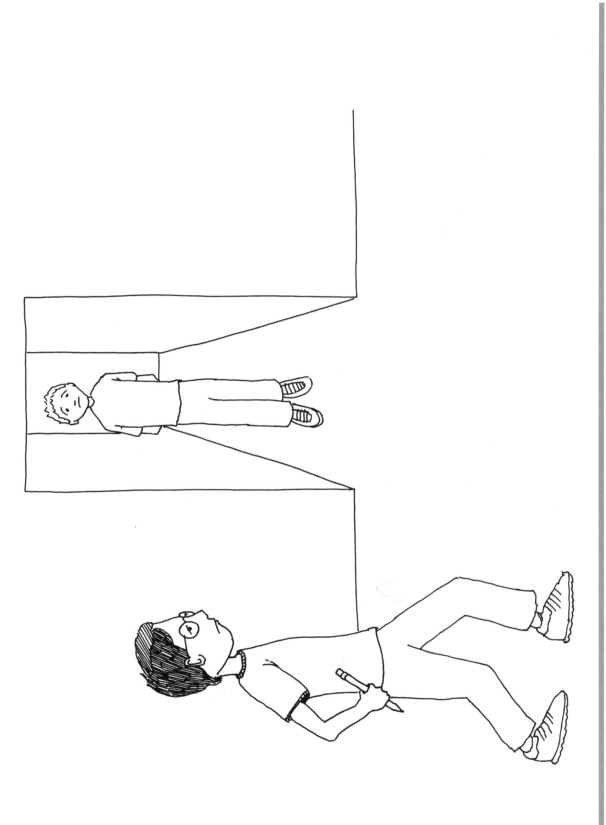

Unit 3: Accident or On Purpose?

ACCIDENT OR ON PURPOSE? #3B

Unit 3: Accident or On Purpose?

232

ACCIDENT OR ON PURPOSE? #4A

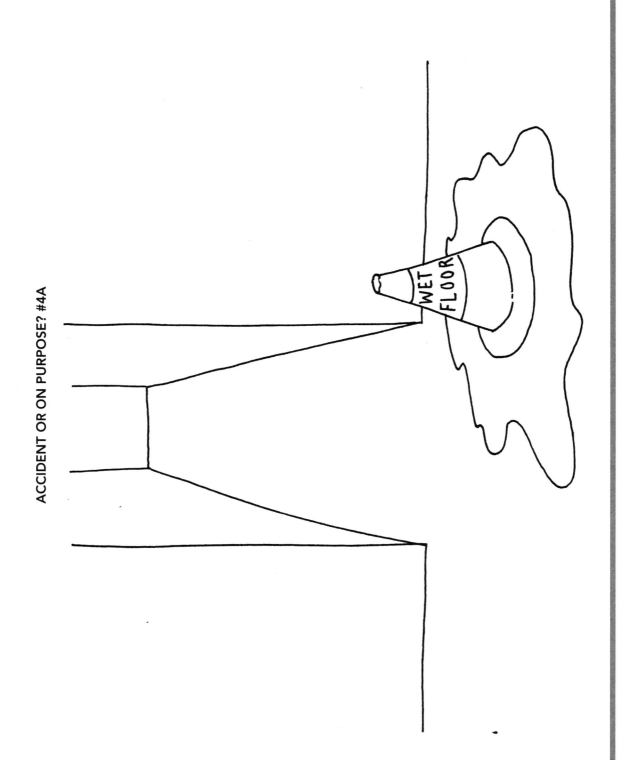

Unit 3: Accident or On Purpose?

Unit 3: Accident or On Purpose?

237

Unit 3: Accident or On Purpose?

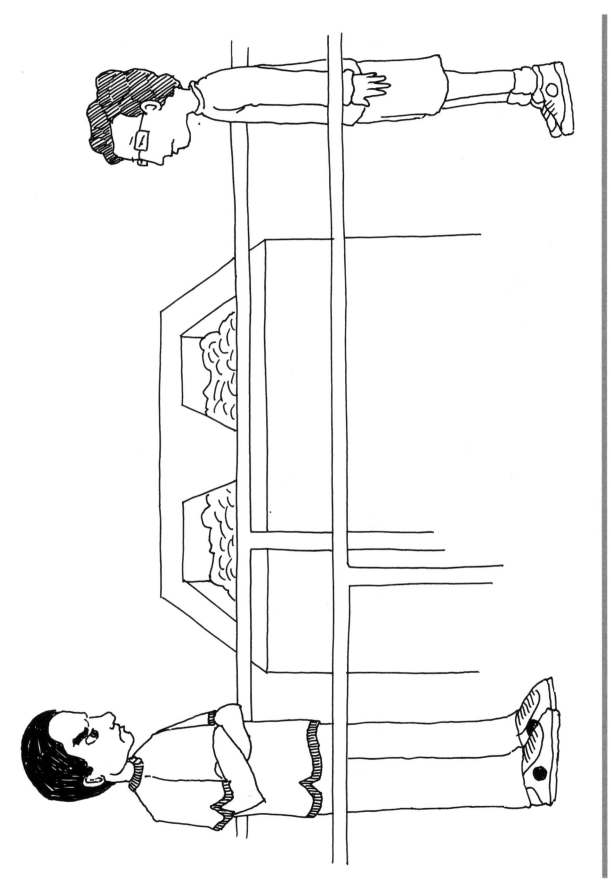

Unit 3: Accident or On Purpose?

Identifying Intention

PURPOSE

To review the concept of intention using the categories of "Accident" and "On Purpose"

To practice the identification and use of relevant cues to determine of intent

STUDENTS WILL

Identify intention (decide if the events happened by accident or if they were done on purpose) in the video clips shown

MATERIALS

- Video clips (Suggested videos: *Hercules; The Borrowers; Honey, We Shrunk Ourselves; All Dogs Go to Heaven; Toy Story; Fantasia*)

- TV/VCR

- Role-play footprints

- Tape

PRESENTATION OF LESSON

Discussion

Review the meaning of the words *accident* (when you didn't mean for something to happen) and *on purpose* (when you meant for something to happen). Use the following example: "I was at the grocery store and when the woman next to me grabbed a box of cereal off the shelf, another one fell off and hit me in the shoulder. Do you think the woman meant to hit me with the cereal box? How do you know? What do you think I was feeling? What could the woman have done in that situation to make me feel better?"

Movie Title	Description of Clip	Clip Location
Hercules	**Hercules accidentally knocks over the marketplace.** Focus on Hercules' expression and on where he is looking as he runs into the columns.	23:18–24:09
The Borrowers	**A boy accidentally closes his sister in the freezer.** This clip may need some explanation ("The two characters are very small, and the brother is holding open the freezer door for his sister."). Focus on the boy's body language and what he says.	8:53–9:59
Honey, We Shrunk Ourselves	**Two men shrink a statue on purpose, then accidentally shrink themselves.** Compare and contrast the two actions. Focus on their words and facial expressions.	21:58–24:19
All Dogs Go to Heaven	**Two dogs purposely knock a third dog off the pier.** Focus on what the mean dogs say and the tone of their laughter.	16:35–17:24
Toy Story	**Buzz Lightyear gets knocked out the window.** Woody (the cowboy) tries to run Buzz over with the car (on purpose), but the fact that Buzz ended up falling out the window was accidental. Focus on Woody's facial expressions.	37:30–38:40
Fantasia	**Mickey purposely brings a broom to life but accidentally ends up flooding the castle.** Focus on Mickey's facial expressions and body language.	29:41–end

Video Activity

Explain to students that today you are going to be watching short clips from different movies and it will be the students' job to decide whether what happened was an accident or on purpose.

The following focus questions will help students attend to contextual cues in the video clips. More than one student can answer the same question. (These questions are also available in the Lesson Reproducible section following this lesson if you want to pass them out to your students.)

Video Clip Focus Questions

Hercules
Things to look for:

1. Where Hercules is looking as he bumps into the columns

2. Hercules' facial expression after he knocks over the marketplace

3. What Hercules does and says before he bumps into the man with the pots

Post-clip questions:

1. Did Hercules knock over the marketplace on purpose or by accident?

2. Did Hercules knock over the man with the pots on purpose or by accident?

The Borrowers
Things to look for:

1. What the boy says as the freezer door closes

2. The boy's body language as the freezer door closes

Post-clip questions:

1. Did the boy shut his sister in the freezer on purpose or by accident?

Honey, We Shrunk Ourselves
Things to look for:

1. What the man said when he was warned that the machine was "revving up"

2. How the men looked when they realized they were small

Post-clip questions:

1. Did the two men shrink the statue on purpose or by accident?

2. Did the two men shrink themselves on purpose or by accident?

All Dogs Go to Heaven
Things to look for:

1. What the dogs say as they push the car down the pier

Post-clip questions:

1. Did the dogs knock Charlie off on purpose or by accident?

Toy Story
Things to look for:

1. The cowboy's facial expression when he decides to drive the car

2. The cowboy's facial expression when Buzz Lightyear gets knocked out the window

Post-clip questions:

1. Did the cowboy run Buzz over with the car on purpose or by accident?

2. Did the cowboy knock Buzz out the window on purpose or by accident?

Fantasia
Things to look for:

1. Mickey's facial expression and body language when the broom came to life

2. What Mickey did while the broom was filling the basin with water

3. Mickey's facial expression and body language when he realized the room was flooded

Post-clip questions:

1. Did Mickey bring the broom to life on purpose or by accident?

2. Did Mickey flood the room on purpose or by accident?

Wrap-Up

Ask students for examples of things that have happened to them that were either accidents or that were done on purpose. Use one of the students' examples as the basis of a role play. Discuss with students the kinds of cues that they used to determine intent.

ALTERNATIVE PRESENTATIONS

Fundamental

You may need to show each clip more than once, especially at the beginning. Show the clip a second time and pause the video to freeze the action. Key questions might include

• What does [the character's] face look like?

• Is he or she laughing?

• Did [the character] look sorry after it happened?

This process will help students identify cues.

Challenging

Discuss with students the idea that we need to take personal responsibility for our actions. Even when we do something by accident, we may need to apologize or otherwise make amends. And if we have done something on purpose, we need to admit what we have done and accept the consequences. Key questions might include

- Have you ever said something was an accident and it really wasn't?

- What does it mean to take responsibility for what we have done?

THROUGHOUT THE DAY

- Point out instances when accidents and events that were done on purpose occur in the classroom. Also point out the cues students should be noticing that reveal a person's intention.

LESSON REPRODUCIBLE

Hercules

Things to look for:
1. Where Hercules is looking as he bumps into the columns
2. Hercules' facial expression after he knocks over the marketplace
3. What Hercules does and says before he bumps into the man with the pots

Post-clip questions:
1. Did Hercules knock over the marketplace on purpose or by accident?
2. Did Hercules knock over the man with the pots on purpose or by accident?

The Borrowers

Things to look for:
1. What the boy says as the freezer door closes
2. The boy's body language as the freezer door closes

Post-clip question:
1. Did the boy shut his sister in the freezer on purpose or by accident?

Honey, We Shrunk Ourselves

Things to look for:
1. What the man said when he was warned that the machine was "revving up"
2. How the men looked when they realized they were small

Post-clip questions:
1. Did the two men shrink the statue on purpose or by accident?
2. Did the two men shrink themselves on purpose or by accident?

All Dogs Go to Heaven

Things to look for:
1. What the dogs say as they push the car down the pier

Post-clip question:
1. Did the dogs knock Charlie off on purpose or by accident?

Toy Story

Things to look for:
1. The cowboy's facial expression when he decides to drive the car
2. The cowboy's facial expression when Buzz Lightyear gets knocked out the window

Post-clip questions:
1. Did the cowboy run Buzz over with the car on purpose or by accident?
2. Did the cowboy knock Buzz out the window on purpose or by accident?

Fantasia

Things to look for:
1. Mickey's facial expression and body language when the broom came to life
2. What Mickey did while the broom was filling the basin with water
3. Mickey's facial expression and body language when he realized the room was flooded

Post-clip questions:
1. Did Mickey bring the broom to life on purpose or by accident?
2. Did Mickey flood the room on purpose or by accident?

Is This Mean?

UNIT 3

PURPOSE

To distinguish between actions that are intended to be mean and actions that are not intended to be mean

STUDENTS WILL

Identify the intention of a role play character as being mean or not mean using contextual cues

MATERIALS

- Stoplight poster #2

- Chart paper and a marker or chalkboard and chalk

- Pictures ("Pulling Hair," "Making Fun")

- Is This Mean? Role-Play Situations list

- Role-play footprints

- Tape

PRESENTATION OF LESSON

Discussion

Review with students Steps #1–4 on Stoplight poster #2. Write Step #4 on the chalkboard or chart paper, and ask students what kinds of things the group has been working on that help them figure out what is going on (body language, identifying emotions, tone of voice, accident/on purpose). Write down student responses (add to the list as needed). Explain to students that today you are going to talk about figuring out when someone is being mean. Figuring out if someone is being mean is an important part of figuring out what is going on.

Pictures Activity

Show and discuss each of the pictures. Key questions might include

- Was he or she being mean? How can you tell?

- What do you think each of the girls/boys is feeling? How can you tell?

It should be pretty clear to your students that someone was being mean in the two pictures. In each picture the boys have mean looks on their faces, and the other person is clearly upset. Explain to students that sometimes it's hard to tell if someone is being mean. Sometimes we don't have enough information to decide if a person is being mean. If we can't tell, we need to look for more clues before we act.

Tell your students that you will be performing role plays and that their job is to decide whether you are being mean. If they can't tell whether you're being mean, you should help your students look for more clues.

Role-Play Activity

With a volunteer, role play situations from the Is This Mean? Role-Play Situations list in which one person may be being mean to another. After each role play, discuss with students how they came to their conclusion about whether you were being mean. Key questions might include

- What was going on?

- What was I doing when . . .?

- How did my face look when . . .?

- Did I have a mean expression?

- What might be another explanation for my behavior besides that I was being mean?

If a student says that he or she is unable to determine someone's intent, discuss what the student could do to find out more information.

Wrap-Up

Add the question, Are they being mean? to the list of things that help us figure out what is going on and review the importance of paying attention to the clues around us. (One way to figure out what is going on is to pay attention to what other people are doing and feeling. This can give us important information about what to do.)

ALTERNATIVE PRESENTATIONS

Fundamental

Perform only the second and third role plays on the list and be less ambiguous as to your intention. For example, in Role Play #2, be sure to say, "Oooops!" after bumping the other person. In Role Play #3, use a mean voice when you speak to the person. Then compare and contrast the mean and not mean situations, writing down the cues that the students used to come to their conclusion (e.g., tone of voice, dialogue, body language).

Challenging

After each role play, discuss with students what could be added to the role play that would change its meaning. For example, in the first role play, you could change the number of markers that are visible or laugh meanly with your friend after you say no. Both of these additional cues could change students' decision as to whether you are being mean. Reenact each role play with additional cues and discuss.

THROUGHOUT THE DAY

- When students are involved in an altercation, they should be encouraged to think about what happened and figure out if the other person involved was being mean. This will help students better understand social situations and to respond appropriately to them.

LESSON REPRODUCIBLES

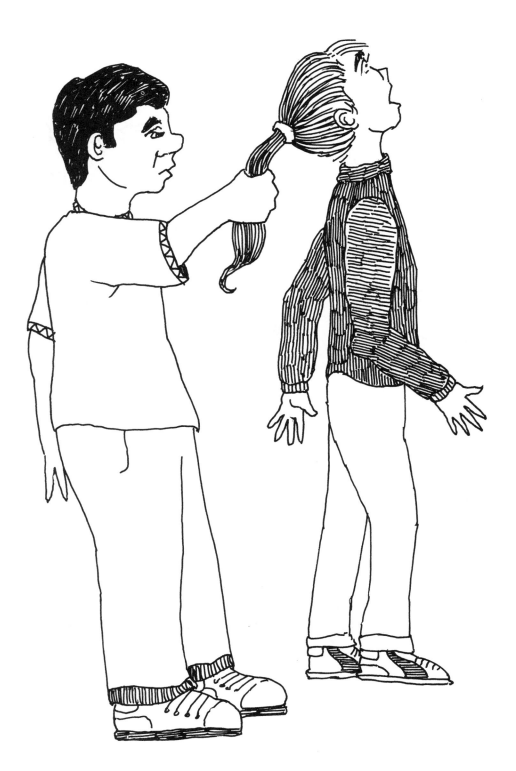

Role-Play Situations

Role Play #1:

You and a friend are coloring. Someone else comes up and asks if she can join you. You say no. Your reason is that there aren't enough markers to go around.

Role Play #2:

Two students are listening to the teacher give a math lesson. When the teacher asks a question, one student excitedly raises his hand. When he raises his hand, he knocks his friend's pencil off her desk.

Role Play #3:

You announce that you are going outside to look for your coat that you left outside on the playground. Someone asks if he can come with you. You say no because you don't like him.

Role Play #4:

At the end of the school day, students are told to get their coats and bags from the closet to go home. One student shoves two other students in order to get his things. The students who get shoved bump into other students in front of them.

Role Play #5:

Students are waiting in line to use the bathroom, and one student steps out of line to get a drink of water. When the student goes back to get in line, the other students close the space so she can't get in.

Role Play #6:

Students are outside on the playground playing tag. The student who is "It" runs into another student when trying to tag someone else.

Role Play #7:

Students are sitting in the cafeteria eating lunch. One student begins waving hard at his friend across the room. He waves so hard that he knocks the elbow of the student sitting next to him, whose milk spills on the table.

How to Tell
When Someone Is Busy

PURPOSE

To distinguish between people who are busy and people who are not busy

To make appropriate judgments about when and how to approach others

STUDENTS WILL

Identify situations that indicate whether someone is busy or not busy

Make assessments about when and how it is appropriate to approach someone

MATERIALS

- Role-play footprints

- Tape

- Chart paper and a marker or chalkboard and chalk

- Busy Role-Play Situations list

- *Promoting Social Success* game board (color and laminate, as desired)

- Game cards

- Game pieces (any small objects, such as figurines or colored paper clips; one for each student)

PRESENTATION OF LESSON

Discussion

Review the previous lesson with students. Remind your students that you talked about figuring out if other people were being mean in the last lesson. Tell them that today you are going to talk about being busy. Sometimes when people are busy and don't talk to us or pay attention to us like we think they should, we think that they are being mean.

Ask the students what it means to be busy and how they know when someone is busy. Role play the following situation: Have a volunteer pretend to be talking on the telephone. Approach them and repeatedly ask them questions, displaying increasing frustration.

Discuss the situation with students. Key questions might include

- What was [volunteer's name] doing?

- Was he or she being mean when he or she didn't answer me?

- How can you tell when someone is busy?

On the chalkboard or chart paper, write down the cues that students generate for determining when someone is busy. Additional discussion questions might be

- When is the best time to try and talk to someone?

- What can you do if you need to talk to someone, but they are busy?

Role-Play Activity

From the Busy Role-Play Situations list, role play the right and wrong ways to handle situations in which someone is busy.

Board Game Activity

Explain to students that you are going to play a board game. The rules of the game are as follows: To start, each student can choose which stack of cards to draw from because the start box does not have an "A" or a "?" Then, taking turns, each student will draw a card. If they land on a "?" space, they should draw a "?" card. The card will have a question on it. If they answer the question correctly, they get to move forward the number of spaces indicated on the card. If they land on an "A" space, they should draw an "A" card. The card will have an action or activity they are to perform. If they do so correctly, they can move forward the number indicated on the card. Each student gets only one draw per turn. If the student lands on a "Short Cut" box, he or she moves the game piece to the place indicated by the arrow. If your group is too large to play on one game board, you can set up multiple games or have students take turns playing while those who are not playing look on.

As students are playing the game, discuss their answers. Have students who answered correctly explain their answers to the rest of the group. If they answered incorrectly, try to explain the concept to them or have another student explain it.

Wrap-Up

As a closing activity, ask students to review what they learned today about people who are busy. Summaries should include some mention of how to tell if someone is busy and what to do if someone looks busy.

ALTERNATIVE PRESENTATIONS

Fundamental

Some of the game questions might be too difficult for students. Have students play in pairs or teams and encourage them to discuss their answers as they go. Provide guidance and clarification as needed, and play the game multiple times to practice the concepts.

Challenging

The game activity should be challenging for most students. Have students come up with their own role-play situations and act out the right and wrong way to handle these situations.

THROUGHOUT THE DAY

- Students should be encouraged to make judgments about when someone is or is not busy in the classroom and to modify their behavior appropriately. It is helpful to show positive reinforcement when students exhibit appropriate behavior and to provide explicit coaching when they make poor judgments.

LESSON REPRODUCIBLES

Role-Play Situations

Role Play #1:

Your teacher is busy talking to another teacher, but you want to ask her a question. Show the right and wrong ways to handle this.

Role Play #2:

Your mother is busy talking on the telephone, but you really want to tell her about your basketball game. Show the right and wrong ways to handle this.

Role Play #3:

You are out at recess and your friend has hurt himself. He is bleeding! The teacher is busy talking to another adult, but you really need to tell her about your friend. Show the right and wrong ways to handle this.

Role Play #4:

Your friend is busy taking a test, but you really want to show her your new game. Show the right and wrong ways to handle this.

Role Play #5:

A group of kids are busy playing basketball. They are in the middle of a game, but you really want to join them. Show the right and wrong ways to handle this.

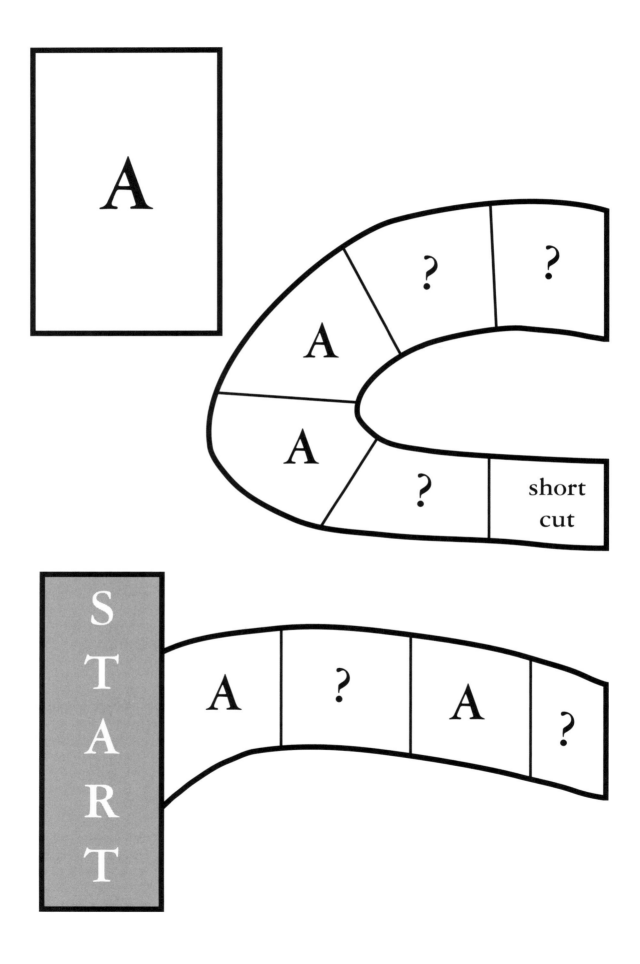

A

? ?

A

A ? short cut

START A ? A ?

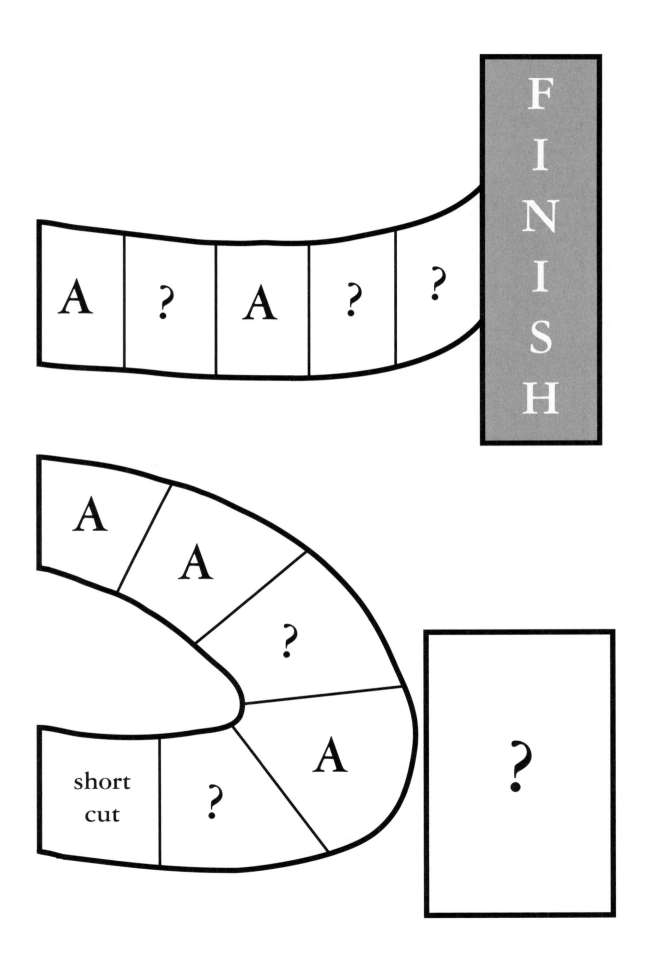

?

Joey is playing catch with three friends.

Is it a good time to ask about his homework?

Value = 3

?

When is a good time to talk to a teacher about a problem you are having?

Value = 4

?

Bobby is playing by himself. You ask him to play checkers with you.

He says, "Go away. Leave me alone."

Is Bobby being rude?

Value = 3

?

Bob is playing basketball by himself.

Is it a good time to ask if he wants to play?

Value = 2

?

It is quiet time in class. You ask your neighbor what time recess is.

She does not say anything.

Is she being rude?

Value = 4

?

You are taking a test in class.

Your friend asks you if you can come over after school.

What would you say to your friend?

Value = 5

?

Marie is studying for a test.

When you ask her to play, she says no.

Is she being mean?

Value = 3

?

The teacher is talking to a student.

You need to use the bathroom.

What would you say to the teacher to be as polite as possible?

Value = 5

?

The fire alarm just went off!

Is this a good time to show the teacher your new doll?

Value = 2

?

You are playing a game with your friend that can only have two players.

How do you tell someone that he or she cannot play without hurting his or her feelings?

Value = 4

?

You are doing an activity for math class. Your friend wants to talk to you.

How do you tell your friend to be quiet in a polite way?

Value = 4

?

If someone does not answer your question, then is the person always being rude?

Value = 3

A

Show the group what someone who does not want to be disturbed looks like.

Value = 3

A

Give three examples of when someone may be too busy to talk to you.

Value = 4

A

Ask your neighbor what time it is in a polite way.

Value = 2

A

Tell someone you are busy in a rude way.

Value = 3

A

Give an example of when it is okay to interrupt.

Value = 4

A

Tell someone you are busy in a polite way.

Value = 2

A

MOVE AHEAD
THREE SPACES

A

Pretend you are talking to another student who is playing a game.

Ask him or her in a polite way if you can play.

Value = 4

A

Show the group what someone who is NOT busy looks like.

Value = 3

A

Give an example of when another student should not be interrupted.

Value = 3

A

Describe a time when you do not want to be disturbed.

Value = 3

A

Give an example of when the teacher is too busy to be disturbed.

Value = 4

Reacting to Other People

UNIT 3

PURPOSE

To discuss and demonstrate in a concrete manner the ways in which we modify
our behavior based on interpersonal cues

STUDENTS WILL

Interpret welcoming/unwelcoming body language and tone of voice and appropriately modify their behavior within the context of a game

MATERIALS

- Dog pictures ("Friendly Dog," "Unfriendly Dog")

- Chart paper and a marker or chalkboard and chalk

- Role-play footprints

- Tape

- Treat for each student (candy or other token)

PRESENTATION OF LESSON

Discussion

Begin with a general question about how students would react if they came
across a dog. Show the "Friendly Dog" picture, and ask the students how they
would react to the dog in the picture. Discuss their responses. Repeat this process with the "Unfriendly Dog" picture, and discuss the different reactions.

   Focus the discussion on human beings and how we also change our reactions to people based on how they look. On the chalkboard or chart paper, write
down three basic emotions: happy, sad, and angry. Using the role-play footprints, demonstrate an appropriate facial expression, body language, and tone

Lesson

of voice for each emotion. Ask students what they might do if they came across people who looked and sounded the way you do. Write these ideas on the chalkboard or chart paper in a list underneath the emotion. Appropriate reactions and/or behaviors might include:

Happy	Sad	Angry
going to play with them	cheering them up	staying away
asking them to help you	listening to their troubles	suggesting they use the
saying hello	offering to play	steps for calming down

Game Activity

Play a modified version of Red Light, Green Light. Have students line up facing you. They will be instructed to take one giant step forward when you demonstrate welcoming body language (arms outstretched with welcoming smile and tone of voice).

When you demonstrate unwelcoming body language (arms folded with angry expression and tone of voice), students will be instructed to either stay still or to take a giant step back (depending on the amount of space available).

Give students a treat when they finally reach you.

Wrap-Up

As a closing activity, have students review what they learned about modifying their behavior. Summaries should include the idea that paying attention to the body language of others can help us act appropriately.

ALTERNATIVE PRESENTATIONS

Fundamental

Students may have difficulty moving from the animal example to regular human emotions. If so, an intermediary step might be to focus on very extreme or stereotypical human appearances. Key questions might include

- What would you do if you saw someone yelling and kicking everything in his or her way? Would you go near that person?

- What would you do if you saw someone who was hurt lying on the ground? Would you ask if he or she needed help?

From these examples you might be able to make the transition to more subtle aspects of human emotion and how people might react to them.

Challenging

Once students are familiar with the welcoming and unwelcoming postures and tones, add other postures and tones that might encourage someone to approach them.

- Neutral expression with arms to the side

- "Busy" body language in which you look to be involved in something else, but with benign intention

- Sad or lonely

Or discourage someone from approaching them.

- "Ignoring" body language with body turned away, hostile intention, and tone of voice

THROUGHOUT THE DAY

- Some students may need encouragement to increase the number of situations in which they approach others. Other students may need assistance in becoming more discriminating about how and when they approach others. Use information about individual students to tailor the lesson in terms of encouraging students to approach others or discouraging students from approaching others.

- Coach students as they evaluate particular situations and make decisions about whether to approach others based on interpersonal cues.

LESSON REPRODUCIBLES

Unit 3: Reacting to Other People

Reviewing Emotional Displays

PURPOSE

To review Step #4 on Stoplight poster #2

To review the identification of several emotions (scared, surprised, happy, confused, sad, angry, disappointed) using facial expression, body language, and dialogue/tone of voice cues

STUDENTS WILL

Identify at least one emotion displayed and provide an explanation as to what cues he or she used to identify that emotion

MATERIALS

- Stoplight poster #2

- Chart paper and a marker or chalkboard and chalk

- Video clips (Suggested videos: *Paulie, Home Alone, George of the Jungle, Men in Black, Home Alone 2, Leave it to Beaver, Home Alone 3, Mouse Hunt*)

- Small feeling faces to match the emotions presented in the video clips (multiple of each for you to fill out a chart)

- Role-play footprints

- Tape

PRESENTATION OF LESSON

Discussion

Briefly review Steps #1–4 on Stoplight poster #2. Remind students that people need to think about things when they're calm so they can figure out what is going on and what to do. Once someone is calm, he or she can ask, "What is going on?"

Explain to students that you will soon be moving on to Step #5 on Stoplight poster #2 but that now you are going to review some of the things you have learned recently. Ask students to review the kinds of things the group has been learning about. Write their responses on the chalkboard or chart paper. The list should include the following:

- Body language

- Tone of voice

- Accident/on purpose

- Mean/not mean

- Busy/not busy

Review with students that one way to figure out what is going on is to pay attention to what other people are feeling. Tell your students that because they have already been working on feelings, that today's activity will be a review. Tell your students that they are going to watch short clips of movies that they may have seen before. After watching each part of the tape, talk with your students about what they've seen.

Video Activity

Show and discuss each of the video clips. Have students answer the following questions for each clip.

- What is going on?

- How can you tell? (Identify cues used in assessing the situation.)

- What are each of the characters feeling?

- How can you tell? (Identify cues used in assessing the emotions.)

Continue until all clips have been presented. As you go, fill out a chart on the chalkboard or chart paper that shows what emotions were displayed in each clip and what cues students used in assessing the situation. Write the names of the movie clips down the left side and label your headings "Emotions" and "Cues." To document the characters' emotions, tape appropriate feeling faces in the "Emotion" column on the chart or write out feeling words that the students identify.

Wrap-Up

Review the chart and ask the students to role play a feeling from their favorite clip. Other group members can guess the emotion being acted out and the clip to which the student is referring.

EMOTIONAL DISPLAYS VIDEO CLIPS

Movie Title	Description of Clip	Clip Location
Paulie	**Paulie flies.** Happy, excited, surprised	1:25:32–1:26:22
Home Alone	**The boy hides.** Scared	31:55–36:17
George of the Jungle	**The couple runs from the lion.** Scared	15:55–16:54
Men in Black	**Will Smith's character sees aliens.** Surprised, confused	36:00–36:36
Home Alone 2	**The kids wake up on Christmas morning.** Surprised, excited, happy	1:53:38–1:54:22
Leave it to Beaver	**The boys get yelled at by their father.** Angry, nervous	27:27–29:19
Home Alone 3	**The mother and son argue.** Angry	34:08–34:55
Mouse Hunt	**The couple argues.** Angry	15:26–15:47

ALTERNATIVE PRESENTATIONS

Fundamental

Have students use their set of small feeling faces cards to help them verbally express the feelings that they have seen.

Challenging

Have students think of other favorite movies and brainstorm lists of emotions present in them. Share the lists, giving examples of when the emotions are displayed in the movie.

THROUGHOUT THE DAY

- Watch a movie and have students point out various emotions depicted.

Reviewing Social Situations

PURPOSE

To review and reinforce the concepts covered in this unit

STUDENTS WILL

Answer questions about a story using the social cues presented

MATERIALS

- Stoplight poster #2

- *Alexander and the Terrible, Horrible, No Good, Very Bad Day* by Judith Viorst

- *Promoting Social Success* game board (from the How to Tell When Someone Is Busy lesson)

- Game pieces (any small objects, such as figurines or colored paper clips; one for each student)

- Using Social Information worksheet

PRESENTATION OF LESSON

Briefly review Steps #1–4 on Stoplight poster #2. Remind students that people need to think about things when they're calm so they can figure out what is going on and what to do. Once someone is calm, he or she can ask, "What is going on?"

Explain to students that next time you meet you will be moving on to Step #5 on Stoplight poster #2 but that today you are going to review some of the things you have learned recently. Ask students to review the kinds of things the group has been learning about, or review the list created in the previous lesson. The list should include things such as body language, tone of voice, accident/on purpose, mean/not mean, and busy/not busy.

Game Activity

Explain to students that you are going to play a game. There will be questions about the book *Alexander and the Terrible, Horrible, No Good, Very Bad Day.* When students answer a question correctly, they will be able to advance on the board the number of spaces you tell them. Read the book through once before beginning the game.

Review Game Questions

Page 1 (read page in a frustrated manner)

- What can you tell by the way I am talking? (tone of voice)   2 spaces

- Alexander dropped his sweater in the sink. Was this an accident, or did he drop it on purpose? How can you tell? (accident/on purpose)   2 spaces

Page 2

- How do you think Alexander was feeling when he didn't get any prize in his cereal? How can you tell? (identifying emotional displays)   2 spaces

- Were Alexander's brothers being mean to him? How can you tell? (mean/not mean)   3 spaces

Page 4

- Is Mrs. Gibson being mean to Alexander? How can you tell? (mean/not mean)   3 spaces

- What feeling is Alexander showing with his body in the picture? (body language)   2 spaces

Page 6

- Who looks the most busy in the picture ? (busy/not busy)   3 spaces

Page 7

- Tell Alexander that he left out 16 in a mean way. Now tell him he left out 16 in a nice way. (tone of voice)   4 spaces

- Would now be a good time to come over to Alexander and ask him if he wanted to play with you? (reactions to others)   3 spaces

Page 8

- Did Paul do something that was mean? (mean/not mean)   4 spaces

- Pretend you are Paul and tell Alexander that you are sorry in a way that sounds like you really mean it. (tone of voice)   3 spaces

---

- Pretend you are Paul and tell Alexander that you are sorry in a way that sounds like you *don't* really mean it. (tone of voice)   3 spaces

Page 9

- What tone of voice would Alexander be using to tell Paul these mean things? Can you demonstrate? (tone of voice)   2 spaces

Page 10

- Did Alexander's mother forget to put dessert in his lunch by accident, or did she not give him a dessert on purpose? (accident/on purpose)   2 spaces

UNIT 3

Page 13

- Does Alexander look angry, happy, or excited? (body language)   3 spaces

- By looking at the picture, can you tell if it would be a good time for Alexander to talk to the dentist? Why? (busy/not busy)   3 spaces

Page 14

- What happened on this page that was an accident and what happened that was on purpose? (accident/on purpose)   4 spaces

- Anthony made Alexander fall, but was Nick mean too? Why? (mean/not mean)   2 spaces

Page 16

- How can you tell Alexander's mom is upset by looking at the picture? (body language)   3 spaces

Page 17

- Would this be a good time to ask Alexander how he was feeling? Why? (reactions to others)   3 spaces

Page 19

- Was the shoe man being mean to Alexander? Why? (mean/not mean)   3 spaces

Page 21

- Alexander looks happy in this picture. Why do you think he looks that way? (identifying emotional displays)   4 spaces

Page 23

- Would Alexander's brothers be able to go out and play right now? Why? (busy/not busy)   3 spaces

- By looking at the picture, can you tell what kinds of things Alexander's mom is saying to him? (body language)   3 spaces

Page 25

- What could you tell Alexander that might make him feel better? (reactions to others)   4 spaces

Page 26

- If Nick knew that Alexander was having a bad day, what could he have done differently? (reactions to others)   4 spaces

ALTERNATIVE PRESENTATION

For all groups

Allow students to confer/discuss answers with other members in the group if they are having difficulty providing an appropriate answer.

THROUGHOUT THE DAY

- Review the concepts covered in this unit with center activities, charades games, and use of photographs and illustrations. Verbally identify your own moods and emotions throughout the day. Coach students to pay attention to the social cues around them through questions and role play.

- Have students complete the Using Social Information worksheet as morning work or homework.

Lesson

LESSON REPRODUCIBLE

Name _____ Date _____

I knew my friend was... (circle one)

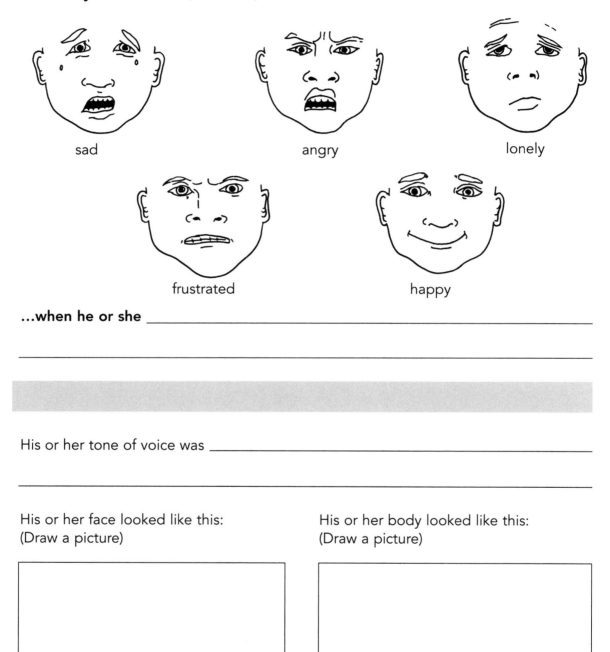

sad

angry

lonely

frustrated

happy

...when he or she _____

_____

His or her tone of voice was _____

_____

His or her face looked like this:
(Draw a picture)

His or her body looked like this:
(Draw a picture)

Planning What to Do

PROBLEM SOLVING

UNIT 4

What Does it Mean to Have Goals?

PURPOSE

To introduce the concept of goals

To identify individual goals

STUDENTS WILL

Identify at least one goal presented in the pictures

Identify one personal goal

MATERIALS

- Chart paper and a marker or chalkboard and chalk

- Stoplight poster #2

- Pictures ("Playing Soccer," "The Race," "Studying for a Spelling Test," "Singing on Stage")

- What Do I Want to Happen? worksheet

- Crayons/markers

- *Promoting Social Success* Parent Newsletter: *Problem Solving*

PRESENTATION OF LESSON

Discussion

Write the word *goal* on the chalkboard or chart paper and show students Stoplight poster #2.

Ask your students if they can tell you what a goal is. Explain that a goal is something that a person wants to happen. Wanting to be a doctor or wanting the help a friend build his or her science project are examples of goals. When people have goals, they try hard to make them happen. Explain to students that today you will be moving on to Step #5 on Stoplight Poster #2, "What do I want to happen?" What we want to happen is our goal.

Ask if any of the students can give an example of a goal, giving a sports reference, if needed (be sure to differentiate between *scoring* a goal and *having* a goal).

Pictures Activity

Show the first picture and ask the students what the goal of the team might be. Continue through the rest of the pictures.

Possible goals
- Picture #1 ("Playing Soccer"): soccer team's goals—to win, to have a good time, to work together, to exercise

- Picture #2 ("The Race"): runner's goals—to win, to beat his opponents, to beat his own record, to exercise

- Picture #3 ("Studying for a Spelling Test"): student's goals—to do well on his spelling test, to learn, to impress the teacher

- Picture #4 ("Singing on Stage"): performer's goals—to sing well, to impress the audience, to get a record deal

Wrap-Up

When you have gone through all of the pictures, ask the students to think of a goal that they have and to draw a picture of themselves trying to reach, or reaching, their goal on the What Do I Want to Happen? worksheet. Have students label the picture at the bottom with a statement explaining their goal.

ALTERNATIVE PRESENTATIONS

Fundamental

When asking students to draw their pictures, offer categories from which they can choose, such as friends, sports, school grades, or games.

Challenging

Discuss with students the role of emotions in reaching a goal. It may be important to use the three calming down steps so that strong emotions do not prevent you from reaching a goal (e.g., getting too excited and competitive during a kickball game might get you benched or prevent you from playing your best, which hinders you from reaching your goal of winning the game).

THROUGHOUT THE DAY

- Each morning, have students answer the question, "What is your goal today?"

- Discuss "friendship goals" for the group.

- Send home the *Promoting Social Success* Parent Newsletter: *Problem Solving*.

UNIT 4

LESSON REPRODUCIBLES

FINISH

Unit 4: What Does it Mean to Have Goals?

Name _____ Date _____

Complete the sentence at the bottom of this page. In the space provided, draw a picture of yourself trying to reach your goal.

My goal is to _____

_____

_____

Identifying Goals

PURPOSE

To review the concept of goals as they apply to different situations

STUDENTS WILL

Identify a goal that is appropriate to a given situation

MATERIALS

- Stoplight poster #2

- Chart paper and a marker or chalkboard and chalk

- Context cards

- Picture ("Boy in Front of Class")

PRESENTATION OF LESSON

Discussion

Review Step #5 on Stoplight poster #2 and the concept of goals as covered in the previous lesson. (A goal is something that we want to happen. When we have a goal, we try hard to make it happen.)

Context Cards Activity

Explain to students that you will be discussing goals and the fact that people have different goals for different situations. On the chalkboard or chart paper, write down the six contexts found on the context cards (recess, math class, gym class, home, trip to the mall, lunch time). Make sure that all students know what these terms mean. Taking turns, have each student pick a card and give an example of an appropriate goal for that context using their past personal experience and the question, "What do I want to happen?" as guides. Model this process once yourself first. ("My goal at recess is to win the kickball game.") Write down each idea. Repeat until all students have had a turn and each context has more than one goal underneath it.

Keep in mind, it may be a challenge for students to come up with multiple goals for the same situation, but this is an important concept—goals can be revised and changed, and often, people have more than one goal in a given situation. For example, goals for lunch time could include

- Having a quiet lunch

- Being able to talk with friends

- Finding a place to sit

Encourage students to focus on friendship and interpersonal goals such as, "I want to get along with Mary," or "I want to avoid fighting during the game."

Wrap-Up

As a closing activity, show the picture of the boy in front of a class. Tell a story about the boy moving to a new area and being very nervous. With the students, run through all of the problem-solving steps from #1 to #4 (e.g., the problem identified in Step #4 may be, "The boy is at a new school and doesn't know anyone. He is feeling very nervous"). For Step #5, brainstorm a list of possible goals for the boy in this situation. What does he want to happen? He may want to

- Make a new friend

- Fit in

- Do well in class

- Stop feeling so nervous

- Talk to someone

- Have someone show him around

ALTERNATIVE PRESENTATIONS

Fundamental

- *In addition to the materials already listed, you will need the pictures used in* What Does it Mean to Have Goals *lesson in this unit ("Playing Soccer," "The Race," "Studying for a Spelling Test," "Singing on Stage").*

Before using the context cards, review with students the four pictures used in the previous lesson. Review the goals of the characters and why those goals are appropriate for those locations.

Challenging

Discuss with students the idea of having multiple, and possibly conflicting, goals. Use the example of a person who wants to finish her art project but also wants to maintain her relationship with a friend. Because there is only one paintbrush available, these goals may be in conflict. Key questions might include

- What does the girl want to happen?

- Which goal is more important?

- Is there a way that she can reach both of her goals?

THROUGHOUT THE DAY

- During social situations or conflicts, coach students using the question, "What do you want to happen?"

- Have students identify a goal for recess (or lunch time, home, and so forth) today. What do they want to happen?

LESSON REPRODUCIBLES

Gym class

What do I want to happen?

Lunch time

What do I want to happen?

Math class

What do I want to happen?

Trip to the mall

What do I want to happen?

Recess

What do I want to happen?

Home

What do I want to happen?

BOY IN FRONT OF CLASS

Practicing Identifying Goals

PURPOSE

To practice identifying situation-appropriate goals in both personal and observed situations

STUDENTS WILL

Identify a goal presented in the videos

Complete the Identify Your Goal worksheet

MATERIALS

- Stoplight poster #2

- Video clips (Suggested videos: *Hercules*, *Toy Story*)

- TV/VCR

- Large version of the Identify Your Goal worksheet on chart paper or chalkboard

- Marker or chalk

- Identify Your Goal worksheet

PRESENTATION OF LESSON

Discussion

Tell students that today you are going to continue to work on identifying goals. Review Step #5 on Stoplight poster #2, along with the concept of a goal. (A goal is something that we want to happen. When we have a goal, we try hard to make it happen.)

General

IDENTIFYING GOALS VIDEO CLIPS

Movie Title	Description of Clip	Clip Location
Hercules	Hercules accidentally knocks over the marketplace.	22:48–24:09
Toy Story	Buzz Lightyear gets pushed out the window.	37:30–38:40

Video Activity

Show the clip from *Hercules,* and together fill out a large version of the Identify Your Goal worksheet for the characters in the clip (answers to numbers 1–3 are the calming down steps from the Stoplight poster #1). In the end, have students come up with multiple goals for Hercules (e.g., finding a friend, becoming better at sports, having people like him).

Show the clip from *Toy Story.* Together, fill out an Identify Your Goal worksheet for the situation presented in the video. Have students generate multiple goals for Woody (e.g., rescuing Buzz, apologizing to Buzz, asking his friends to stop being mad at him).

Worksheet Activity

Have students identify a problem that they currently have or have had in the past. Explain to students that before they can solve their problems, they need to be calm enough to think. Have students show you the three steps they would use to calm down.

Have students fill in the three calming down steps on the Identify Your Goal worksheet and then move on to Steps #4 and #5 for their own problem.

It may be hard to generate multiple goals simultaneously for personal situations, but try to get students to articulate at least two goals. Be sure to model this process yourself with one of your own problems.

Wrap-Up

Have the students share their problems and goals with the group.

ALTERNATIVE PRESENTATIONS

Fundamental

- *In addition to the materials already listed, you will need drawing paper and crayons/markers.*

Have students draw pictures about their problems. Divide a piece of drawing paper in half by folding it and drawing a line down the middle. On the left side of the paper, have the students draw and label a picture of the problem. On the right side of the paper, have them draw and label a picture of their goal. For example, if a student's goal after a fight was to make up and be friends, he or she could draw a picture of him- or herself playing with a friend.

Challenging

Discuss with students the idea of having multiple, and possibly conflicting, goals. Use the example of a person who wants to play basketball but also wants to maintain his relationship with a friend who does not want to play. Because his friend does not want to play basketball, these goals may be in conflict. Key questions might include

- What does the boy want to happen?

- Which goal is more important?

- Is there a way that he can reach both of his goals?

THROUGHOUT THE DAY

- Check in with students to see if they are having success meeting their personal goals or group "friendship goals." Discuss their progress.

LESSON REPRODUCIBLE

Name _____ Date _____

Write down the three calming down steps.

RED LIGHT

1. _____

2. _____

3. _____

Fill in the blanks below using your own problem.

YELLOW LIGHT

4. What is going on? _____

_____

_____

Identify feelings _____

_____

_____

5. What do I want to happen? _____

_____

_____

Generating
Strategies to Solve a Problem

PURPOSE

To generate strategies to solve a problem (reach a stated goal)

STUDENTS WILL

Provide at least one possible strategy to solve a problem

Participate in the role-play activity

MATERIALS

- Stoplight poster #2

- Chart paper and a marker or chalkboard and chalk

- Pictures ("Shauna's Problem" #1–3, "Randal's Problem")

- Role-play footprints

- Tape

PRESENTATION OF LESSON

Discussion

Tell students that today you will be moving on to Step #6 on Stoplight poster #2.

Explain to students that today you will be adding a new step to the problem-solving routine you have been working on. This new step is, "What can I do?" Tell students that once they have decided what they want to happen (Step #5), they need to think of what they can do to make it happen. Point out Step #6 on Stoplight poster #2.

Write the word *strategy* on the chalkboard or chart paper. Explain to students that a strategy is something people can do to solve their problems.

Pictures Activity

Show the "Shauna's Problem" pictures. After looking at all three pictures in order, ask your students to tell you what is going on (Shauna lost the money her mother gave her for lunch), and discuss how Shauna might be feeling. For example, Shauna might be feeling

- sad

- angry

- frustrated

Offer one strategy Shauna could use to solve her problem (e.g., Shauna might call her mother), and have your students brainstorm as many other ideas as they can about what Shauna can do to solve her problem. Shauna might

- tell an adult

- ask the lunch lady for help

- borrow money from a friend

Write these strategies on the chalkboard or chart paper.

When students offer ideas that involve violence or are otherwise inappropriate, explain to them that a *good* strategy is a strategy that solves one problem without creating another. Fighting might solve the problem but it can create other problems such as getting in trouble, getting arrested, having to pay for hospital bills, making an enemy, and so forth.

Repeat the previous procedure with the last picture ("Randal's Problem"). Show the picture to students and tell them that Randal had an argument with his friend. Tell your students that when Randal was upset, he said some mean things to his friend. Since then, Randal used the three steps for calming down and is thinking more clearly. Randal feels badly about how he acted. Ask your students what Randal can do now.

Note: Make sure to save these lists of strategies for a future lesson in this unit (Predicting Consequences) that introduces consequences.

Role-Play Activity

Role play Shauna and Randal's problems. Using the lists the students generated, role play the characters using a variety of strategies to solve their problems.

Wrap-Up

Discuss the strategies that were role played. Are some better than others? Why? Why not?

ALTERNATIVE PRESENTATIONS

Fundamental

• *In addition to the materials already listed, you will need drawing paper and crayons/markers.*

Have students draw a picture of Randal using one of the strategies the group brainstormed.

Challenging

Extend with students the discussion about appropriate strategies. Discuss with them the idea of good and bad strategies. Key questions might include

• How do you figure out if a strategy is good or not?

• Why do you think it's harder to figure out a strategy when you're in the middle of the problem than it is to figure it out other times?

• Why do you think some people use bad strategies?

THROUGHOUT THE DAY

• Continue to encourage students to practice and use problem-solving steps as needed throughout the school day.

• Brainstorm a list of strategies to solve a group problem.

• Hold a problem-solving meeting.

LESSON REPRODUCIBLES

SHAUNA'S PROBLEM #1

Unit 4: Generating Strategies to Solve a Problem

Practicing Generating Strategies

PURPOSE

To apply the first six steps of the problem-solving model to a problem

STUDENTS WILL

Generate multiple strategies to solve a hypothetical problem (reach a stated goal)

Complete worksheets related to the problem-solving steps

MATERIALS

- Stoplight poster #2

- Practicing Generating Strategies worksheet

- Generating Strategies on Your Own worksheet

PRESENTATION OF LESSON

Discussion

Review with students the meaning of the word *strategy* (a strategy is something you can do to solve your problem). Explain to students that you will be practicing generating strategies, but in order to do this correctly, you must also review Steps #1–5 on Stoplight poster #2.

General

Worksheet Activity

Show the picture at the top of the Practicing Generating Strategies worksheet. Ask students what is going on in the picture (Brian missed the ball when he went to kick it, and the other students are laughing at him). Ask your students how Brian might be feeling.

Lesson

Tell students that before they can solve their problem, they need to be calm enough to think. Have students show you the three steps they would use to calm down.

Then, together answer the questions on the worksheet about Brian's problem. At the question next to Step #5, discuss multiple goals but decide on one main goal as a group. At the question next to Step #6, discuss multiple strategies. Encourage students to list as many ideas as they can about what Brian could do to solve his problem.

Have students repeat this process again independently on the Generating Strategies on Your Own worksheet. Remind them to think about what is going on (Danny wants to swing on the swing, but Joe got there first) and how Danny might be feeling.

Wrap-Up

As a closing activity, have students share their worksheets and the strategies that they generated to solve Danny's problem.

ALTERNATIVE PRESENTATIONS

Fundamental

Have students fill in the facial expressions on the worksheet on their own, but create overheads from the worksheets and complete the writing tasks together as a group.

Challenging

Discuss with students whether your students have ever encountered problems similar to the ones Brian and Danny faced. Key questions might include

- How did you feel when this problem happened to you?

- How did you solve your problem?

- Was your strategy successful? Why or why not?

THROUGHOUT THE DAY

- Have students create their own worksheets about a personal problem to exchange with other members of the group.

LESSON REPRODUCIBLES

Practicing Generating Strategies

Name _____ Date _____

Answer the questions about Brian and his friends and the problem they are having.

| Brian | Kristen | Alan |

Step #4: What is going on? _____

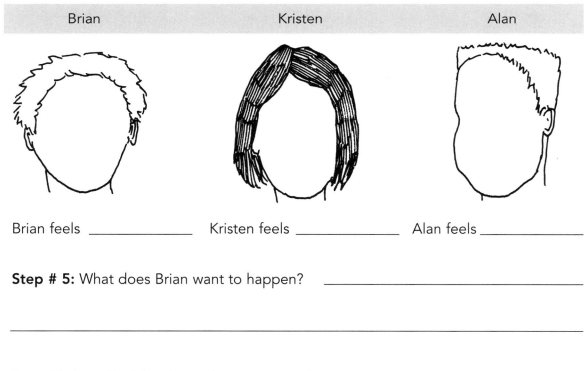

| Brian | Kristen | Alan |

Brian feels _____   Kristen feels _____   Alan feels _____

Step # 5: What does Brian want to happen?   _____

_____

Step #6: List all of the things that Brian can do.   _____

_____

Generating Strategies on Your Own

Name _____ Date _____

Answer the questions below about Danny and his friends and the problem they are having.

Ricky	Joe	Danny

Step #4: What is going on? _____

Ricky	Joe	Danny

Ricky feels _____ Joe feels _____ Danny feels _____

Step # 5: What does Danny want to happen? _____

_____

Step #6: List all of the things that Danny can do. _____

_____

Generating Multiple Strategies

PURPOSE

To provide additional practice in generating multiple strategies to solve a
problem

STUDENTS WILL

Provide at least two strategies for each problem

UNIT 4

MATERIALS

- Stoplight poster #2

- Picture ("Steve and the Basketball Game")

- Steve and the Basketball Game worksheet

- Pencils/pens

- Chart paper and a marker or chalkboard and chalk

- Small rewards such as M&Ms

PRESENTATION OF LESSON

Discussion

Review with students the meaning of the word *strategy* (something you can do
to solve your problem). Explain to students that you will be practicing generating strategies, but in order to do this correctly, you must also review Steps #1–5
on Stoplight poster #2.

General

Game Activity

Explain to students that you will be splitting them up into pairs (or small groups) in order to practice the problem-solving steps. Give each pair a copy of the "Steve and the Basketball Game" picture and worksheet.

Tell students that Steve has a problem, but before he can solve his problem, he needs to be calm enough to think. Have students show you the three steps they would use to calm down. Tell students that once he is calm, Steve has to figure out what is going on (Step #4). Ask students to tell you what is going on in the picture and how Steve might be feeling (Steve really wants to play basketball with the other kids but is feeling lonely and left out while the other kids look so happy and excited). Next, Steve has to figure out what he wants to happen (Step #5). He decides that he wants to join the game so he can feel like he is part of the group. Tell your students that their job is to come up with strategies to solve Steve's problem. What can Steve do? (Step #6)

Once the class has gone over the picture and the first section of the worksheet, each pair should come up with as many good strategies to solve the problem as they can. List these strategies on the chalkboard or chart paper. (Remind students that a good strategy solves one problem without creating another. Fighting might solve the problem but it can create other problems such as getting in trouble with parents, getting suspended from school, having to pay for hospital bills, making an enemy, and so forth.) Students will have to provide a rationale as to why their strategy would be a good, and potentially successful, one. The goal will be to see how many strategies the group can come up with as a whole—each strategy on the group list will earn the students a reward. As a class, discuss Steve's problem, feelings, and goals.

Encourage students to think of creative ideas because the goal of the game is to come up with as many good and different strategies as possible. Give students 10 minutes or so to complete the worksheet.

Once the allotted time is up, have each group share one strategy. Discuss the merits of each strategy and add it to the group list if appropriate. Continue until all pairs have given all of their ideas. Dispense the appropriate number of rewards to each student.

Wrap-Up

As a closing activity, have the students pick their favorite strategy and explain to the group why they feel that strategy would be the best one for Steve to try.

ALTERNATIVE PRESENTATIONS

Fundamental

- *In addition to the materials already listed, you may need a blank audiotape and a tape recorder.*

Pair students with writing difficulties with more advanced students. If this is not possible, allow students to record their ideas on a tape recorder, or assist them with the writing task.

Challenging

Extend the discussion about appropriate strategies. Challenge students to think through their ideas and to come up with the possible consequences resulting from each strategy before adding it to the list. Encourage students to modify their ideas according to the possible consequences.

Have students come up with an additional problem, run through Steps #4–6, and repeat the activity.

THROUGHOUT THE DAY

- Continue to practice the problem-solving steps and emphasize their uses throughout the school day.

- During recess, have a group basketball game. Role play Steve's problem and the strategies he might use to solve his problem.

LESSON REPRODUCIBLES

Name _____ Date _____

In the space provided, write down as many strategies as you can that Steve can use to solve his problem.

The problem is: Steve wants to play basketball with the other kids.

Steve feels lonely and left out.

The other kids feel excited.

Steve's goals are to join the game and feel like he is part of the group.

One strategy is _____

_____

_____

Another strategy is _____

_____

_____

Another strategy is _____

_____

_____

Steve

Another strategy is _____

_____

Write some other ideas on the back of this paper.

Assertive Problem-Solving Strategies

PURPOSE

To practice assertive problem-solving strategies

STUDENTS WILL

Generate assertive statements within role-play situations

UNIT 4

MATERIALS

- Chart paper and a marker or chalkboard and chalk

- Role-play footprints

- Tape

- Assertive Problem-Solving Strategies Role-Play Situations list

- Stoplight poster #2

PRESENTATION OF LESSON

Discussion

Write the word *assertive* on the chalkboard or chart paper. Remind students that you have been talking about what people can do to solve problems. Tell them that being assertive is one thing we can do to reach a goal and solve a problem. Ask if anyone knows what it means to be assertive. Explain that being assertive means you stand up for yourself. You say what you want using good manners. Using the role-play activity that follows, show your students an example of being assertive.

Role-Play Activity

Role play the following situation: A group of students is eating lunch, and you would like to join them. An unassertive strategy is to stand by the table and wait for one of the students to notice you. An assertive strategy is to ask the students directly, perhaps using their names, if you can sit with them.

Discuss the role play with the students. Key questions might include

- What strategy did I use to get what I wanted?

- Was I being polite?

Role play the rest of the situations on the Assertive Problem-Solving Strategies Role-Play Situations list. Encourage students to state what they would like or ask for what they want in a polite manner.

Wrap-Up

Review with students Steps #1–6 on Stoplight poster #2.

ALTERNATIVE PRESENTATIONS

Fundamental

Give the students more guidance in the role play. Have them complete the sentence, "Excuse me, I would like . . .," or "Excuse me, could you please . . .?"

Challenging

Discuss with students situations in which assertive strategies are inappropriate or do not work. What could you have done if the students at the lunch table did not want you to sit down?

THROUGHOUT THE DAY

- Encourage students to use assertive strategies when appropriate.

LESSON REPRODUCIBLE

Role-Play Situations

Role Play #1:

You are at a party, and you want to ask someone to dance.

Role Play #2:

Your teacher is busy talking to another teacher, and you want to tell her it's time for you to go to music class.

Role Play #3:

Your teacher is explaining a math problem to the class, and you don't understand, so you want to ask her to explain it again.

Role Play #4:

You need to use the computer, but another student is using it.

Role Play #5:

You are at a restaurant, and you want to order food.

Role Play #6:

At recess, you want to join in the kickball game.

Role Play #7:

You want to invite someone to go swimming after school.

Role Play #8:

A student is teasing another student, and you want him or her to stop.

Using Compromise as a Strategy

PURPOSE

To introduce compromise as a problem-solving strategy

To practice generating problem-solving strategies that involve compromise

UNIT 4

STUDENTS WILL

Generate at least one appropriate compromise for the conflict situations presented

MATERIALS

- Balance scale and weights

- Worksheets (The Swing, The Computer, Where to Play?, The Line Leader, and The Class Party) or overheads of worksheets and overhead markers

PRESENTATION OF LESSON

Discussion

Begin by introducing the concept of *compromise* as one strategy that is often successful in solving problems. Ask students what they know about compromise, and define the term (a way to solve problems in which each person gives in a little bit).

Describe the following situation to your students: There is only one piece of cake left, and two people want it. Explain to students that the people who want the cake might have to compromise in order for each of them to have some. In a compromise, both people might decide to divide the piece of cake in two. Each person gives in a little so that they can each have some cake instead of no cake at all. Explain to students that this way to solve problems, in which each person gives in a little bit, is a compromise.

Use the balance scale to visually represent compromise. This can be done in several ways. When the scale has all of the weights in place, taking a few off each side can represent "giving up a little bit." When each side gives up a certain amount, things are still *balanced* and *fair*. A more literal demonstration involves thinking of each side of the scale as a person who wants all the markers (weights). Giving one person all the markers makes things unbalanced and unfair. A compromise would be for the two sides to share the markers, thus creating a balanced scale.

Worksheet Activity

Show the first worksheet (The Swing). Describe the problem that is occurring and ask the students to come up with a compromise in which each side gives up a little but which is satisfactory to both. Write their solutions in the space marked "Compromise." If several suggestions are given, you might want to decide on the best one as a group, or acknowledge that all of them would be appropriate. Repeat this procedure with the next three worksheets (The Computer, Where to Play?, and The Line Leader).

Ask students to fill out the final worksheet (The Class Party) themselves.

Wrap-Up

Have students share their answers for The Class Party worksheet with the class.

ALTERNATIVE PRESENTATIONS

Fundamental

* *In addition to the materials already listed, you will need drawing paper and crayons/markers.*

Students who are unable to complete the worksheet on their own with a written description can draw a picture depicting the selected compromise. If students are unable to come up with appropriate compromises on their own, ask them to pick from possible solutions below and on the next page for each worksheet (the appropriate compromises are in *italics*).

The Swing
Melissa runs and tells the teacher.
Juan pushes Melissa off the swing.
Melissa swings for 10 minutes, then Juan swings for 10 minutes.

The Computer
John tells Tannika that he won't be her friend if he can't use the computer.
Tannika and John share the computer.
Tannika walks away crying.

Where to Play?

Justin goes to Rob's house today, and Rob will go to Justin's house tomorrow.
The boys both play alone.
Rob plays at Justin's house.

The Line Leader

Nina gets to be the line leader this time, Julie gets to be the line leader next time.
Both students go to the back of the line.
Julie gets to be the line leader.

The Class Party

The class cancels the party.
The girls and boys agree to get both pizza and ice cream, but less of each.
The teacher decides to get popcorn.

Challenging

* *In addition to the materials already listed, you will need role-play footprints and tape.*

Have students role play a situation that involves compromise. Break the students into groups and give them a problem they must solve with a compromise. If possible, use problems that your students have encountered in the past. Encourage students to discuss possibilities, support the ideas of others, and to make sure that all parties are satisfied with the compromise.

THROUGHOUT THE DAY

* Be aware that students may have the tools to solve interpersonal conflicts without the input of an adult. At every opportunity, teachers should give students the chance to come up with an acceptable compromise together, or the teacher should coach/guide students in this process.

* Have students come up with compromises concerning the sharing of group chores and the sharing of group resources such as markers, crayons, and so forth.

* Hold a problem-solving meeting.

LESSON REPRODUCIBLES

Name _____ Date _____

In the space provided, write a compromise for the characters in the picture.

Problem:

Melissa wants to use the swing.   Juan wants to use the swing.

Compromise:

_____

_____

_____

_____

Name _____ Date _____

In the space provided, write a compromise for the characters in the picture.

Problem:

John wants to use the computer.   Tannika wants to use the computer.

Compromise:

_____

_____

_____

_____

_____

Name _____ Date _____

In the space provided, write a compromise for the characters in the picture.

Problem:

Justin wants Rob to come
over to his house.

Rob wants Justin to come
over to his house.

Compromise:

_____

_____

_____

_____

_____

_____

Name _____ Date _____

In the space provided, write a compromise for the characters in the picture.

Problem:

Nina and Julie reached the door at the same time.

Nina wants to be first. Julie wants to be first.

Compromise:

_____

_____

_____

_____

_____

Name _____ Date _____

In the space provided, write a compromise for the characters in the picture.

Problem:

The girls want to have pizza
at the class party.

The boys want to have ice
cream at the class party.

Compromise:

_____

_____

_____

_____

Predicting Consequences

PURPOSE

To introduce the question, "What happens if . . .?" as a way to understand consequences

To practice the prediction of consequences for a variety of situations

STUDENTS WILL

Apply the question, "What happens if . . .?" to strategies for a hypothetical problem

Offer at least one plausible outcome for a situation

MATERIALS

* List of strategies from the Generating Strategies to Solve a Problem lesson in this unit

* Pictures from the Generating Strategies to Solve a Problem lesson in this unit

* Role-play footprints

* Tape

* Chart paper and a marker or chalkboard and chalk

* Drawing paper

* Crayons/markers

PRESENTATION OF LESSON

Discussion

Review the list of strategies and the pictures from the Generating Strategies to Solve a Problem lesson.

Ask your students if they remember Shauna, the girl in the pictures. Remind students that when you talked about Shauna before, you came up with a lot of great ideas to solve her problem. Tell students that today they are going to try to help Shauna more by asking a new question, "What happens if . . .?" to determine which idea to solve her problem is best. One way to figure out which idea is best is to think about what might happen if you did a certain thing.

Role-Play Activity

For each strategy on the list from the Generating Strategies to Solve a Problem lesson, ask students what might happen if Shauna tried that strategy. Role play the situation. Role play Shauna using the strategy and role play the consequences of that strategy.

Strategy Selection

Begin the process of strategy selection by picking the best strategy based on the consequences of each. Have students vote for the strategy that had the most favorable outcome.

Repeat this process with the picture of Randal and his friend. Remind students that Randal had an argument with his friend and because he was upset, he said some mean things to her. After using the three steps for calming down, Randal began thinking more clearly and felt badly about how he acted.

Wrap-Up

As a closing activity, have students draw a picture of Shauna or Randal using the best strategy to solve their problems.

ALTERNATIVE PRESENTATIONS

Fundamental

Role play two possible strategies for the characters to use. Have students pick the best strategy from only those two possibilities.

Challenging

- *In addition to the materials listed, you will need a TV/VCR and the* Toy Story *video clip from the* Identifying Intention *lesson.*

Discuss with students the idea that sometimes our actions have unexpected consequences. Perhaps use as an example the video clip from *Toy Story* that you showed in the Identifying Intention lesson. In this clip, Woody wanted to knock over Buzz Lightyear but ended up knocking him out the window by mistake. Key questions might include

- Can you tell me about a time something unexpected happened as a result of something you did?

- How can we remind ourselves to think about what might happen?

THROUGHOUT THE DAY

- Question students about the consequences of their actions.

- Have students answer the question, "What happens if . . .?" in regard to a group problem.

UNIT 4

Practicing Strategy Selection

PURPOSE

To practice the evaluation and selection of strategies based on possible
consequences

STUDENTS WILL

Generate at least one strategy to solve a problem

Predict at least one possible consequence of using a particular strategy

MATERIALS

- Role-play footprints

- Tape

- Practicing Strategy Selection Role-Play Situations list

- Chart paper and a marker or chalkboard and chalk

PRESENTATION OF LESSON

Discussion

Review with students what you covered in the previous lesson. Students were
asked to predict what happens if a particular strategy is used. Thinking about
consequences helps us choose the best way to solve a problem.

Role-Play Activity

Explain to students that today you are going to be doing some role plays. The
role plays have to do with picking good strategies to solve a problem.

Read the first-role play situation from the Practicing Strategy Selection Role-
Play Situations list. Have students think of three possible ways to solve the prob-

lem, and write them on the chalkboard or chart paper under the heading "Strategies." Students will act out each of these strategies. Before beginning the role play, explain that the rest of the students' job is to watch what happens when each strategy is used and to decide if the strategy solved the problem.

Have students discuss what happened when the student used each strategy. Write down the consequences next to the strategy (make a separate list of "Consequences"). Repeat this process for each role play. Conclude by having students pick the strategy with the best consequence (the strategy that best solved the problem), and mark it on the chalkboard with a star or smiley face.

Wrap-Up

As a closing activity, review with students the importance of thinking about consequences. Key questions might include

- Why is it important to think about what might happen before you do something?

- Why is it important to pick the best strategy?

- What can you do if the strategy you picked does not work?

ALTERNATIVE PRESENTATIONS

Fundamental

Compare two strategies—one successful and one unsuccessful—instead of three.

Challenging

Have students come up with their own role-play situations. After generating three possible strategies, have students predict ahead of time the consequences of using each one. Role play the strategy and the consequences.

THROUGHOUT THE DAY

- Verbally coach students to think through the consequences of their actions using versions of the following questions: "What are you going to do?" or "What do you think will happen if you do that?"

- Discuss with students the consequences of their lunch room or recess behavior.

LESSON REPRODUCIBLE

Role-Play Situations

Role Play #1:

The teacher is busy talking to another student, but you need help with your work. How can you solve this problem?

Role Play #2:

You don't have anyone to play with at recess, and you are feeling lonely and left out. How can you solve this problem?

Role Play #3:

You want a drink of water, but someone is hogging the water fountain. How can you solve this problem?

Role Play #4:

Someone is teasing you because you got a bad grade on a math test. How can you solve this problem?

Role Play #5:

Your best friend always wants to play with someone else. Your feelings are hurt. How can you solve this problem?

Role Play #6:

The student next to you is always getting you in trouble by being noisy and talking to you when you are trying to work. How can you solve this problem?

Role Play #7:

Someone is playing too roughly out at recess, and you are not having fun anymore. How can you solve this problem?

Promoting Social Success: A Curriculum for Children with Special Needs by Gary N. Siperstein & Emily Paige Rickards
© 2004 by Paul H. Brookes Publishing Co. Inc. All rights reserved.
www.brookespublishing.com   1-800-638-3775

Introducing the
Green Light Action Steps

PURPOSE

To introduce the concepts of evaluation and revision through Steps #7 and #8 of Stoplight poster #2

STUDENTS WILL

Evaluate the outcome of several problem-solving plans

MATERIALS

- Stoplight poster #2

- Role-play footprints

- Tape

- Introducing the Green Light Role-Play Situations list

PRESENTATION OF LESSON

Discussion

Tell students that you are moving on to Steps #7 and #8 on Stoplight poster #2. Show students Stoplight poster #2, and point out Steps #7 and #8.

Tell your students that once they have picked the best strategy ("What can I do?"), they need to try their plan and see how it goes. They need to ask themselves if things worked out the way they wanted them to. Did they reach their goals?

Role-Play Activity

Explain to students that today you will be doing some role plays. Each group of students will role play a problem and three possible strategies to solve the problem from the Introducing the Green Light Role-Play Situations list. One of the strategies will successfully solve the problem. The rest of the class will answer the question, "How did it go?" concerning the outcome of each plan. The class will vote for the best outcome (one in which the person reached his or her goal) using a "thumbs up" or "thumbs down" response.

Remember, a good strategy is a strategy that solves one problem without creating another (fighting might solve the problem, but it can create others such as getting in trouble, getting arrested, having to pay for hospital bills, making an enemy, and so forth).

Wrap-Up

Review with students Steps #1–8 on Stoplight poster #2.

ALTERNATIVE PRESENTATIONS

Fundamental

Compare one successful and one unsuccessful strategy for each problem.

Challenging

Ask students to predict the outcome of using the strategy prior to the role play.

THROUGHOUT THE DAY

- Reinforce the concepts of evaluation and revision by encouraging students to make repeated attempts to reach their goals using a variety of strategies. The question, "How did it go?" can act as a prompt for students to reflect on their strategy and its results.

- Have students evaluate the outcome of a group problem they have tried to solve.

LESSON REPRODUCIBLE

Role-Play Situations

Role Play #1:

What is going on? I have lost my best friend's new toy. I feel upset and guilty. My friend feels angry.

What do I want to happen? I want to make up with my friend.

What can I do?
- Talk to my friend and aplogize.
- Blame it on someone else.
- Talk about something else and hope that my friend forgets about the toy.

Role Play #2:

What is going on? A student is making fun of me because of the clothes that I wear. I am feeling angry and embarrassed. The other student is laughing.

What do I want to happen? I want her to stop laughing at me and be nice.

What can I do?
- Make fun of her, too.
- Tell the teacher and get her in trouble.
- Ask her to stop teasing me, then walk away.

Role Play #3:

What is going on? I am in a bad mood because my mom yelled at me this morning. I do not want to do my work. I am feeling angry and upset. The teacher is getting frustrated with my behavior.

What do I want to happen? I want to feel better.

What can I do?
- Yell at the person next to me.
- Crumple up my work.
- Tell the teacher how I feel and ask for help.

Role Play #4:

What is going on? I keep getting in trouble out at recess because we play a rough game of football. I am feeling frustrated, and I am not having fun anymore.

What do I want to happen? I want to have fun at recess.

What can I do?
- Tell my friends that I want to play something else.
- Yell at my friends.
- Keep playing the game and hope that we don't get in trouble.

Role Play #5:

What is going on? My friend always hogs all the magic markers. I am feeling upset. She is feeling happy that she has all the colors.

What do I want to happen? I want to draw with the markers.

What can I do?
- Grab the markers from her.
- Ask her to share half the markers with me.
- Tell on her to the teacher.

Role-Play Situations, continued

Role Play #6:

What is going on? My friend took my ruler without asking to borrow it. I am feeling upset and angry. He is using it to do his work.

What do I want to happen? I want my ruler back.

What can I do?

- Let him have the ruler.
- Grab it back from him.
- Tell him that I want the ruler back and that he should ask to borrow it next time.

How Did it Go?

PURPOSE

To evaluate the success of problem-solving plans based on outcomes

STUDENTS WILL

Answer the question, "How did it go?" as it pertains to several poems

MATERIALS

- Stoplight poster #2

- Chart paper and a marker or chalkboard and chalk

- Shel Silverstein's *Where the Sidewalk Ends* and *Falling Up*

- Problem Solving and Consequences worksheet

PRESENTATION OF LESSON

Discussion

Review with students Steps #7 and #8 on Stoplight poster #2 along with the content of the previous lesson.

Remind your students that once they have picked the best strategy ("What can I do?"), they need to try their plan and see how it goes. They need to ask themselves if things worked out the way they wanted them to? Did they reach their goals? If not, they need to ask themselves what to do next.

Write the categories, "Goal," "How Did it Go?" and "New Plan" on the chalkboard or chart paper. Tell students that you will be reading some poems out loud in order to see how things work out for the people in the poems.

Poems Activity

Set the stage for each poem by identifying the goal for each character—write these under the "Goal" column. For example, the first poem is about a little boy named Jimmy. Jimmy's goal is to have fun watching a lot of TV. Read each poem aloud to your students and tell them to listen to see if things work out for each character.

Goals

- "Jimmy Jet and his TV Set," page 28, *Where the Sidewalk Ends*
  Goal: To have fun watching a lot of TV

- "Headphone Harold," page 161, *Falling Up*
  Goal: To have fun listening to music

- "Melinda Mae," page 154, *Where the Sidewalk Ends*
  Goal: To eat a whale

- "Yuck," page 151, *Falling Up*
  Goal: To clean off the "yuck"

Keep in mind that these are general goals, not necessarily goals in a problem-solving context; these examples are meant to familiarize students with the ideas of evaluation and revision in a general way.
     After you read each poem, ask students to identify what happened in the poem.

- Jimmy turned into a TV set because he watched so much TV—people watched him instead of him watching TV.

- Harold may have gotten run over by the train.

- Melinda ate the whale.

- The boy got stuck to everything.

Encourage students to identify these outcomes as either positive or negative. Ask the students

- Do you think that things worked out the way [the character] wanted them to?

- Did [the character] reach his or her goal?

Draw either a smiling face or a frowning face under the category "How Did it Go?" on the chalkboard or chart paper depending on whether the character reached his or her goal.

- Jimmy did not reach his goal. (frowning face)

- Harold did not reach his goal. (frowning face)

- Melinda reached her goal. (smiling face)

- The boy did not reach his goal. (frowning face)

Focus the discussion on what the characters who did not reach their goals could do now (new strategy selection). Write this new strategy on the chalkboard or chart paper under "New Plan." Possibilities include

- Jimmy could just pick some of his favorite shows, watch only shows after school, watch only on weekends, and so forth.

- Harold could listen while in one place, listen inside, use a radio without head-phones, be more careful to look around him, and so forth.

- The boy could wait until it dries, wash it off in the shower, wipe it with a towel, and so forth.

Wrap-Up

Review with students Steps #1–8 on Stoplight poster #2.

ALTERNATIVE PRESENTATIONS

Fundamental

Limit the number of poems used in the lesson to two—one with a successful outcome and one with an unsuccessful outcome. Compare the two outcomes.

Challenging

Discuss with students times when their strategies have failed to solve a problem. What did they do next?

THROUGHOUT THE DAY

- Reinforce the concepts of evaluation and revision by encouraging students to make repeated attempts to reach their goals using a variety of strategies. The question, "How did it go?" can act as a prompt for students to reflect on their strategies and their results.

- Have students complete the Problem Solving and Consequences worksheet as morning work or homework.

Problem Solving and Consequences

Name _____ Date _____

Think of a problem you have had or are having right now. Draw a picture or write a few sentences describing this problem in the box labeled "Problem." Follow the arrows until you have completed each box.

Problem
(write or draw)

What I wanted to happen
(write or draw)

What I did
(write or draw)

What happened
(write or draw)

Good or bad?

Something I could have done
(write or draw)

What would have happened
(write or draw)

What to Do If We Don't Reach Our Goal

PURPOSE

To develop the students' ability to evaluate the outcome of a plan and decide how they should proceed if they have failed to reach a goal

STUDENTS WILL

Choose an appropriate course of action when a problem-solving plan fails

Give appropriate rationale for the chosen course of action

MATERIALS

- Chart paper and a marker or chalkboard and chalk

- Give Up/Try Again signs (cut in half before handing out to students)

- Pictures ("Can I Play Basketball?" "Can I Go to the Circus?" "Can My Friend Come Over?" "Can We Be Friends?")

- Role-play footprints

- Tape

PRESENTATION OF LESSON

Discussion

Review with students the work they have done so far on selecting strategies to achieve goals and on evaluating the outcome of problem-solving plans.

Remind your students that once they have picked the best strategy ("What can I do?"), they need to try their plan and see how it goes. They need to ask themselves if things worked out the way they wanted them to? Did they reach their goal? If not, what should they do then? Give up? Try again? Change their plan?

Write the words *give up* and *try again* on the chalkboard or chart paper. Explain to students that sometimes the best thing to do when your strategy doesn't work is to give up. Other times it is better to try again.

Explain to students the following examples:

- If Ming asks her father for permission to go to her friend's house and her father says no because the family is all going to Ming's grandmother's house, it is probably best to give up. Ming probably can't change her family's plans. Asking again later won't help.

- If Juan asks his mother to drive him to the store and she says no because she is washing the car right now, it might be a good idea to try asking her again later when she is not so busy.

Tell your students that the reasons for saying no should give them a clue as to whether they should give up or try again.

Pictures Activity

Give each student one Give Up sign and one Try Again sign. Explain that you will be showing them pictures of someone who has gone through Steps #1–7 on Stoplight poster #2 and now they are asking themselves, "How did it go?" Unfortunately, their strategies didn't work, and they must figure out what to do now.

Explain to students that they will be deciding whether the person in the picture should give up or try again by holding up the appropriate sign.

Show and explain the pictures. After each picture, ask students, "What should she or he do? Give up? Or try again?" Be sure to discuss student responses. There are a variety of correct answers, but the key is for their answers to be socially adaptive and for the students to provide a reasonable rationale for their answer.

Picture Explanations

- Can I Play Basketball?
  What is going on? Larry doesn't have anything to do out at recess. He feels left out.
  What do I want to happen? Larry wants to play basketball with the other kids.
  What can I do? Larry decides that he should go up to one of the boys and ask if he can play.
  Try my plan: He goes up to one of the players and says, "Can I play basketball with you guys?"
  How did it go? The player responds, "We're playing 3-on-3 right now, so if you play the teams will be uneven. Sorry."
  What should he do? Give up? Try again? *(try again later)*

- Can I Go to the Circus?

  What is going on? Marvin doesn't know if he has enough money to buy tickets to the circus that is in town. He is feeling confused.

  What do I want to happen? Marvin really wants to go see the tigers.

  What can I do? He decides to call the circus and find out how much the tickets cost.

  Try my plan: Marvin calls the circus.

  How did it go? When he calls, he is told that the tickets are sold out—there are no tickets left.

  What should he do? Give up? Try again? (*give up*)

- Can My Friend Come Over?

  What is going on? Julie is bored and lonely.

  What do I want to happen? She wants to have someone to play with.

  What can I do? She decides to ask her friend Cathy to come over.

  Try my plan: She dials Cathy's number.

  How did it go? The phone is busy.

  What should she do? Give up? Try again? (*try again later*)

- Can We Be Friends?

  What is going on? A new boy has moved into Malik's neighborhood.

  What do I want to happen? Malik wants to become friends with John.

  What can I do? He decides to ask John if he wants to go swimming after school at the pool.

  Try my plan: He talks to John and shows him the pool.

  How did it go? John tells Malik that he can't go because he doesn't know how to swim.

  What should he do? Give up? Try again? (*try again—suggest different activity*)

Wrap-Up

As a closing activity, have students role play one of the previous situations. Encourage students to calm down and verbalize the problem-solving steps as they act out the situation and decide to either give up or try again.

ALTERNATIVE PRESENTATIONS

Fundamental

Compare and contrast two situations. Discuss one situation in which the best idea is to give up and one situation in which the best idea is to try again. What makes these situations different from each other? Role play the situations.

Challenging

Have students choose between three options instead of two. If they choose *try again,* they will have to decide if the person should try the *same* strategy again or whether they should try a *different* strategy. Have students explain why the same strategy or a different strategy would most likely work.

THROUGHOUT THE DAY

- Encourage students to revise their plans when they are unsuccessful in reaching their goals.

- Have students make and display posters that remind them to "Try, try, again!"

LESSON REPRODUCIBLES

Give Up

- - - - - - -

Try
Again

CAN I GO TO THE CIRCUS?

CAN WE BE FRIENDS?

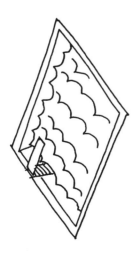

Applying the
Problem-Solving Steps

PURPOSE

To apply the eight problem-solving steps to a problem situation

STUDENTS WILL

Demonstrate their ability to apply the problem-solving steps to a situation by
completing a worksheet

MATERIALS

- Stoplight poster #2

- Cutting in Line worksheet

- Role-play footprints

- Tape

- Teasing Nicole worksheet

PRESENTATION OF LESSON

Discussion

Review with students the problem-solving steps on Stoplight poster #2 and explain that today they are going to practice using all eight of the steps.

Worksheet Activity

Show the picture at the top of the Cutting in Line worksheet, and tell students
that you want them to pretend that they are Joel.

Tell them that before they can solve their problem, they need to be calm enough to think. Have students show you the three steps they would use to calm down.

Then, together answer the questions on the worksheet about Joel's problem (he was first in line, but Peter cut in front of him). At the question next to Step #5 ("What does Joel want to happen?"), discuss multiple goals but decide on one main goal as a group. At the question next to Step #6 ("What can Joel do?"), discuss multiple strategies. Encourage students to list as many ideas as they can about what Joel could do to solve his problem.

Role-Play Activity

Explain to students that in order to fill out question #8 ("How did it go?"), the group will have to role play the problem situation. Emphasize that the job of the student pretending to be Joel is to follow the problem sheet as closely as he or she can (e.g., acting out the problem, using the steps for calming down, figuring out feelings, enacting a strategy).

Once the role play has ended, the group will need to decide if the strategy used effectively solved the problem. Together, fill out question #8 ("How did it go?"). If the strategy was unsuccessful, repeat the role play using a new strategy and then evaluate its success.

Wrap-Up

Have students repeat this process again independently on the Teasing Nicole worksheet (Amanda is teasing Nicole because she has trouble reading). Then come together to share answers and enact the role play.

ALTERNATIVE PRESENTATIONS

Fundamental

Complete both worksheets as a group or do away with the writing activity and practice the problem-solving steps using the role plays only.

Challenging

Have students come up with their own problem situations and repeat the process.

THROUGHOUT THE DAY

- Have students fill out a similar worksheet for a group problem.

- Hold a problem-solving meeting.

LESSON REPRODUCIBLES

Name _____ Date _____

Answer the questions about Joel and his friends and the problem they are having.

Peter   Joel   Rachel   Manny

Step #4: What is going on? _____

_____

| Peter | Joel | Rachel | Manny |

Peter feels _____ Joel feels _____ Rachel feels _____ Manny feels _____

Step # 5: What does Joel want to happen? _____

_____

Step #6: What can Joel do? _____

_____

Step #7: Try my plan _____

Step #8: How did it go? _____

_____

Name _____ Date _____

Answer the questions about Nicole and her friend and the problem they are having.

Nicole	Amanda

ALPHABET

Step #4: What is going on? _____

_____

Nicole	Amanda

Nicole feels _____   Amanda feels _____

Step # 5: What does Nicole want to happen? _____

_____

Step #6: What can Nicole do? _____

_____

Step #7: Try my plan _____

Step #8: How did it go? _____

_____

Reviewing Problem-Solving Skills

PURPOSE

To identify problems encountered by students

To practice applying the problem-solving steps to real-life situations

STUDENTS WILL

Identify personal problem situations

Complete a problem-solving worksheet

MATERIALS

- Stoplight poster #2

- Chart paper and a marker or chalkboard and chalk

- A Problem I Had worksheet

- Role-play footprints

- Tape

PRESENTATION OF LESSON

Discussion

Review with students the problem-solving steps that you have covered on Stop-light poster #2 (Steps #1–8). Explain that today you are going to talk about problems in school that make students upset or angry.

Explain to students that everyone experiences problems that get them upset, and today they are going to use the problem-solving steps to help them with these problems. Tell students that you have problems, too. For example, you may tell them there was a time you went to lunch and the people you were going to eat with didn't save you a seat. Explain that this hurt your feelings and that you were a little angry with them.

Ask students to identify times when they had a problem at school and write their responses on the chalkboard or chart paper.

Worksheet Activity

Once multiple situations have been identified, have each student pick one problem that they have experienced. Each student will be filling out an A Problem I Had worksheet about their problem. Model this process yourself first with the problem that you described previously. Assist students in filling out their problem-solving sheets through Step #6 (encourage students to generate multiple strategies to solve their problems, to think through the consequences of each one, and to select the best strategy).

Role Play Activity

Explain to students that in order to fill out question #8 ("How did it go?"), the group will have to role play the problem situations. Have each student act out his or her problem situation, with you and the other students playing important roles. Emphasize that the students' jobs are to follow the problem sheet as closely as they can (e.g., acting out the problem, using the steps for calming down, figuring out feelings, enacting a strategy). Model this process yourself first with the problem on your own worksheet.

Once the role play has ended, the group will need to decide if the strategy they used effectively solved the problem. Together, fill out question #8 ("How did it go?"). If the strategy was unsuccessful, repeat the role play using a new strategy and then evaluate its success.

Wrap-Up

After each student has acted out his or her problem situation, discuss how he or she felt and how well the problem-solving steps worked. Encourage the students to use the same strategy in the classroom when the situation actually arises.

ALTERNATIVE PRESENTATIONS

Fundamental

Instead of having the students do the writing activity, have the group work on each problem together verbally, focusing on one student at a time.

Challenging

Discuss with students ways for them to remember the problem-solving steps during recess, lunch, and during other school activities. Together, generate ideas for helping students remember to use the problem-solving steps.

THROUGHOUT THE DAY

- Encourage students to use the problem-solving steps, and the particular strategy practiced in today's lesson, when the problem they chose arises during the school day.

- As a homework assignment, have students fill out a similar worksheet for a problem that occurs outside of school.

- Hold a problem-solving meeting.

Name _____ Date _____

Think of a problem you had and complete the following questions.

Situation _____

_____

RED LIGHT

    1. Stop

    2. Keep Hands to Yourself

    3. Take a Deep Breath

YELLOW LIGHT

    4. What is going on? _____

       _____

       How am I feeling? _____

       _____

       How are other people feeling? _____

       _____

    5. What do I want to happen? _____

       _____

    6. What can I do? _____

       _____

GREEN LIGHT

    7. Try your plan!

    8. How did it go? _____

       _____

Making and Keeping Friends

SOCIAL KNOWLEDGE

UNIT 5

What Makes a Good Friend?

PURPOSE

To identify the qualities that make a person a good friend

To identify those qualities in oneself

To identify ways to improve those qualities in oneself

STUDENTS WILL

Contribute at least one suggestion to the discussion

Apply the ideas to him- or herself using the Ways I Am a Good Friend worksheet

UNIT 5

MATERIALS

* Chart paper and marker or chalkboard and chalk

* *The Giving Tree* by Shel Silverstein

* Ways I Am a Good Friend worksheet

* Friendship worksheet

* *Promoting Social Success* Parent Newsletter: *Friendship*

PRESENTATION OF LESSON

Discussion

Brainstorm with students the qualities that make a good friend and write these on the chalkboard or chart paper. Examples of these qualities may include being honest, being trustworthy, being kind, and having shared interests. Focus on helping and sharing as two important aspects of friendship.

Story Activity

Read *The Giving Tree*. When finished, ask the following two key questions:

- How was the tree a good friend to the boy?

- How was the boy a good friend to the tree?

Answers to the second question especially may vary. The discussion may touch on the fact that the boy did not give concrete things back to the tree, but he did give his time and friendship.

Worksheet Activity

Have students fill out both columns of the Ways I Am a Good Friend worksheet. Use the initial brainstorm list as a guide. Make sure to fill one out yourself.

Wrap-Up

Share your worksheet with students and have students share their answers with the group.

ALTERNATIVE PRESENTATIONS

Fundamental

- *In addition to the materials already listed, you will need a tape recorder and a blank audiotape.*

Allow students to record their answers for the worksheet on a tape recorder. Conclude with a game that focuses on helping behavior. This is an adaptation of the Hot/Cold game in which one person leaves the room while another hides an object. Students who remained in the room will help the individual find the object by clapping as he or she moves around the room. Clapping should be soft when the student is far away from the object (cold) and should become louder as the student moves closer to the object (hot).

Challenging

Discuss with students ways in which they help each other. Have students identify times during the school day when they can make an extra effort to help each other. Have students incorporate helping and sharing behaviors into the list of group rules and the group schedule.

THROUGHOUT THE DAY

- Use the students' Ways I am a Good Friend worksheets to help you provide positive reinforcement when students demonstrate ways they are good friends. Reward any improvements in friendly behavior that you observe.

- Have students complete the Friendship worksheet as morning work or homework.

- Send home the *Promoting Social Success* Parent Newsletter: *Friendship.*

Lesson

General

UNIT 5

LESSON REPRODUCIBLES

Name _____ Date _____

Fill out the columns below.

Ways I am a good friend	Things I need to work on

Name _____ Date _____

From the choices below, circle all of the ways you were a good friend, and draw a picture of yourself being a good friend.

I was a good friend today. I

gave a compliment   told my friend how I felt   knew how my friend was feeling

listened to my friend   shared   forgave my friend

other _____

Here is a picture of me being a good friend.

```




```

Parent/Teacher initials _____ Date _____

The Ups and Downs of Friendship

PURPOSE

To recognize that friendships sometimes involve both happy and sad emotions

STUDENTS WILL

Identify at least one event in the book that caused either happy or sad emotions

MATERIALS

- *We Are Best Friends* by Aliki

- Chart paper and a marker or chalkboard and chalk (write a line down the center of the chalkboard or chart paper with a happy face on one side and sad face on the other)

- Drawing paper

- Crayons/markers

PRESENTATION OF LESSON

Discussion

Tell students that today's lesson is going to be about friendships. Explain to them that being friends with someone is usually a very good thing. Most of the time people are happy when they are with their friends, but sometimes being friends with others can make people sad, too. For example, fighting with a friend or having a friend move away might make people feel very sad and lonely. Explain that in today's lesson, you are going to read a story about friends named Robert and Peter and what happens when Robert moves away to a new house.

Story Activity

Read the story to the students. Ask the students to categorize different events in the story that involved happy or sad emotions. Write the events under the appropriate column on the chalkboard or chart paper.

Drawing Activity

Have students pick either a happy or sad thing that they have experienced within a friendship and draw a picture of it.

Wrap-Up

Have students share their drawings with the group.

ALTERNATIVE PRESENTATIONS

Fundamental

- *In addition to the materials already listed, you will need index cards with happy and sad events from the book drawn on them (you will need to draw these) and tape.*

Rather than asking for the students to spontaneously generate happy and sad events from the book, have index cards with main events drawn on them that the students can tape in the correct column on the chart paper.

Challenging

- *In addition to the materials already listed, you will need role-play footprints and tape.*

Role play some of the students' experiences with the ups and downs of friendship. Discuss and role play strategies for dealing with these ups and downs.

THROUGHOUT THE DAY

- Remind students whose friendships are experiencing periods of trouble that these ups and downs are normal. Discuss with them ways in which both students can feel better about the friendship.

- Remind students to use their set of small feeling faces to show you how they are feeling.

The Importance of Trust

PURPOSE

To build on the What Makes a Good Friend? lesson

To discuss the importance of intimacy and trust within friendships

STUDENTS WILL

Participate in the discussion on friendships

Determine whether a particular act would strengthen or weaken a friendship

MATERIALS

- Brainstorm list from the What Makes a Good Friend? lesson

- *We Are Best Friends* by Aliki (optional)

- Multiple lengths of string

- The Importance of Trust cards

PRESENTATION OF LESSON

Discussion

Review with students the brainstorm list from the What Makes a Good Friend? lesson. If ideas such as talking or sharing personal information are not on the list, make a point of adding them. Discuss the fact that many friendships are based on knowing things about each other, and mutual sharing of personal information can strengthen the bond between friends. You might want to use examples from *We Are Best Friends* by Aliki, or you can generate your own.

Ask students if they ever fight with their brothers or sisters. Remind students that if they tell their friend about their problems with their brothers or sisters, their friend could maybe help them with the problem or at least try to make them feel better if they are upset. Tell your students that these kinds of things make friendships stronger.

Explain to students that today you are going to talk about things that can strengthen and weaken friendships. Discuss with them the idea that although sharing personal information with a friend can strengthen a friendship, it is important for friends to be trustworthy.

Ask students if they have ever had a friend tell others an important secret. Tell them that this will create problems and weaken the friendship because they won't be able to trust their friends with personal information in the future.

Ask students for other ideas of things that either strengthen or weaken friendships.

String Activity

Using two volunteers, show students that they can visually represent friendships by using lengths of string. When friendships are strong (multiple lengths of string connecting the two people, twisted into a strong rope), the bond between the two people is strong. When the friendship is weakened (take away some of the lengths of string), the connection between two people is more easily broken.

While your volunteers are up front, have the rest of the students pick from a pile of The Importance of Trust cards and decide whether the act on the card will strengthen or weaken the friendship. Add or take away the lengths of string depending on their decision. Each student should have the chance to read a card and make the decision. If a friendship "ends" because there are no more strings connecting the two people, continue with a new "friendship" and two new volunteers.

Wrap-Up

Have students identify a "friendship goal." Each student should select one strategy for strengthening a friendship (e.g., being a good listener, keeping a secret, sticking up for a friend) that they can try to implement with a friend.

ALTERNATIVE PRESENTATIONS

Fundamental

• *In addition to the materials already listed, you will need drawing paper, crayons/markers, and a stapler.*

Have students draw a picture depicting a friendship. Staple short lengths of string to blank sheets of paper, and ask students to draw themselves on one end of the string and a friend on the other. Ask them to write about, or draw a picture depicting, some of the aspects of their friendship. What are the shared interests or qualities of their friendship that tie them to that person?

Challenging

Discuss with students their own friendship experiences along with the issue of trust. Key questions might include

- What are some of the things you look for in a friend?

- What kinds of things have happened to make your friendships stronger or weaker?

- How does it make you feel when a friendship becomes weaker?

THROUGHOUT THE DAY

- Check in with students to see if they have implemented their strategies to strengthen their friendship.

- Students may be unaware of the consequences of their behavior. Assist students by pointing out the consequences of certain actions on the students' friendships. This can include positive feedback ("I noticed that you were being extra nice to [group member] today because he is having a hard time. You're being a good friend."), as well as negative feedback ("I noticed that you were teasing [group member] again. You know that she might not want to be your friend anymore if you keep teasing her.").

UNIT 5

LESSON REPRODUCIBLES

Amy told Barry about a time when she got upset. Barry gave Amy some advice to help her.	Amy apologized when she saw that she hurt Barry's feelings.
When someone was teasing Jenny, Gail stuck up for Jenny.	Sometimes Gail won't let Jenny play with her.
Quentin talked about his parent's divorce. Jason listened.	Jason and Quentin shared their music CDs and tapes with each other.

Amy laughed at Barry for being upset.	Barry told Amy about a problem he was having.
Jenny and Gail have fun together when they jump rope.	Amy asked Barry to play on the jungle gym during recess. Barry said, "Yes."
Gail told Jenny that her new haircut was ugly.	Jenny lied to Gail about what she got on the math test.

Mike got mad when Paul played with someone else.

Tara shared her crayons and markers with Liz.

Tara told Liz she looked pretty.

Jason told Quentin about his own parent's divorce, and they talked about how to deal with it.

Paul did not tease Mike about his feelings.

Tara told every- one else Liz's secret.

Jason gave Quentin good advice about his parents.

Paul and Mike talked about how they felt.

Liz didn't return Tara's markers.

Jason tried to cheer Quentin up.

Paul noticed that Mike was upset.

Tara and Liz shared secrets with each other.

Give and Take

PURPOSE

To understand the importance of equality and reciprocity within a friendship

STUDENTS WILL

Participate in the discussion on friendships

Identify at least one relevant example from the book as it pertains to the discussion

UNIT 5

MATERIALS

- Chart paper and a marker or chalkboard and chalk

- Balance scale and weights

- *The Giving Tree* by Shel Silverstein, *Let's Be Enemies* by Janice Udry, or *The Rat and the Tiger* by Keiko Kasza

PRESENTATION OF LESSON

Discussion

Discuss with students the importance of both giving and taking within a friendship. Ask students what kinds of things friends do to make a friendship equal. Create a list on the chalkboard or chart paper. Ideas might include

- Taking turns during a game

- Using compromise as a strategy

- Making sure one person isn't always "the boss"

- Playing at each other's houses

Scale Activity

Using the scale and weights, visually demonstrate the importance of balance in friendships in terms of sharing things, doing favors, being "the boss" (making decisions), and so forth. Show that when one person is doing more for the other, or when one person is bossing the other around, the friendship becomes *unbalanced* and *unstable*. When the friends give in equal amounts, or get to make decisions with equal frequency, the friendship scale is more balanced and fair.

Story Activity

Read the book you feel is most appropriate for your group.

For *The Giving Tree*, make a list of the ways each character was either a good or bad friend to the other. Be sure to include concrete (shared apples) as well as more abstract (spending time together) demonstrations of friendship. Read the book again, and allow students to put weights on either end of the scale as the boy and the tree demonstrate their friendship, and discuss whether the friendship was balanced.

For *Let's Be Enemies* or *The Rat and the Tiger*, make a list of the reasons one character gets mad at the other (incidences of being too "bossy"). Read the story a second time, allowing the students to place a weight on either end of the scale every time one of the characters got to make a decision (or each time a character was too bossy) in the story. Discuss whether the friendship was balanced.

ALTERNATIVE PRESENTATIONS

Fundamental

- *In addition to the materials already listed, you will need role-play footprints and tape.*

Role play the characters in the story. Have students in the audience use the scale as the role play progresses.

Challenging

- *In addition to the materials already listed, you will need role-play footprints and tape.*

Discuss the idea that although it is important that friendships be balanced, keeping score can also be a problem. Role play a situation in which one friend berates another for not having an equal score ("Last week you got to be first twice. This week I need to be first twice," or "You don't come over to my house as much as I go to yours. You owe me at least two times."). Discuss the situation and the problems that might arise from keeping score.

THROUGHOUT THE DAY

- Point out and discuss areas of inequality within friendships or instances of score keeping that you observe during the school day.

UNIT 5

Encouraging Empathy

PURPOSE

To encourage empathetic thinking

STUDENTS WILL

Identify possible feelings and thoughts of characters in the book

MATERIALS

- Chart paper and a marker or chalkboard and chalk

- *Huge Harold* by Bill Peet

- Role-play footprints

- Tape

PRESENTATION OF LESSON

Discussion

Write the phrase, "Put yourself in his or her shoes" on the chalkboard or chart paper. Ask students if they have ever heard this expression before or if anyone has ever told them to put themselves in someone else's shoes. Discuss with students the fact that we don't literally put on a pair of shoes, but the expression asks us to try and figure out how the other person might feel or what he or she might be thinking. For example, if Paul is teasing Johnny, the teacher might ask Paul to "put himself in Johnny's shoes" to see how much Paul liked being teased that way. Explain to students that Paul would need to imagine what he would feel like if he were in Johnny's place.

Story Activity

Tell students that you will be reading a book then asking them to put themselves in the characters' shoes. They will be doing this by physically stepping on the role-play footprints.

Read *Huge Harold.* When you are finished reading the book from beginning to end, focus on page 7 and the picture of Harold in the woods. Ask a volunteer from the group to put him- or herself in Harold's shoes by stepping on the footprints and answering questions about how he or she might feel if he or she were in the same situation as Harold. Also ask the student what kinds of things he or she might be thinking. The key is to focus on how the student would feel or think (based on personality, previous experience, and so forth) as a way to understand the feelings and thoughts of others.

Continue this exercise with different students and different situations in the book. Remember to ask students to stand on the footprints as they answer the questions.

- Page 14: How would you feel if you were in the cows' shoes and found a big rabbit on your food?

- Page 18: How would you feel if you were in Howard's shoes and had been running away from people all day?

- Page 22: How would you feel if you were in Howard's shoes and there was a big thunderstorm?

- Page 26: How would you feel if you were in the boys' shoes and came across a giant rabbit?

- Page 36: How would you feel if you were in Howard's shoes and finally saw a big warm barn?

- Page 46: How would you feel if you were in Howard's shoes and you found out you were really good at something?

- Page 47: How would you feel if you were in Howard's shoes and everyone was being nice to you?

ALTERNATIVE PRESENTATIONS

Fundamental

Figurative language may be a difficult concept for some students. If so, present the lesson in different terms using phrases such as, "How would you feel if . . .?" instead of "Put yourself in his or her shoes."

Challenging

Have students answer questions about situations that occur in school in which empathetic thinking would be appropriate (e.g., teasing, ignoring someone else, having few friends). Have them put themselves in the shoes of the person being teased or ignored, and discuss how the person might be feeling.

THROUGHOUT THE DAY

- Have students design and post signs reminding each other to "Put yourself in his or her shoes" to discourage teasing and unfriendly behavior.

- Remind students to use their set of small feeling faces to let you know how they are feeling.

Communicating with Friends

PURPOSE

To identify and discuss conflicts that result from miscommunication

To discuss ways to prevent similar conflicts from arising in real-life situations

STUDENTS WILL

Identify at least one action that could have avoided a conflict or resolved a conflict sooner

UNIT 5

MATERIALS

- *The Hating Book* by Charlotte Zolotow

- Chart paper and a marker or chalkboard and chalk

- Telephone Game cards

PRESENTATION OF LESSON

Discussion

Explain to students that today you are going to be talking about misunderstandings that happen between friends. Explain to students that misunderstandings are when one person doesn't understand what is going on. Sometimes people hurt their friends' feelings by mistake because they aren't communicating or talking to each other very clearly.

Story Activity

Read *The Hating Book* and then ask the students what happened to make the friends stop talking to each other. Discuss the feelings of the different characters during the argument and how it hurts when friends are not there for you or when they change their behavior toward you.

Ask the students to each give an idea of what either girl in the story could have done to prevent the conflict (e.g., only tell the girl to her face that she looked neat, make sure their message is understood, trust that a friend wouldn't say something mean) and resolve the conflict sooner (e.g., follow the mother's advice and ask what the problem was, ask another friend if she knows what's wrong). Write the list on the chalkboard or chart paper.

Game Activity

Have students sit in a circle. The first student picks a Telephone Game card and reads it to him- or herself. The first person whispers the message to the second person, and each person whispers the message to the next person in line until it reaches the last person. The last person says the (now probably distorted) message out loud. Compare the message on the card to the message heard by the last person.

Wrap-Up

Discuss with students how the message became distorted as it got passed down the line. Make the connection between the problem in the book and the distorted telephone message in the game. Both are examples of miscommunication.

ALTERNATIVE PRESENTATIONS

Fundamental

- *In addition to the materials already listed, you will need role-play footprints and tape.*

Role play with students a scene from the story in which the main character says her friend looks neat. Other students relay the conversation incorrectly and the conflict arises. Role play the same situation again but with clearer communication.

Challenging

Have students give examples of real-life situations in which communication mix-ups have happened to them. Have students make up their own Telephone Game messages.

THROUGHOUT THE DAY

- Encourage students to communicate clearly with one another. Model this clear communication yourself in terms of your expectations, reactions, and student appreciation.

LESSON REPRODUCIBLE

Silly Simon ate three apple pies for dessert.

I had hamburgers and baked beans for dinner last night.

The cat next door has big black eyes.

The boat has four white wild sails.

Dealing with Rejection

PURPOSE

To identify strategies for dealing with rejection by a peer or friend

STUDENTS WILL

Generate at least one possible strategy to pursue when rejected by a peer

Identify areas of personal strength

MATERIALS

- Role-play footprints

- Tape

- Chart paper and a marker or chalkboard and chalk

- Dealing with Rejection Role-Play Situations list

- My Good Qualities worksheet

- Crayons/markers

PRESENTATION OF LESSON

Discussion

Discuss with students how it feels when someone does not want to be a friend. Explain to students that today you're going to talk about a situation that every-one has to deal with at some point: Sometimes when you ask someone to do something, they say no. Or, someone that you like will tell you that he or she doesn't want to be your friend. Tell students that this can really hurt our feelings and can make us feel very sad or bad about ourselves. But today you're going to talk about how to feel better about it.

Role-Play Activity

With a volunteer, role play the following situation: You ask a person in your class to play at your house after school. The person laughs and says, "No way!"

Have students brainstorm a list of things the student can do if someone does not want to play or does not want to be a friend. Discuss with students what the person can do to make him- or herself feel better and where he or she might be able to find support or friendship. Write these strategies on the chalk-board or chart paper. Possible answers include

- Asking someone else to play

- Asking the other person to do a different activity

- Finding a fun activity and inviting others to participate

- Asking an adult for advice

Role play the situations on the Dealing with Rejection Role-Play Situations list, and use the strategies generated by students to determine what the characters can do.

Drawing Activity

Ask students to think of good qualities in themselves (e.g., being kind, having a big smile, being a good artist). Have students decorate the figure on the My Good Qualities worksheet in a way that depicts the positive qualities in themselves.

Wrap-Up

Discuss with students the idea that even if someone does not want to play with them or be their friend, their good qualities don't change and they are still good and interesting people. Have students share their drawings with the group.

ALTERNATIVE PRESENTATIONS

Fundamental

Discuss appropriate responses to rejection. Generate verbal responses that are assertive without being hostile ("I'm sorry that I bothered you," "My feelings are a little hurt by what you said," or "Okay, maybe some other time then").

Challenging

Discuss with students how the group can become more friendly. What can the students do as a group to make sure that members do not feel rejected?

THROUGHOUT THE DAY

- Acknowledge situations when students said no in an appropriate way or when someone handled rejection well.

UNIT 5

LESSON REPRODUCIBLES

Role-Play Situations

Role Play #1:
Characters: teacher, Ana, Martha, Jonelle

Ana, Martha, and Jonelle are all in the same class. Ana and Martha are best friends. During math time, the teacher asks Ana to pick a partner to work with. Ana chooses Jonelle. Martha feels angry and sad that Ana didn't choose her. What can Martha do?

Role Play #2:
Characters: teacher, Leah, Carla, Andy, Ricardo

Andy recently moved here from another country. He is just learning to speak English. In his new class, none of the students speak his language. When the teacher asks him a question and he answers her, Leah, Carla, and Ricardo laugh at the way he talks. Andy feels embarrassed and hurt. What can Andy do?

Role Play #3:
Characters: Joyce, Patrick, Donald

Patrick and Donald play checkers together almost every day during snack time. One day during snack time, Patrick is playing checkers with Joyce. Donald asks if he can join them. Patrick says, "Sorry, only two people can play at a time." Donald feels left out. What can Donald do?

Role Play #4:
Characters: Mickey, Carlos, Alex, Martin

Mickey, Carlos, Martin, and Alex are good friends. They meet every day after school to play soccer in the park. One afternoon, Carlos and Mickey are waiting for Alex. Alex arrives wearing a new shirt that is bright yellow. Mickey says, "Oooh, what an ugly color! I hate yellow!" Carlos and Martin start to laugh. Alex's feelings are hurt, and he feels left out. What can Alex do?

Role Play #5:
Characters: Rebecca, Jessie, Amanda

Jessie and Rebecca are best friends. They play together a lot, but Amanda is constantly asking if she can play with them. Jessie doesn't mind it sometimes, but other times she wants Amanda to leave them alone. How can she get Amanda to leave them alone without hurting Amanda's feelings? What can Jessie do?

Promoting Social Success: A Curriculum for Children with Special Needs by Gary N. Siperstein & Emily Paige Rickards
© 2004 by Paul H. Brookes Publishing Co. Inc. All rights reserved.
www.brookespublishing.com   1-800-638-3775

Name _____ Date _____

Color and label the figure below to show your good qualities.

Sharing Hurt Feelings with Friends

PURPOSE

To help students understand the importance of sharing feelings with their friends, especially when upset

STUDENTS WILL

Generate effective strategies for communicating with a friend when their feelings are hurt

Communicate their feelings to the group

UNIT 5

MATERIALS

- *Jamaica and Brianna* by Juanita Havill

PRESENTATION OF LESSON

Discussion

Discuss with the students the idea that sometimes people's feelings are hurt and we don't know it. We can try to pay attention to how they look and to what is happening, but sometimes we won't know that their feelings are hurt. This means that sometimes people won't know that our feelings are hurt. So, it is important to share our feelings with people to be sure they know how we feel.

Story Activity

Tell the students you are going to read a book about two friends who find out how important it is to share their feelings with each other. Read *Jamaica and Brianna*. Turn to page 16. Discuss with students why Brianna said that cowboy boots weren't "in" and why Jamaica said that pink boots were ugly.

Explain to students that sometimes when we are upset and our feelings are hurt, we say mean things. We might try to hurt someone else's feelings to make ourselves feel better. But that usually doesn't work. Instead of feeling better, we've just made someone else feel bad, too.

Turn to pages 21 and 22. Discuss with students how it helped both girls when they were honest with each other about their feelings.

Wrap-Up

Have each child share how he or she is feeling by showing a feeling face to the group.

ALTERNATIVE PRESENTATIONS

Fundamental

- *In addition to the materials already listed, you will need role-play footprints and tape.*

Have students practice communicating their feelings. Role play the situation on page 16 of the story, and have students communicate Jamaica and Brianna's feelings in a clear and direct way.

Challenging

Discuss with students the importance of trying to understand someone else's point of view when they are lashing out. Often, the person who is being mean feels badly about him- or herself and, therefore, is putting all those feelings onto someone else. How can students handle someone who lashes out?

THROUGHOUT THE DAY

- Model appropriate sharing of feelings by displaying your own feeling faces.

- Encourage students to vocalize their hurt feelings during conflicts.

- Remind students to use their set of small feeling faces to show how they are feeling.

Unit 5: Sharing Hurt Feelings with Friends

Coping with Teasing

PURPOSE

To identify emotional reactions to teasing

To generate coping strategies for dealing with teasing

STUDENTS WILL

Generate at least one strategy for dealing with teasing

MATERIALS

- Chart paper and a marker or chalkboard and chalk

- Video clips (Suggested videos: *Hercules, Cinderella, The Big Green, The Pebble and the Penguin, Space Jam*)

- TV/VCR

- Drawing paper

- Crayons/markers

PRESENTATION OF LESSON

Discussion

Review the content of the last few lessons with students. Remind students that you have been talking about what makes a good friend and how people can communicate and share their hurt feelings with friends. Tell students that today you are going to talk about teasing and how it can make people feel. Some teasing can be friendly, but a lot of teasing is mean and can hurt people's feelings.

Ask students for examples of times they have been teased. Discuss how teasing can make people feel. Key questions might include

- Why do you think people tease each other?

- How does it make you feel when someone is teasing you?

- What can you do when someone is teasing you?

On the chalkboard or chart paper, write a list of strategies that students can use to deal with teasing.

TEASING VIDEO CLIPS

Movie Title	Description of Clip	Clip Location
Hercules	**A group of boys teases Hercules.** The boys do not allow him to play, make excuses, and call him names.	22:48–23:18
Cinderella	**The step-sisters tease Cinderella about going to the ball.** They mimic her and use a sarcastic tone of voice.	35:37–36:17
The Big Green	**One team teases the other.** The well-dressed team laughs at the other team and calls them names.	31:19–32:21
The Pebble and the Penguin	**A group of penguins tease another penguin who is uncoordinated.** They laugh and point at him.	18:01–18:25
Space Jam	**Bugs Bunny teases aliens.** Bugs teases the aliens by pretending not to be Bugs Bunny (this is a good example of teasing that is more humorous than hurtful, but it is also a more subtle kind of teasing than the other examples).	16:49–17:29

Video Activity

Show and discuss each of the video clips. Key questions might include

- How did (the character's name) feel when she or he was being teased?

- How can you tell?

- What do you think (the character's name) should do to handle the situation?

Have students refer to the list of strategies they created for an appropriate strategy.

Wrap-Up

As a closing activity, have students draw a picture of a time they were being teased. Encourage them to show in the picture how being teased made them feel and what they did, or could have done, to handle the situation.

ALTERNATIVE PRESENTATIONS

Fundamental

• *In addition to the materials already listed, you will need role-play footprints and tape.*

Role play situations in which a person is being teased. Focus on how that person might be feeling, and practice using the strategies from the list to handle the situation.

Challenging

Discuss the role of teasing in friendships with students. Key questions might include

• Is teasing always mean?

• Do you ever tease your friends?

• Will people want to be your friend if you tease them?

THROUGHOUT THE DAY

• Have students make posters to hang in the classroom as reminders not to tease each other; the posters might also display the class rule about teasing.

• Hold a problem-solving meeting.

The Importance of Forgiveness

PURPOSE

To recognize forgiveness as an important characteristic of friendship

STUDENTS WILL

Identify reasons why forgiveness is an important aspect of friendship

Generate examples from their own life when they have forgiven someone

MATERIALS

- Chart paper and a marker or chalkboard and chalk

- *Matthew and Tilly* by Rebecca C. Jones

PRESENTATION OF LESSON

Discussion

Write the word *forgive* on the chalkboard. Ask students if they know what the word means. Explain to students that today you're going to talk about forgiveness. When you forgive someone, you stop blaming him or her for something he or she did. Sometimes, in order to keep a friend, you have to forgive him or her for something that has happened. Tell your students that you are going to read a story about two friends, Matthew and Tilly, and see what happened that made Tilly forgive Matthew.

Story Activity

Read the story to students and discuss the role of forgiveness. Key questions might include

- Why was Tilly angry? (Matthew broke her purple crayon.)

- What happened next? (They played alone, both kids missed each other, they were lonely, and so forth.)

- What did Matthew do to try to make things better? (He said he was sorry.)

- What did Tilly do then? (She said she was sorry, too, and she forgave Matthew.)

- Why do you think Tilly wanted to forgive Matthew? (She wanted to be his friend, she was lonely/sad, and so forth.)

- Why do you think it is important to forgive your friends sometimes?

Wrap-Up

Have students share a time when they have had to forgive someone and how they felt about it.

ALTERNATIVE PRESENTATIONS

Fundamental

If students have difficulty coming up with situations in which they had to forgive someone, use the following examples: "Your brother eats the last piece of your birthday cake" and "Your friend loses your favorite book." Ask each student if he or she thinks he or she could forgive someone for that action and how it might make him or her feel.

Challenging

Discuss the issue of whether something happens on purpose or by accident and if that changes how easy it is to forgive someone. For example, would Tilly have been so quick to forgive Matthew if he had broken the crayon on purpose?

THROUGHOUT THE DAY

- Help students identify situations when forgiveness is warranted.

Keeping Friends

PURPOSE

To generate ideas about how to sustain friendships

STUDENTS WILL

Identify ways to actively participate in and maintain friendships

MATERIALS

- *Best Friends Together Again* by Aliki

- Drawing paper

- Crayons/markers

UNIT 5

PRESENTATION OF LESSON

Discussion

Explain to students that today you're going to talk about friends and how to keep friends, especially if you are now separated. Key questions might include

- Have any of you had a friend that moved away to a new place?

- If yes: Did you see him or her again?

- If no: What do you think you could do to let him or her know you would still like to be his or her friend?

Story Activity

Ask students if they remember the story you read about Robert and Peter (*We Are Best Friends* in The Ups and Downs of Friendship lesson in this unit)? Remind students that Peter moved away, and Robert was very sad that he left. Tell them that today they'll find out what happens when Peter comes back to visit.

Read students *Best Friends Together Again.* Ask students what both Robert and Peter did to stay friends (e.g., wrote letters, visited). Ask students to think of things that they could do to keep their friends. Possible responses for friends who are far away include

- Calling them on the telephone

- Planning a visit

- E-mailing

- Writing a letter

Possible responses for friends who are close by include

- Playing with them after school

- Having a sleep-over

- Playing with them at recess

- Going to the movies together

Writing/Drawing Activity

Have students write or e-mail a letter to a friend or draw a picture to give or send to a friend.

Wrap-Up

Have students share their letters or drawings with the group.

ALTERNATIVE PRESENTATIONS

Fundamental

- *In addition to the materials already listed, you will need role-play footprints and tape.*

Role play the different ways Robert and Peter can keep in touch with each other.

Challenging

Discuss with students the idea of making new friends while keeping the old ones. Key questions might include

- How did Peter feel about Robert's new friend Will?

- What did Robert mean when he said that, "Will is just like a best friend . . . But he's not an oldest best friend, like us?"

THROUGHOUT THE DAY

- Create a group mailbox in which students can put letters or cards for each other.

The Importance of Compliments

PURPOSE

To understand the importance of compliments within social interactions

To develop compliments for others in the group

STUDENTS WILL

Evaluate a list of statements and choose which ones are compliments

Verbalize the reasons for their choices

Formulate compliments and deliver them to others in the group

UNIT 5

MATERIALS

- Compliments Role-Play Situations list

- Role-play footprints

- Tape

- Pen and paper

- Chart paper and a marker or chalkboard and chalk

PRESENTATION OF LESSON

Discussion

Begin the lesson by complimenting one of the students in the group. Then ask students to describe what you did. Have the student identify how the compliment made him or her feel, and relay to the students how you felt when you gave the person the compliment (it made you feel good, too). Tell students that this is called a *compliment*. A compliment is when we say something about another person that makes him or her feel good.

Tell the students that they are going to learn how to compliment others really well. It is first important to figure out what makes a good compliment. A good compliment acknowledges effort or achievement, is specific, and should create positive feelings in the person receiving the compliment. Either read or write out (on the chalkboard or chart paper) the following pairs of statements, and have students choose which one is a compliment and then explain why.

1. I know that you worked really hard on that drawing. It looks great. (compliment)
2. You drew a picture.

1. Your shirt is purple and gray.
2. I like the colors on your shirt; they are very pretty. (compliment)

1. You shared your pencil with me.
2. You are really good at sharing. (compliment)

Role-Play Activity

Explain to students that you will be role playing situations from the Compliments Role-Play Situations list that involve complimenting another person. Have the students take turns being the one to come up with an appropriate compliment. You may want to have the students generate the compliment before they start the role play to ensure that the compliment is appropriate and that students do not have to come up with compliments on the spot.

Wrap-Up

Explain to students that they are going to practice giving compliments to each other. Gather students in a circle. Have each student pick a person in the group to compliment (be sure that the compliments are distributed evenly). Go around the circle and share the compliments. The individual speaking should talk directly to the person he or she is complimenting, and the person receiving the compliment should thank him or her.

ALTERNATIVE PRESENTATIONS

Fundamental

Students may have difficulty with the discussion about what makes a good compliment. Begin, rather than end, the lesson with the complimenting of each other. Refine the definition of a compliment as you go through this activity.

Challenging

- *In addition to the materials already listed, you will need one list of everyone's name in the group for every student and pens/pencils.*

Discuss with students good compliments (ones that acknowledge appearance or material possessions) and great compliments (ones that acknowledge effort or achievement). Why is one type better than the other? Distribute the list with the names of every student in the group. Have students write down one compliment for each student in the group. Review the compliments to help students to make them as strong as possible. Have the students take turns sharing their compliments with each other.

THROUGHOUT THE DAY

- Have students compliment each other at the end of every day.

- Have students make a mailbox in which members in the group can mail each other compliments.

- Hold a problem-solving meeting.

UNIT 5

LESSON REPRODUCIBLE

Role-Play Situations

Role Play #1: Compliments can help us make new friends.

You are in a new after-school group, and you do not know anyone there. You notice that one student is wearing the same kind of shoes that you are. What could you say to that student to make him or her feel good?

Role Play #2: Compliments can help someone feel better.

One of your friends is upset because the teacher told her she had to stay inside to do her work but that she will be able to come out before recess is over. What could you say to her to make her feel good?

Role Play #3: Compliments help us keep our friends and let them know that we care about them.

Your friend just won a gold medal for getting the highest bowling score. What could you say to make him feel good?

Role Play #4: Giving a compliment can often help us feel better, too.

You are in a bad mood. You feel left out and angry. The other students are drawing cool pictures. What can you say to one of the students?

Role Play #5: Compliments make other people feel good about themselves.

One of your classmates got a 100% on her math test. What could you say to her to make her feel good?

Promoting Social Success: A Curriculum for Children with Special Needs by Gary N. Siperstein & Emily Paige Rickards
© 2004 by Paul H. Brookes Publishing Co. Inc. All rights reserved.
www.brookespublishing.com   1-800-638-3775

GENERAL REPRODUCIBLES

Body Language Photographs

ANGRY #2

CONFUSED #1

EXCITED #2

FRUSTRATED #1

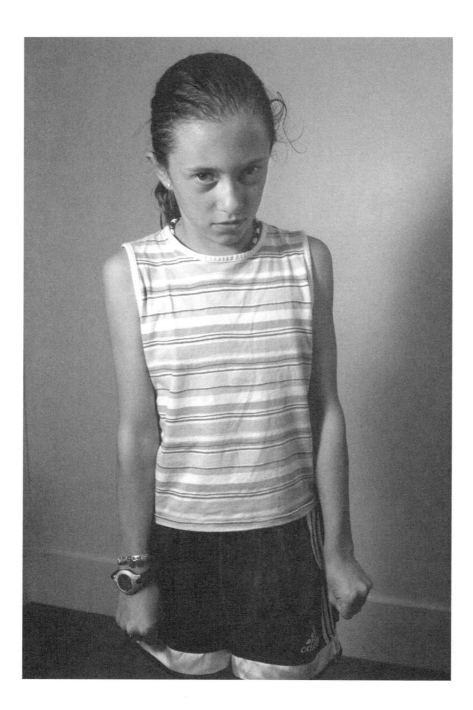

HAPPY #1

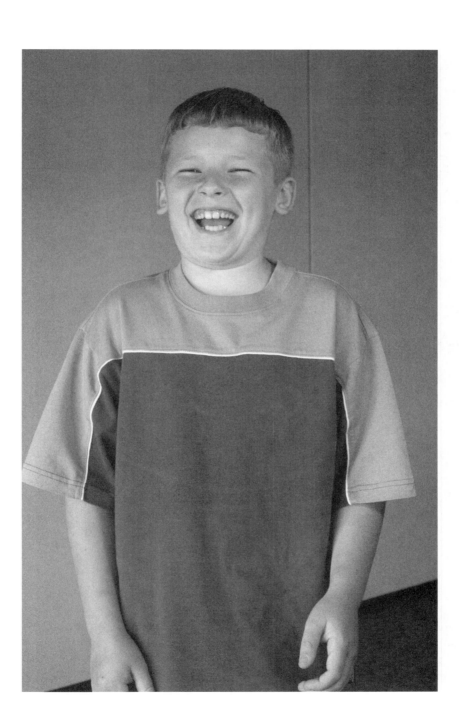

HAPPY #2

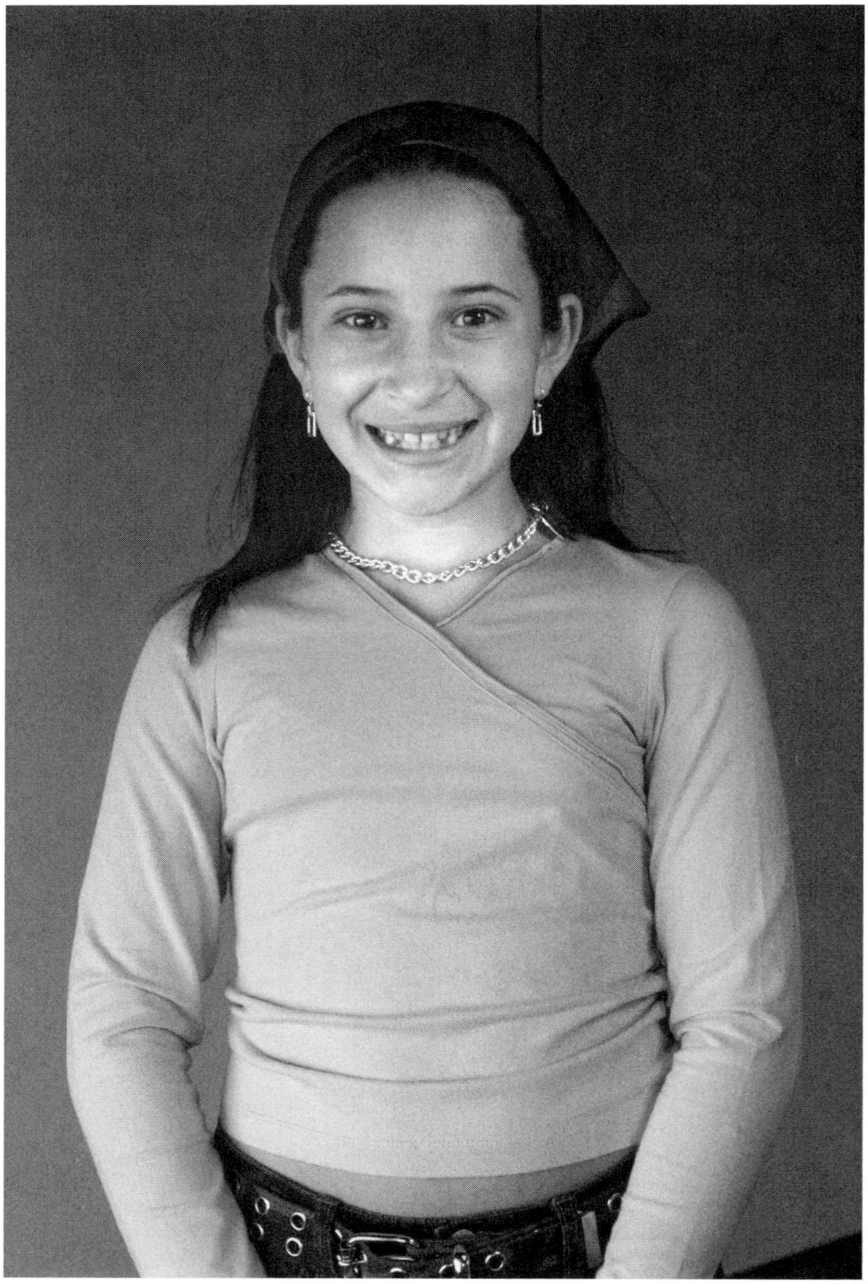

NERVOUS #1

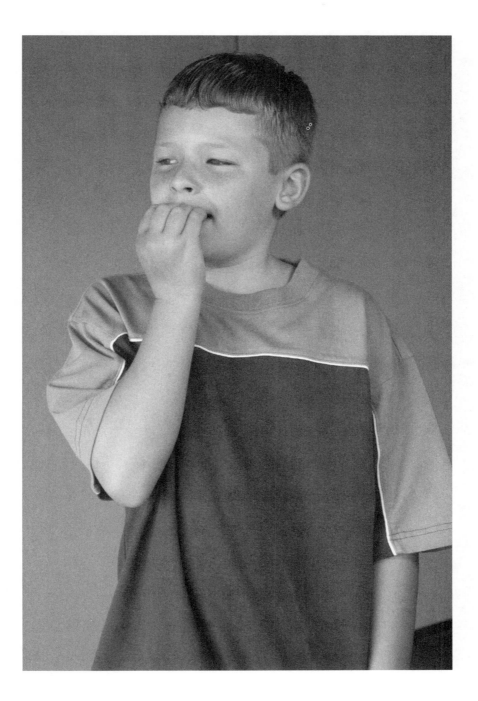

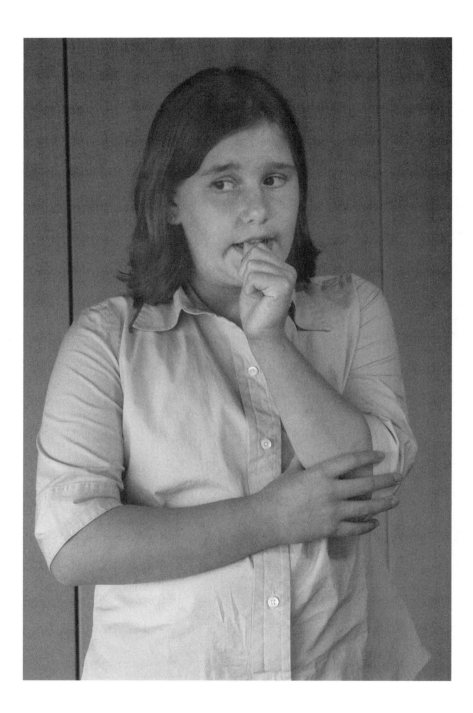

SAD #1

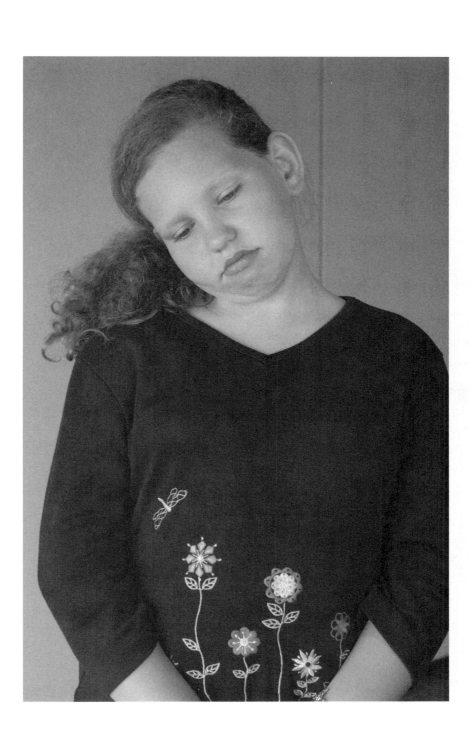

SAD #2

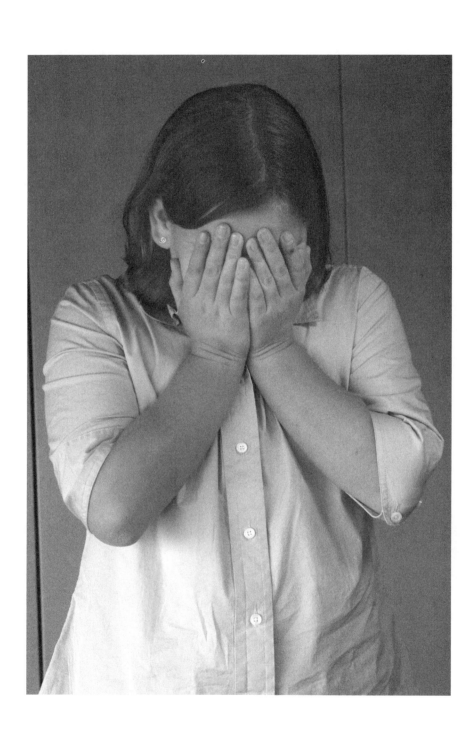

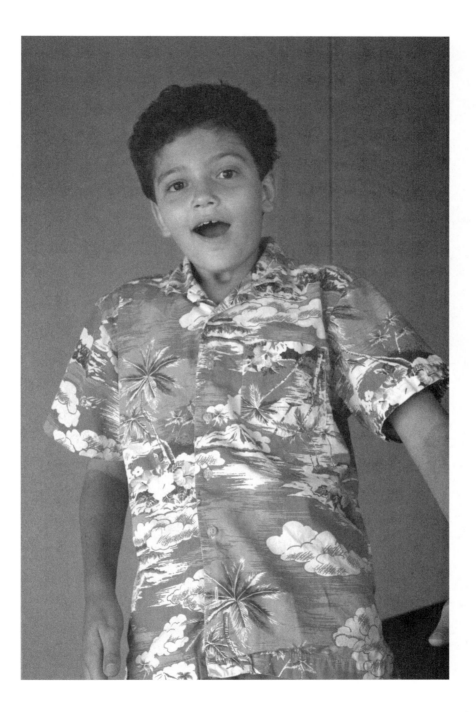

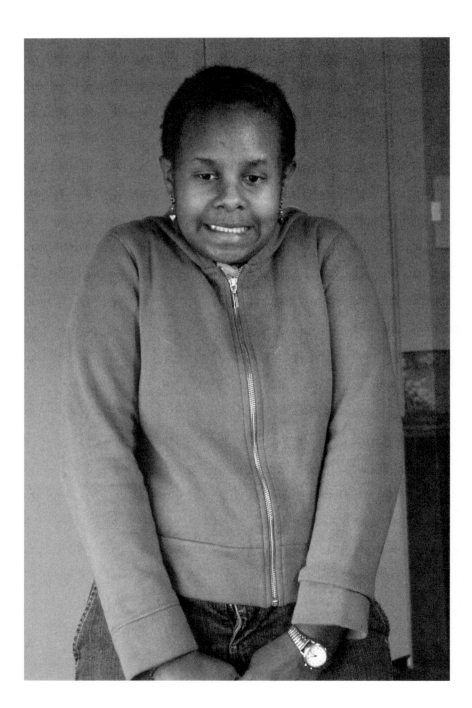

SURPRISED #1

SURPRISED #2

Large Feeling Faces

Happy

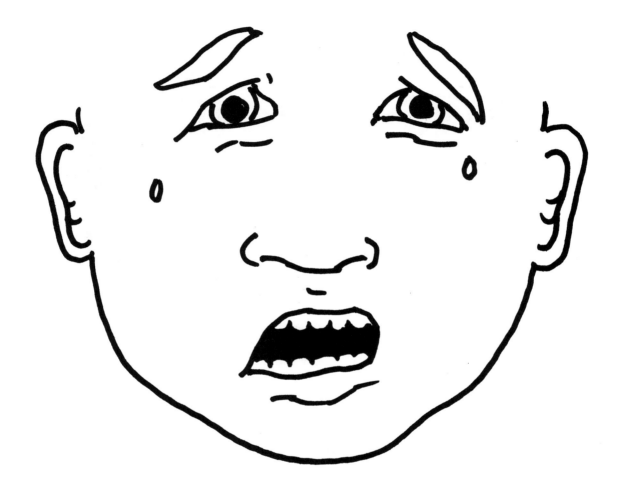

Sad

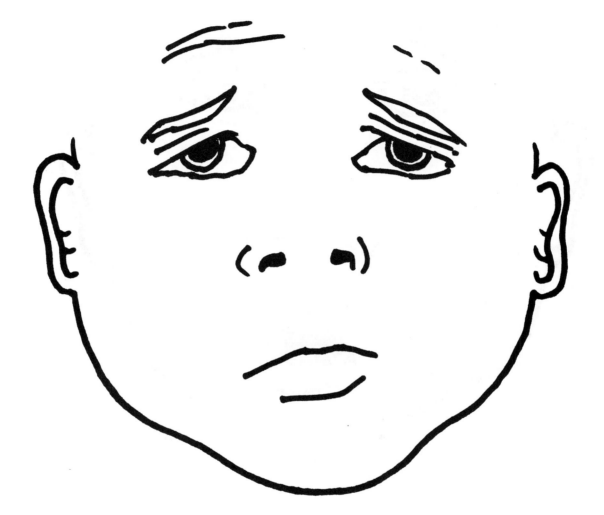

Lonely

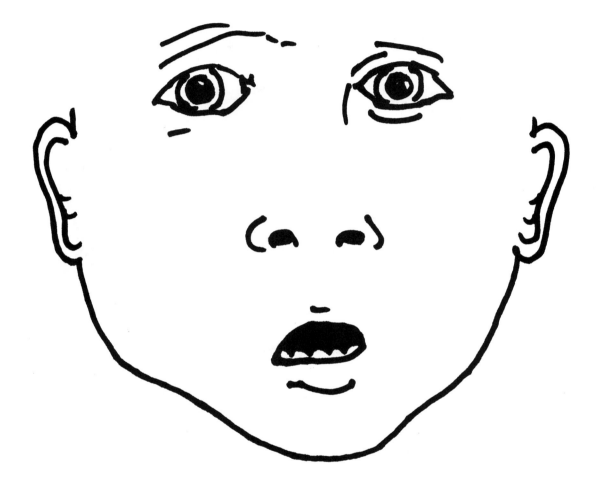

Confused

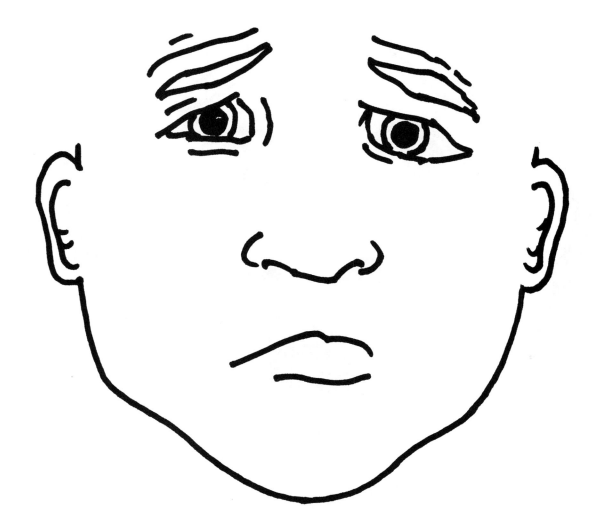

Nervous

Scared

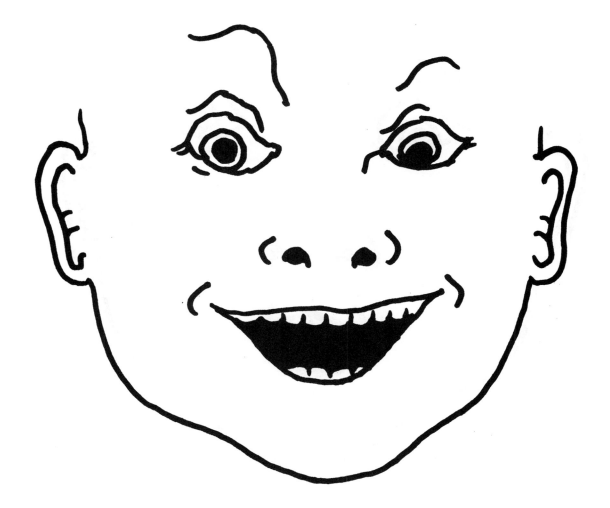

Excited

Surprised

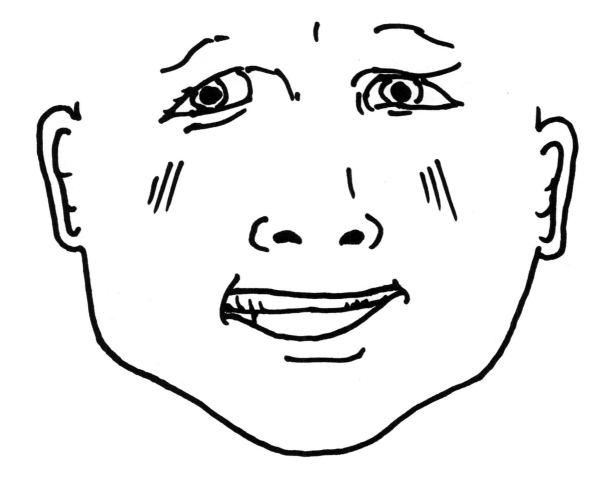

Embarrassed

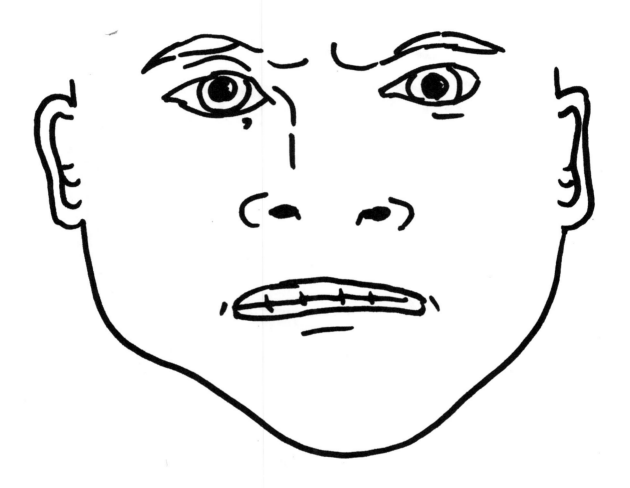

Frustrated

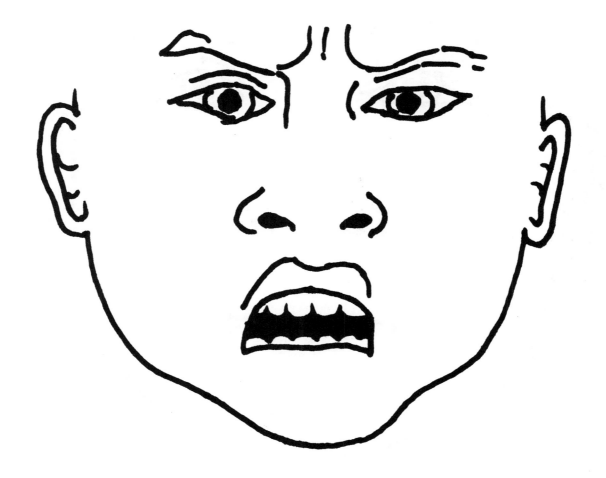

Angry

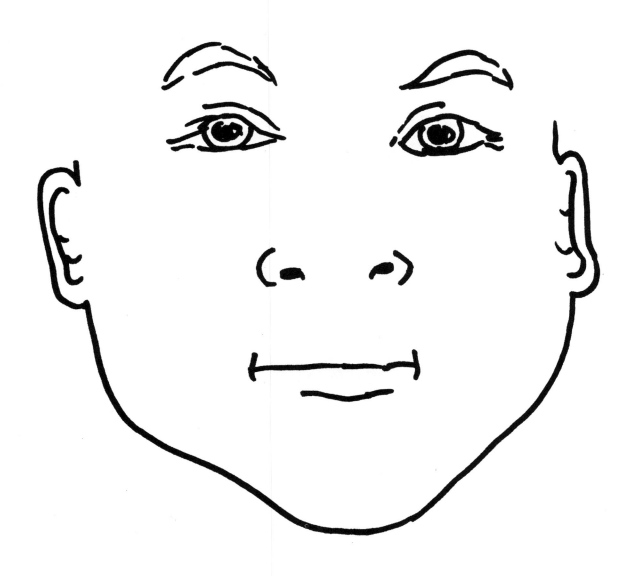

Calm

Small Feeling Faces

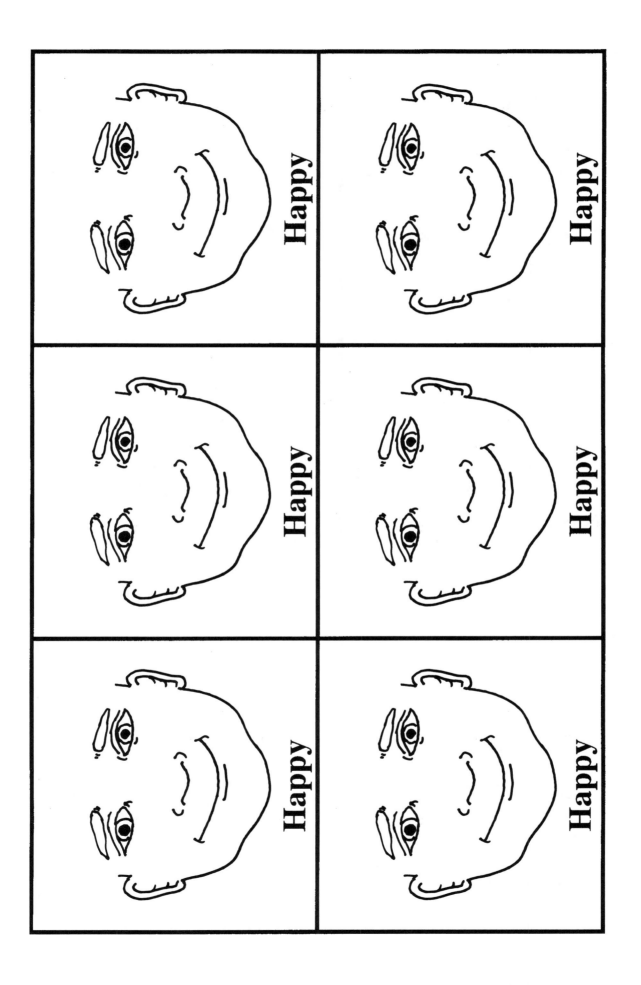

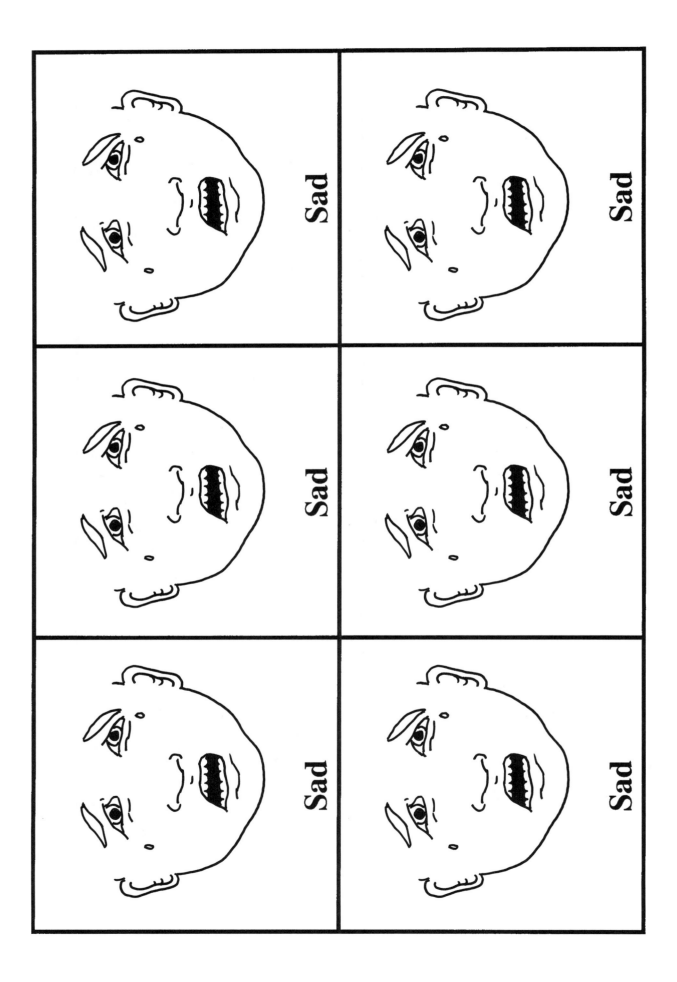

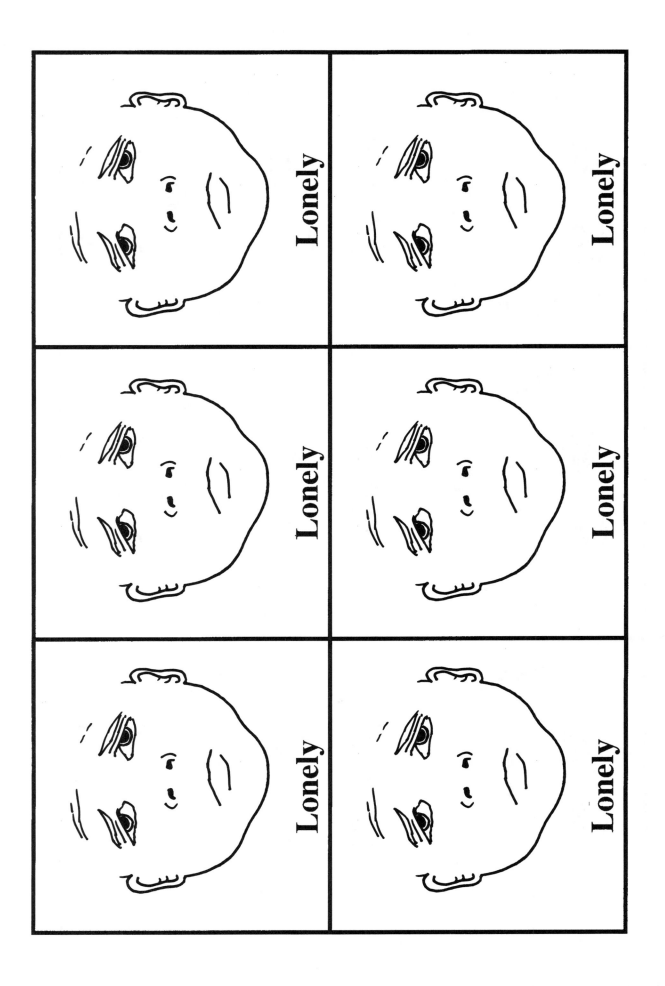

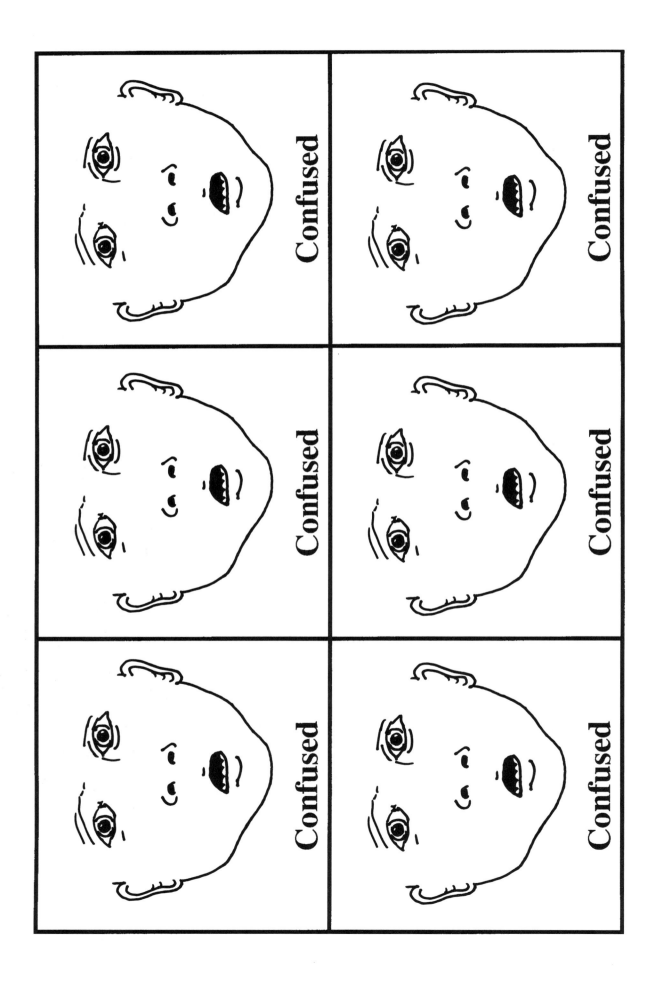

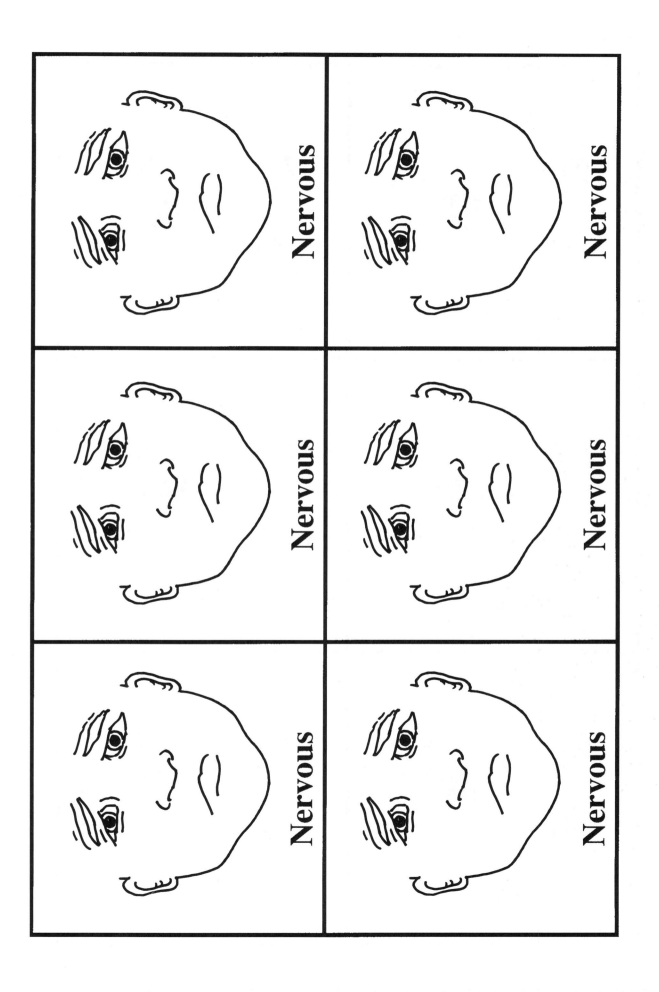

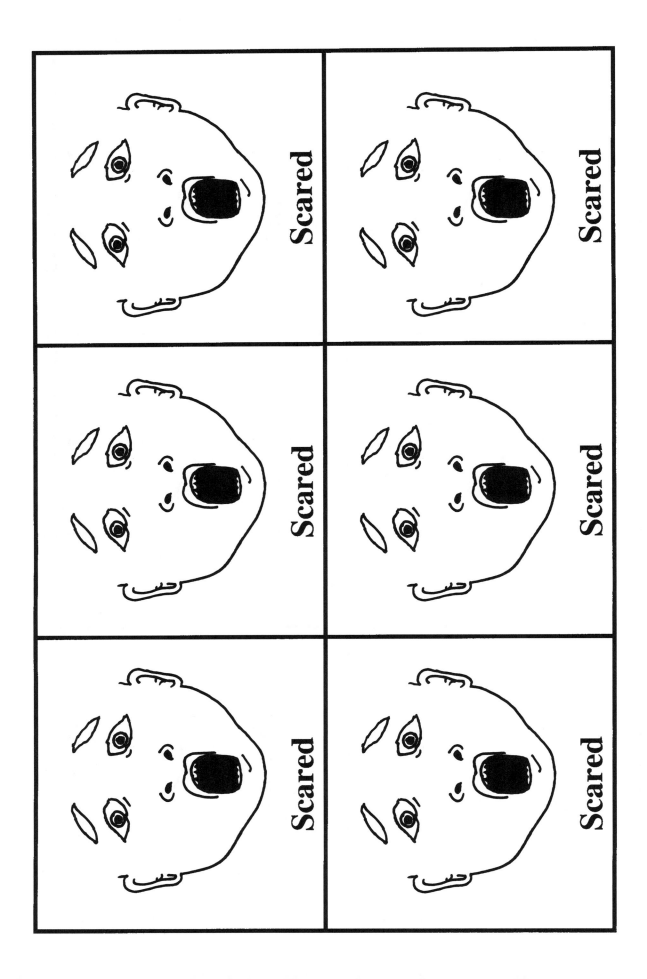

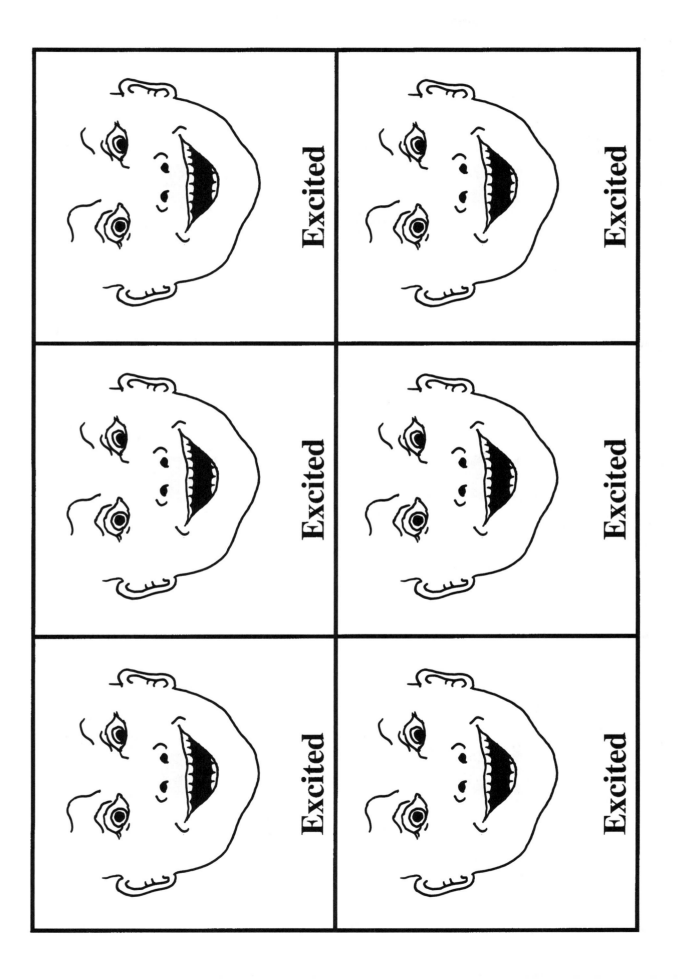

Excited

Excited

Excited

Excited

Excited

Excited

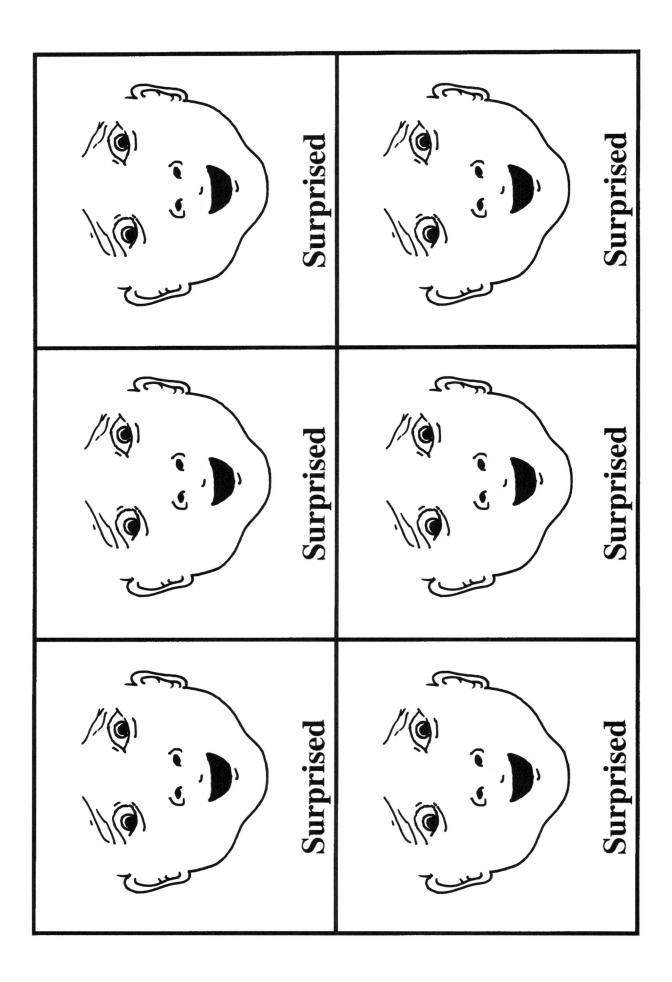

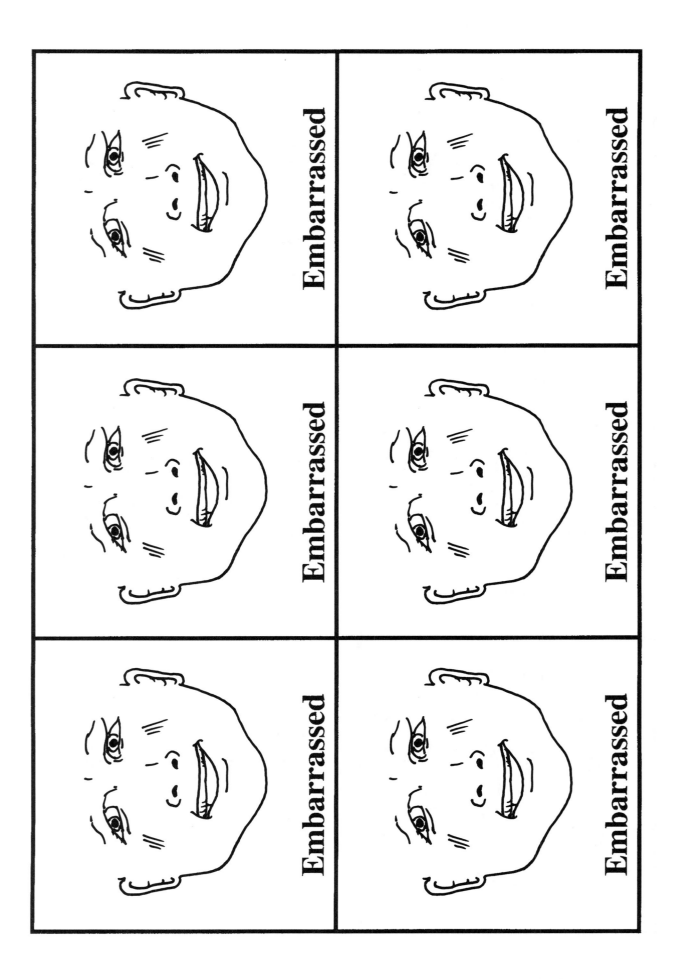

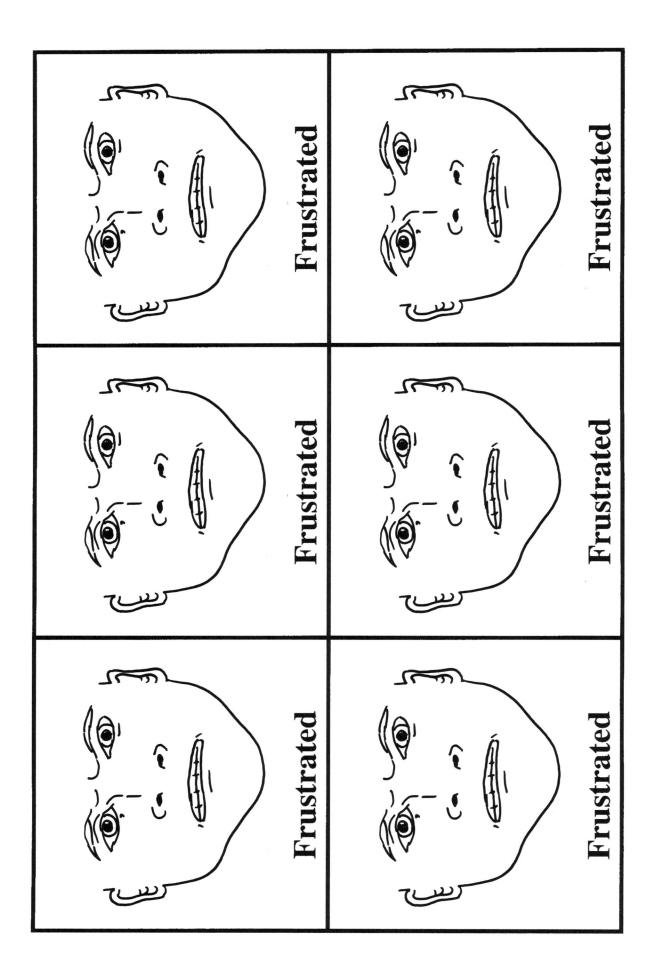

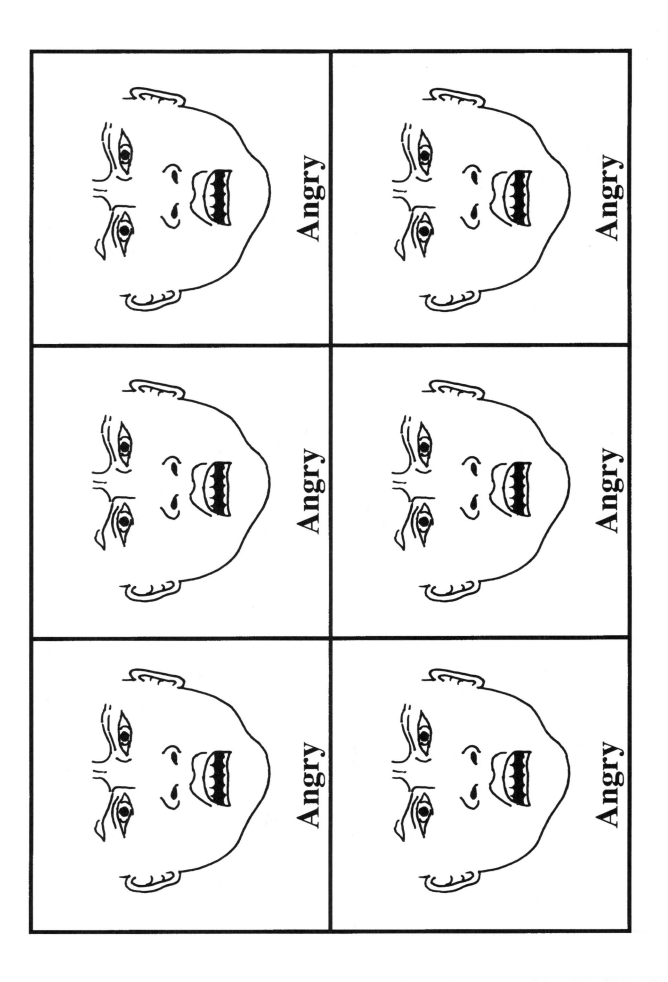

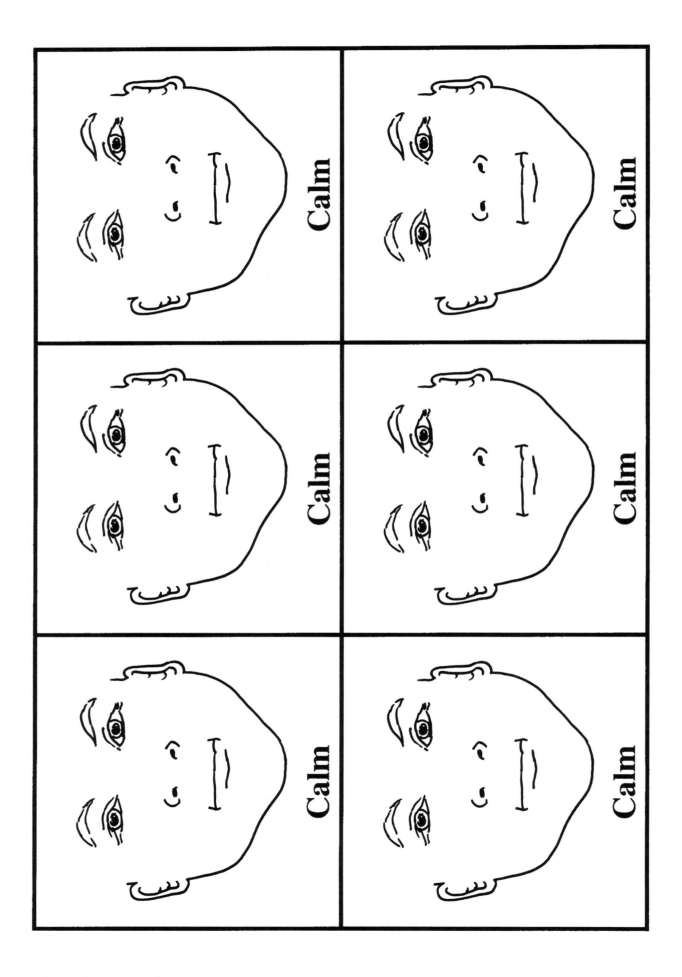

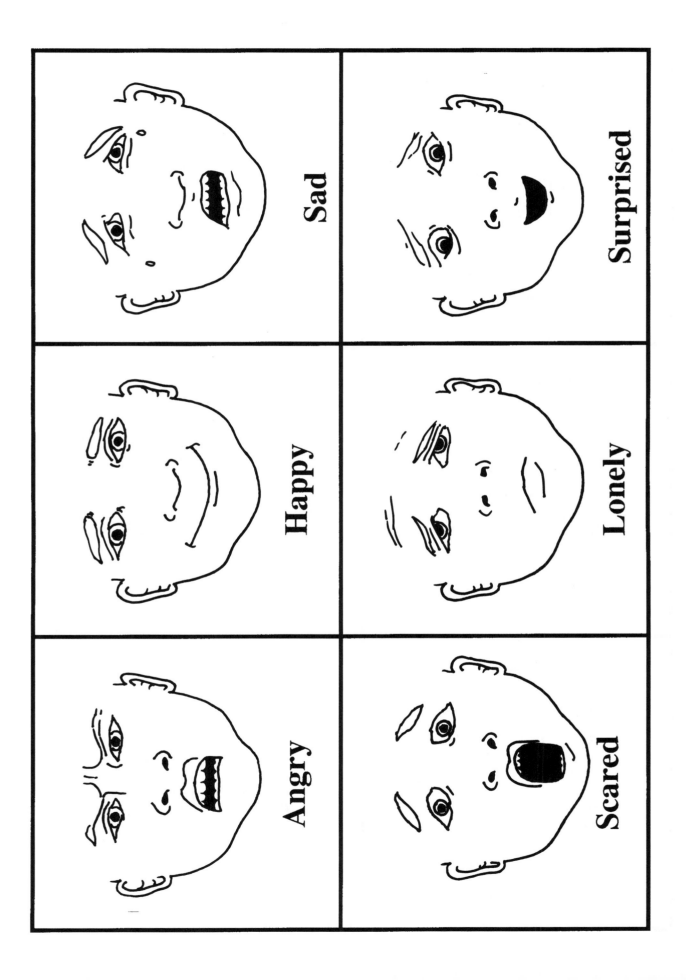

Sad

Surprised

Happy

Lonely

Angry

Scared

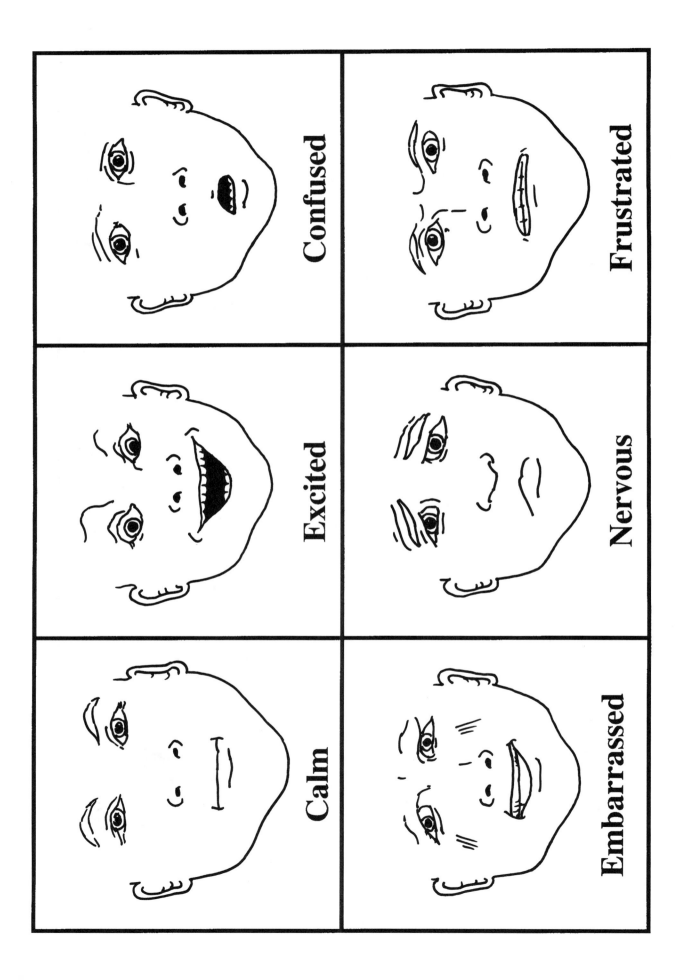

Confused

Frustrated

Excited

Nervous

Calm

Embarrassed

Parent Newsletters

Introducing the Program

Helping your child be successful!

The *Promoting Social Success* Program

Your child is beginning a new program at school. The *Promoting Social Success* program teaches children the social skills they need in order to be successful at school and at home. Teaching children social skills is very important. Social skills are essential for both academic success and healthy self-esteem.

Many children have difficulty making friends and may act out in ways that interfere with their learning. However, the *Promoting Social Success* program can help your child get along with others and control his or her behavior.

This program teaches children to

1. Better understand and deal with their emotions
2. Calm down when upset or overexcited
3. Accurately "read" social situations
4. Problem solve independently
5. Be a good friend

You will receive updates about what your child is learning and what you can do with your child to reinforce these skills at home.

It is fun to have friend.

The First Unit

After several introductory lessons, students will begin working on lessons about emotions and behavior. Lessons ask students to identify a variety of emotions (e.g., happy, sad, angry, frustrated, excited, confused) in both themselves and in others.

Being aware of their own emotions, and the emotions of others, helps children control their behavior. The first step to calming down is recognizing when you are upset! Students are taught three steps to help them calm down. The next newsletter will discuss each step.

Parents are a child's most important teachers! Your support of this program will benefit your child and his or her social development in countless ways. Thank you for your cooperation!

What Can You Do?

With your child...

- Find a picture of someone who looks excited (or sad, angry, and so forth).

- Make a list of things to do when you are lonely.

- Read a book and identify the feelings of all the different characters.

- Draw a picture of something you love.

- Play Feeling Charades. Act out emotions and have the other person guess which one you are showing.

The Calming Down Steps

Calming down steps help kids think clearly!

The Three Steps for Calming Down

Children often act in impulsive ways. Feelings of anger or excitement can be overwhelming. Teaching children to monitor their emotions and to calm down when these emotions are running high can help them to control their behavior and make better choices.

With this goal in mind, *Promoting Social Success* lessons teach children three steps to help them calm down. Using a red traffic light symbol to cue our students, we ask them to:

1. Stop

2. Keep hands to yourself

3. Take a deep breath

People use many methods to help themselves relax. Some people count to 10, and some picture themselves on a deserted beach.

It is fun to have friend.

We believe that these three steps are a good tool for kids who need help calming themselves. The steps are simple, easy to remember, and can be done as easily in the mall as they can in math class.

With practice, students can become proficient at recognizing when they need to calm down and at performing the three steps independently.

Practicing at Home

You are your child's most important teacher. Reinforcing skills at home is an essential part of your child's learning. And learning to calm down is a skill that will benefit your child both academically and socially.

What Can You Do?

With your child...

• Post the Stoplight Poster #1 on the refrigerator.

• Coach your child to perform the three steps when he or she is upset.

• Play an exciting game, then practice calming down using the three steps.

• Use the words *feeling, angry,* and *calm* in a sentence.

Promoting Social Success: A Curriculum for Children with Special Needs by Gary N. Siperstein & Emily Paige Rickards
© 2004 by Paul H. Brookes Publishing Co. Inc. All rights reserved.
www.brookespublishing.com   1-800-638-3775

Figuring Out Social Situations

Helping kids "read" social situations!

Paying Attention to Cues

Your child is learning how to better interact with other people. When we talk to someone, we notice the facial expression and body language of the other person. We pay attention to their tone of voice. We look around us and modify our behavior according to the environment. Many kids, however, have difficulty "reading" these kinds of social cues and adapting their behavior accordingly.

Promoting Social Success lessons are teaching children to pay attention to the details of social interactions. Specifically, lessons ask students to notice:

1. Facial expressions

2. Body language

3. Tone of voice

4. Environmental cues

Learning to pay attention to social situations helps children behave in more appropriate ways.

Interpreting Social Cues

How many times have you heard

"He pushed me!"

"She's being mean to me!"

Many children have difficulty interpreting social situations. They are likely to say that someone is being mean, when in fact the person's intentions were innocent. They are likely to interpret an accident as being done on purpose.

Noticing social cues is not enough. The next step is to interpret these cues accurately.

Promoting Social Success lessons are teaching children how to

1. Decide if something was an accident or if it was done on purpose

2. Figure out when a person is being mean

3. Decide when and how to approach a person who appears busy

4. Deal with teasing

What Can You Do?

With your child...

• Find a picture of someone who looks busy.

• Think of a time you hurt someone by accident.

• Go "people watching." What might other people be feeling? How can you tell?

• Say something in an excited (or sad, angry, and so forth) tone of voice.

• Make faces in the mirror.

It is fun to have friend.

Promoting Social Success: A Curriculum for Children with Special Needs by Gary N. Siperstein & Emily Paige Rickards
© 2004 by Paul H. Brookes Publishing Co. Inc. All rights reserved.
www.brookespublishing.com   1-800-638-3775

Problem Solving

Helping your child become a problem solver!

Solving Social Problems

Problem-solving skills are an important part of a child's academic and social success. One of the goals of the *Promoting Social Success* program is to help kids become good problem solvers. Too often, children have problems that they do not know how to resolve on their own. And too often, children rely on parents and teachers to intervene in their disputes with other children.

Your child's class is beginning a unit that will give students the skills to resolve conflicts. Lessons focus on figuring out a goal, coming up with a strategy, trying a plan, and evaluating how things went.

The *Promoting Social Success* program teaches students to ask themselves:

- What do I want to happen?

- What can I do?

- How did it go?

Practicing these steps when problems arise will help your child think through the situation and become a better problem

solver. The more your child practices, the better he or she will be able to handle dilemmas that arise.

What Can You Do?

With your child . . .

- Post the Stoplight Poster #2 on the refrigerator.

- Practice the problem-solving steps.

- Look up the word *goal* in the dictionary.

- Make a goal for the week. Try to reach this goal.

- Discuss how to handle teasing.

- Read a book about someone who solved a problem.

- Make a list of all the things you could do to solve a problem.

- Ask someone you know how they solved a problem.

- Look up the word *compromise* in the dictionary.

- Ask someone for help with a problem you have.

- Find a picture of someone who has a problem.

It is fun to have friends.

Friendship

Helping children to be good friends!

Making and Maintaining Friendships

Friendships are some of the most important relationships in our lives. They provide us with emotional support, companionship, and, most of all, fun! Most of us can't imagine life without our friends. But many children lack the social skills necessary to make and maintain friendships. And as a result, they miss out on these important relationships.

Your child's class is beginning a unit that teaches students how to be a good friend. Below are some of the topics dealt with in these lessons:

1. Helping and sharing

2. Empathy

3. Hurt feelings

4. Forgiveness

5. Dealing with rejection

6. Trust

7. Give and take

It is fun to have friend.

Lessons ask students to identify the characteristics of a good friend and provide strategies for making and maintaining relationships that are fulfilling and enjoyable.

The skills addressed in this unit assist both students who are experiencing social difficulties and students who are experiencing social success.

Focusing on friendship helps create a classroom atmosphere that is accepting and supportive. And a friendly classroom is a place kids and adults can look forward to being in every day!

What Can You Do?

With your child . . .

• Read a book about friendship.

• Look up the words *friend* and *friendship* in the dictionary.

• Talk about the kinds of things that make a person a good friend.

• Invite a friend to play.

• Tell how you solved a problem in one of your friendships.

• Write a letter to a friend.

• Draw a picture for a friend.

• Talk about any problems your child might be having making friends.

Role-Play Footprints

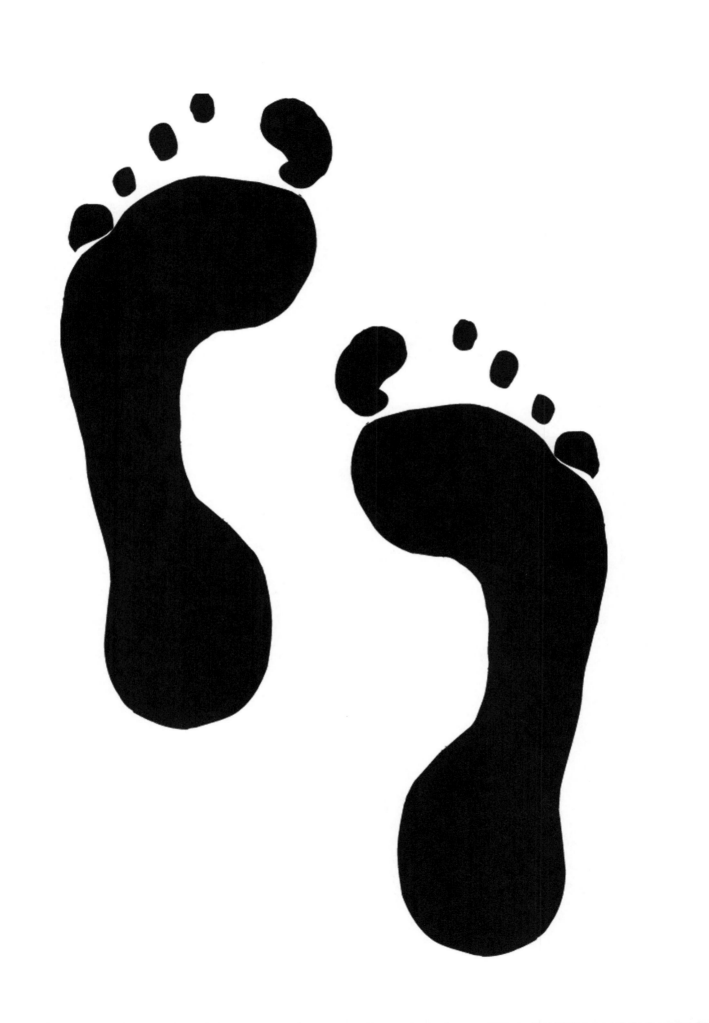

Stoplight Posters

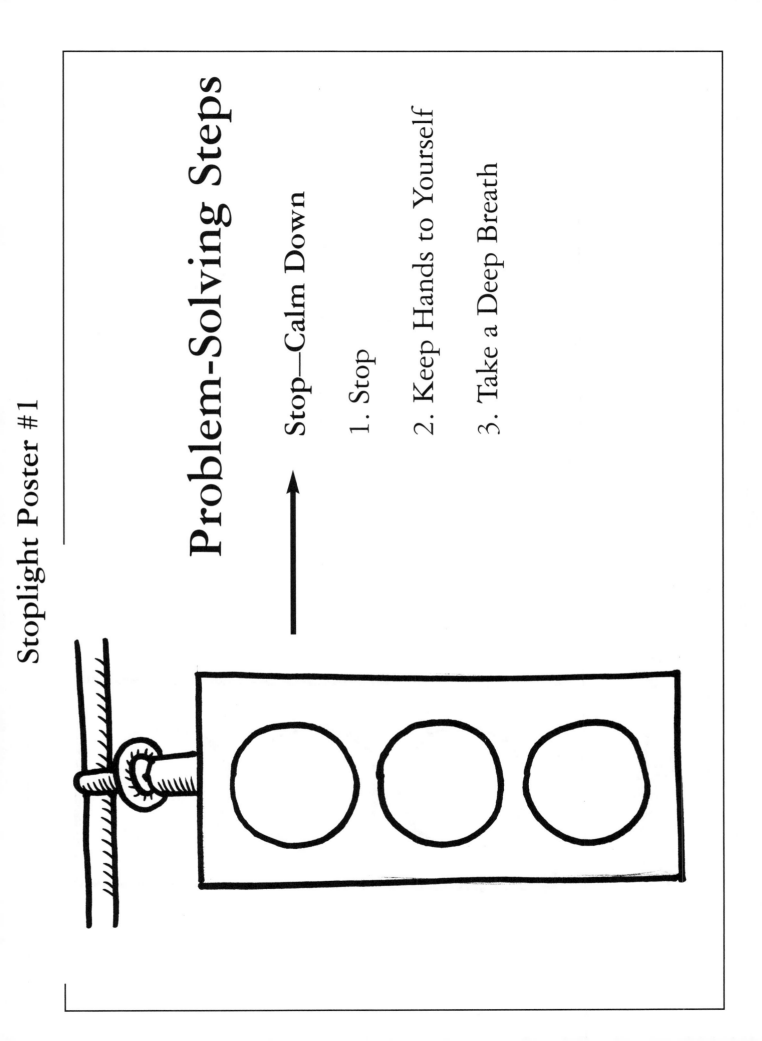

Stoplight Poster #1

Problem-Solving Steps

Stop—Calm Down

1. Stop

2. Keep Hands to Yourself

3. Take a Deep Breath

Stoplight Poster #2

Problem-Solving Steps

Stop—Calm Down
1. Stop
2. Keep Hands to Yourself
3. Take a Deep Breath

Slow Down—Think
4. What is going on?
5. What do I want to happen?
6. What can I do?

Go
7. Try my plan
8. How did it go?

BIBLIOGRAPHY

Books are wonderful tools to engage students in conversations about feelings, friendship, and problem solving. Below is a list of books, arranged by topic, that will help you spark lively discussions and reinforce concepts presented in the *Promoting Social Success* curriculum. Many of these books can be used in place of books mentioned in specific *Promoting Social Success* lessons.

KEY

A – More advanced in length and vocabulary

E – Easier chapter book

L – Longer than the typical easy/picture book

I – Illustrations are particularly engaging

P – Parents may find these books more applicable

B – Applicable to both teachers and parents

T – Teachers may find these books more applicable

Y – More appropriate for younger students

ACCIDENT/ON PURPOSE

This subject area deals with events that happen by accident but are perceived by others as happening on purpose, along with how these differences are resolved.

A Bear for Christmas by Holly Keller. Greenwillow Books; New York; 1986. (P)

Curious George by H.A. Rey. Houghton Mifflin; Boston; 1941. (B, Y)

Keeping a Christmas Secret by Phyllis Reynolds Naylor. Atheneum Books; New York; 1989. (B)

Rosie & the Yellow Ribbon by Paula DePaolo. Little, Brown, & Co.; Boston; 1992. (B, I)

ADOPTION

Although the curriculum does not specifically cover this topic, the following books offer insight and information to children learning or asking about adoption (their own or others').

Abby by Jeannette Franklin Caines. Harper & Row; New York; 1973. (I, P)

Adoption is For Always by Linda Walvoord Girard. A. Whitman Co.; Niles, IL; 1986. (P)

Somebody Else's Child by Roberta Silman. F. Warne Co.; New York; 1976. (E, P)

BEHAVIOR CHANGE

The characters of these books realize that one of the ways to change a situation is to change their behavior.

Miss Nelson is Missing by Harry Allard and James Marshall. Scholastic; New York; 1977. (I, T)

Mona the Vampire by Sonia Holleyman. Delacourt Press; New York; 1991. (B, I)

Sometimes I Feel Like I Don't Have Any Friends (But Not So Much Anymore): A Self-Esteem Book to Help Children Improve Their Social Skills by Tracy Zimmerman and Lawrence Shapiro. Center for Applied Psychology Inc.; King of Prussia, PA; 1996.

Sometimes I Like to Fight, but I Don't Do It Much Anymore: A Self-Esteem Book to Help Children with Difficulty Controlling Their Anger by Lawrence Shapiro. ChildsWork/ChildsPlay; Secaucus, NJ; 1995.

There's a Boy in the Girl's Bathroom by Louis Sachar. Alfred Knopf Paperbacks; New York; 1987.

BULLIES

These books give readers insight as to how to deal with bullies.

Arthur's April Fool by Marc Tolon Brown. Little, Brown, & Co.; Boston; 1983. (B, Y)

King of the Playground by Phyllis Reynolds Naylor. Atheneum Books; New York; 1991. (B, I)

There's a Boy in the Girl's Bathroom by Louis Sachar. Alfred Knopf Paperbacks; New York; 1987.

Why Is Everybody Always Picking on Me: A Guide to Handling Bullies by Terrence Webster-Doyle. Atrium Society; Middlebury, VT; 1991. (B, especially chapters 5 and 6.)

DEALING WITH DISABILITIES

The characters of the following books either have a disability or know someone with a disability. The books offer insightful illustrations as to what disabilities are and how it feels to have one.

Arnie and the New Kid by Nancy Carlson. Viking; New York; 1990. (B)

The Balancing Girl by Alexander Rabe. Dutton; New York; 1981. (B)

Howie Helps Himself by Joan Fassler. A. Whitman Co.; Chicago; 1974. (B, I)

I Have a Sister: My Sister Is Deaf by Jeanne Whitehouse. Harper & Row; New York; 1977. (B)

My Buddy by Audrey Osofsky. H. Holt.; New York; 1992. (T)

My Sister Is Different by Betty Ren Wright. Raintree Children's Books; Milwaukee; 1981. (P)

DEATH AND LOSS

This category covers death of a family member, death of a pet, death of a friend, divorce, and having a pet run away. Although, these issues are not covered in our curriculum, these books offer insight in how to deal with such losses and the emotions that arise.

Eleanor, Arthur and Claire by Diana Engel. Macmillan; New York; 1992. (I, P)

The Foundling by Carol Carrick. Seabury Press; New York; 1977. (L, P)

Goodbye, Max by Holly Keller. Greenwillow Books; New York; 1987. (P)

Granddad Bill's Song by Jane Yolen. Philomel Books; New York; 1994. (I, P)

I Had a Friend Named Peter by Janice Cohn. W. Morrow; New York; 1987. (P)

Jim's Dog Muffins by Miriam Cohen. Greenwillow Books; New York; 1984. (P)

Murphy and Kate by Ellen Howard. Simon & Schuster Books for Young Readers; New York; 1995. (P)

Mustard by Charlotte Towner Graebeer. Macmillan; New York; 1982. (A, P)

My Mother's House, My Father's House by C.B. Christiansen. Atheneum Books; New York; 1989. (B, Y)

Nana Upstairs & Nana Downstairs by Tomie de Paola. Putnam's; New York; 1997. (P)

Nonna by Jennifer Bartoli. Harvey House; New York; 1975. (L, P)

Petey by Tobi Tobias. Putnam; New York; 1978. (L, P)

Saying Goodbye to Daddy by Judith Vigna. A. Whitman; Niles, IL; 1991. (P)

The Tenth Good Thing About Barney by Judith Viorst. Atheneum; New York; 1971. (P)

Tough Boris by Mem Fox. Harcourt, Brace & Jovanovich; San Diego; 1994. (P)

Under the Blackberries by Rachel Pank. Scholastic; New York; 1992. (I, P)

When Lucy Went Away by G. Max Ross. Dutton; New York; 1976. (P)

Where is Daddy? The Story of a Divorce by Beth Goff. Beacon Press; Boston; 1969. (P, Y)

Whiskers Once and Always by Doris Orgel. Viking Kestrel; New York; 1986. (A, P)

You Hold Me and I'll Hold You by Jo Carson. Orchard Books; New York; 1992. (P)

EMOTIONS

Alone/Loneliness

These books contrast the feelings of being alone and feeling lonely, emphasizing that these emotions are different and are not necessarily related.

Annie and the Wild Animals by Jan Brett. Houghton Mifflin; Boston; 1985. (B)

I Like Being Alone by Betty Ren Wright. Raintree Children's Books; Milwaukee; 1981. (B)

Our Snowman by M.B. Goffstein. Harper & Row; New York; 1986. (B)

Anger

These books focus on the reasons for anger and the expression of anger.

Mean Soup by Betsy Everitt. Harcourt, Brace & Co.; San Diego; 1992. (Y, P)

Now Everybody Really Hates Me by Jane Read Martin & Patricia Marx. Harper-Collins; New York; 1993. (I, B)

When I'm Angry by Jane Aaron. Golden Books; New York; 1998. (P; includes Parent Guide)

Courage

The following books focus on characters who overcome a lack of courage.

Cowardly Clyde by Bill Peet. Houghton Mifflin; Boston; 1979. (B, I)

My Brother John by Kristine Church. Tambourine Books; New York; 1991. (B, Y)

Curiosity

Although curiosity is not an easy subject, this book addresses the idea that we like to know what will happen next through a story about a family that feels as though something unusual is going to happen.

Something is Going to Happen by Charolotte Zolotow. Harper & Row; New York; 1988.

Disappointment

The following book deals with a boy who realizes what is really important after being greatly disappointed.

The Luckiest Kid on the Planet by Lisa Campbell Ernst. Bradbury Press; New York; 1994. (B)

Embarrassment

These books show how the main characters deal with feeling embarrassed.

Jim Meets the Thing by Miriam Cohen. Greenwillow Books; New York; 1981. (B, Y)

A Letter to Amy by Ezra Jack Keats. Harper & Row; New York; 1968. (B, Y)

Officer Buckle and Gloria by Pebby Rathmann. Putnam's; New York; 1995.

Quiet! There's a Canary in the Library by Don Freeman. Golden Gate Junior Books; San Carlos, CA; 1969. (B, I)

Sabrina by Martha G. Alexander. Dial Press; New York; 1971. (B)

Fear

These books cover a wide range of feelings of fear, including being scared and being nervous.

All Alone After School by Muriel Stanek. A Whitman; Niles, IL; 1985. (B, L)

Because of Lozo Brown by Larry L. King. Viking Kestrel; New York; 1988. (B, I, Y)

The Bravest Babysitter by Barbara Greenberg. Dial Press; New York; 1977.

Fang by Barbara Shook Hazen. Atheneum Books; New York; 1987. (B, I)

Ghost's Hour, Spook's Hour by Eve Bunting. Clarion Books; New York; 1987. (B)

Goggles! by Ezra Jack Keats. Macmillan; New York; 1969. (B, Y)

Harriet's Recital by Nancy L. Carlson. Carolrhoda Books; Minneapolis; 1982. (B, Y)

The Highest Balloon on the Common by Carol Carrick. Greenwillow Books; New York; 1977.

Huge Harold by Bill Peet. Houghton Mifflin; Boston; 1961. (B, I)

Ira Sleeps Over by Bernard Waber. Houghton Mifflin; Boston; 1972. (P, Y)

Left Behind by Carol and Donald Carrick. Clarion Books; New York; 1988. (I, T)

Lost in the Storm by Carol Carrick. Seabury Press; New York; 1974. (B)

There's a Monster Under My Bed by James Howe. Aladdin Paperbacks; New York; 1986. (I, P, Y)

Thunder Cake by Patricia Polacco. Philomel Books; New York; 1990. (B, I)

When I'm Afraid by Jane Aaron. Golden Books; New York; 1998. (P)

Frustration

These books deal with feeling frustrated with other people or about certain events.

Alexander and the Terrible, Horrible, No Good, Very Bad Day by Judith Viorst. Aladdin Paperbacks; New York; 1972. (B, I)

Everybody Knows That! by Susan Pearson. Dial Press; New York; 1978. (B)

A Little Touch of Monster by Emily Lampert. Atlantic Monthly Press; Boston; 1986. (B)

Stevie by John Steptoe. Harper & Row; New York; 1969. (P)

General Emotions

These books deal with various emotions together.

The Feelings Book: Expressing Emotions Creatively: A Guide for Children and Grownups by Caryn Frye Boddie. Cordillera Press; Evergreen, CO; 1998. (B)

Today I Feel Silly and Other Moods that Make My Day by Jamie Lee Curtis. HarperCollins; New York; 1998. (B, I)

Guilt

These books deal with feeling guilt after an unfortunate incident occurs, either by accident or due to carelessness.

Lilly's Purple Plastic Purse by Kevin Henkes. Greenwillow Books; New York; 1996. (B, I)

Marvin Redpost: Alone in His Teacher's House by Louis Sachar. Random House; New York; 1994. (A, B)

Too Many Tamales by Gary Soto. Putnam; New York; 1992. (B, I)

Jealousy

These books deal with feeling jealous of other people's situations.

Benjy and the Barking Bird by Margaret B. Graham. Harper & Row; New York; 1971. (B, Y)

Happy Birthday, Crystal by Shirley Gordon. Harper & Row; New York; 1981. (B, L)

I Wish I Was Sick Too! by Franz Brandenberg. Greenwillow Books; New York; 1976. (P)

Little Monster Did It! by Helen Cooper. Dial Books for Young Readers; New York; 1996. (P; This book is especially helpful for dealing with jealousy toward a new baby.)

Much Bigger Than Martin by Steven Kellogg. Dial Press; New York; 1976. (B, Y)

Why Couldn't I Be An Only Kid Like You, Wigger? by Barbara Shook Hazen. Atheneum Books; New York; 1975. (B, I)

Pride

This book offers a wonderful illustration of a child feeling proud due to a specific event.

Annabelle Swift, Kindergartner by Amy Schwartz. Orchard Books; New York; 1988.

Sadness

These books deal with the feeling of sadness related to events other than death.

Fishing by Diana Engel. Macmillan; New York; 1993. (B, I)

Sylvester and the Magic Pebble by William Steig. Simon & Schuster; New York; 1969. (B, I)

Selfishness

This book deals with selfishness and greed by illustrating what can happen when a group of people allow greed to take control.

Chestnut Cove by Tim Egan. Houghton Mifflin; Boston; 1995. (B)

Surprise

These books deal with feeling surprised.

No Jumping on the Bed by Tedd Arnold. Dial Books for Young Readers; New York; 1987. (B, I)

The Wednesday Surprise by Eve Bunting. Clarion Books; New York; 1989.

FRIENDSHIP

These books deal with the many aspects of friendship, including how to be a good friend, having a friend move away, and making new friends.

Amber Brown Is Not a Crayon by Paula Danziger. Putnam's; New York; 1994. (A, B)

Annie Bananie by Leah Komaiko. Harper & Row; New York; 1987. (B, I, Y)

Best Friends Together Again by Aliki. Greenwillow Books; New York; 1982. (B)

Blumpoe the Grumpoe Meets Arnold the Cat by Jean Davies Okimoto. Joy Street Books; Boston; 1990. (B, I, L)

Chester's Way by Kevin Henkes. Greenwillow Books; New York; 1988. (B)

Crystal is My Friend by Shirley Gordon. Harper & Row; New York; 1978. (B, L)

Don't be Mad, Ivy by Christine McDonnell. Dial Press; New York; 1981. (B, E)

Eli by Bill Peet. Houghton Mifflin; Boston; 1978. (B)

Gabrielle and Selena by Peter Desbarats. Harcourt, Brace & World; New York; 1968. (B, I)

George and Martha by James Marshall. Houghton Mifflin; Boston; 1972. (B, Y)

The Giving Tree by Shel Silverstein. HarperCollins; New York; 1964.

Good Friends are Hard to Find by Fred Frankel. Perspective Publishing; Los Angeles; 1996. (P; especially chapters 2, 3, 4, 6, 18, 23)

Happy Birthday, Crystal by Shirley Gordon. Harper & Row; New York; 1981. (B, L)

Happy Birthday, Ronald Morgan! Patricia Reilly Giff. Viking Kestrel; New York; 1986. (I, T)

The Hating Book by Charlotte Zolotow. HarperTrophy; New York; 1969. (B)

Horrible Harry in Room 2B by Suzy Kline. Puffin Books; New York; 1997. (B, E, I)

How to Be a Friend: A Guide to Making Friends and Keeping Them by Laurie Krasny Brown and Marc Brown. Little, Brown & Co.; Boston; 1998. (B, I, L)

Ira Says Goodbye by Bernard Waber. Houghton Mifflin; Boston; 1988. (B)

Jamaica and Brianna by Juanita Havill. Houghton Mifflin; Boston; 1993. (B, I)

Jeremy Bean's St. Patrick's Day by Alice Schertle. Lothrop, Lee & Shepard Books; New York; 1987. (B)

Let's Be Enemies by Janice May Udry. Harper & Row; New York; 1961.

Lilly's Purple Plastic Purse by Kevin Henkes. Greenwillow Books; New York; 1996. (B, I)

Matthew and Tilly by Rebecca C. Jones. Puffin Unicorn/Penguin Group; New York; 1991. (This book gives a good example of forgiveness, in terms of friendship.)

Maude and Sally by Nicki Weiss. Greenwillow Books; New York; 1983. (B)

My Best Friend by Pat Hutchins. Greenwillow Books; New York; 1993. (B, Y)

My Best Friend Moved Away by Joy Zelonky. Raintree Children's Books; Milwaukee; 1980. (L, P)

My Outrageous Friend Charlie by Martha G. Alexander. Dial Books for Young Readers; New York; 1989. (B, I, Y)

Peach and Blue by Sarah S. Kilborne. Alfred Knopf Paperbacks; New York; 1994.

The Rat and the Tiger by Keiko Kasza. Putnam & Grosset Group; New York; 1993. (B, I)

Rosie and Michael by Judith Viorst. Atheneum Books; New York; 1974. (B, I)

Somebody Else's Child by Roberta Silman. F. Warne; New York; 1976. (B, E)

Somebody Loves You, Mr. Hatch by Eileen Spinelli. Bradbury Press; New York; 1991. (B, I)

Starting School With an Enemy by Elisa Carbone. Alfred Knopf Paperbacks; New York; 1998. (A, B)

There's a Boy in the Girl's Bathroom by Louis Sachar. Alfred Knopf Paperbacks; New York; 1987.

Three Cheers for Tacky by Helen Lester. Houghton Mifflin; Boston; 1994. (I, T)

We Are Best Friends by Aliki. Greenwillow Books; New York; 1982. (B, I)

Yo! Yes? by Chris Raschka. Orchard Books; New York; 1993. (B, I)

GOALS

These books deal with the determination, planning, and perseverance needed to reach both long-term and short-term goals.

Amanda and the Giggling Ghost by Steven Kroll. Holiday House; New York; 1980. (B)

The Case of the Stolen Bagels by Hila Colman. Crown Publishers; New York; 1977. (B, L)

Howie Helps Himself by Joan Fassler. A. Whitman; Chicago; 1974. (B, I)

Sometimes It Happens by Elinor Lander Horwitz. Harper & Row; New York; 1981. (B, L)

There's a Party at Mona's Tonight by Harry Allard. Doubleday; Garden City, NY; 1981. (B, I, Y)

What's the Matter, Sylvie, Can't You Ride? by Karen Born Anderson. Dial Press; New York; 1981. (B)

MANNERS

These books deal with appropriate and inappropriate manners.

The Bad Good Manners Book by Babette Cole. Dial Books for Young Readers; New York; 1996. (I, P)

Elbert's Bad Word by Audrey Wood. Harcourt, Brace & Jovanovich; New York; 1988. (I, P)

PROBLEM SOLVING

The books in this section illustrate the different steps to solve a problem.

Arthur's April Fool by Marc Brown. Little, Brown & Co.; Boston; 1983. (B, Y)

The Bad Dreams of a Good Girl by Susan Shreve. Alfred Knopf Paperbacks; New York; 1982. (A, B)

Bootsie Barker Bites by Barbara Bottner. G P Putnam's Sons; New York; 1992. (B)

The Case of the Stolen Bagels by Hila Colman. Crown Publishers; New York; 1977. (B, L)

Growing Pains: Helping Children Deal with Everyday Problems Through Reading by Maureen Cuddigan and Mary Beth Hanson. American Library Association; Chicago; 1988. (P)

Herbie's Troubles by Carol Chapman. Dutton; New York; 1981. (B)

I Like Being Alone by Betty Ren Wright. Raintree Children's Books; Milwaukee; 1981. (B)

I'm Telling You Now by Judith Delton. Dutton; New York; 1983. (P, Y)

Josie's Troubles by Phyllis Reynolds Naylor. Atheneum Books; New York; 1992. (A, B)

King of the Playground by Phyllis Reynolds Naylor. Atheneum Books; New York; 1991. (B, I)

Starting School With an Enemy by Elisa Carbone. Alfred Knopf Paperbacks; New York; 1998. (A, B)

There's an Alligator Under My Bed by Mercer Mayer. Dial Books for Young Readers; New York; 1987. (B, I, Y)

SELF-RELIANCE AND INDIVIDUALITY

These books give insight on the importance of being self-reliant and responsible for one's self, as well as encouraging readers to enjoy who they are.

All Alone After School by Muriel Stanek. A. Whitman; Niles, IL; 1985. (B, L)

Three Cheers for Tacky by Helen Lester. Houghton Mifflin; Boston; 1994. (B, I)

TEASING

Books in this section include both playful and mean-spirited teasing for comparison purposes.

Arnie and the New Kid by Nancy Carlson. Viking; New York; 1990. (B)

Bet You Can't by Penny Dale. Lippincott; New York; 1987. (B, I, Y)

But Names Will Never Hurt Me by Bernard Waber. Houghton Mifflin; Boston; 1976. (B)

Hundred Dresses by Eleanor Estes. Harcourt, Brace & Co.; San Diego. 1944.

Jeremy Bean's St. Patrick's Day by Alice Schertle. Lothrop, Lee & Shepard Books; New York; 1987. (B)

Merry Christmas, Space Case by James Marshall. Dial Books for Young Readers; New York; 1986. (B)

The Red Racer by Audrey Wood. Simon & Schuster Books for Young Readers; New York; 1996. (I, P)